READING THE FUNNIES

My priority at that time of writing had to lie with following the pace of my sentiments and thoughts, which I ruefully admit was sometimes obsessive. Still, I hope with all my heart that I provided interested readers with some helpful suggestions and (for younger readers, especially) information, and that the cost in patience may not prove prohibitive.

My thanks to the Guggenheim Foundation, whose grant, in 1978, provided wheels and a track for the undertaking.

— Donald Phelps

FANTAGRAPHICS BOOKS

7563 Lake City Way
Seattle, WA 98115
www.fantagraphics.com

edited by Gary Groth
art directed by Preston White
promotion by Eric Reynolds
published by Gary Groth & Kim Thompson

First Fantagraphics edition: March, 2001.

ISBN 1-56097-368-4

Printed in Canada

Reading the Funnies

Essays on Comic Strips

Donald Phelps

FANTAGRAPHICS BOOKS
SEATTLE, WASHINGTON

CONTENTS

BANG

INTRODUCTORY NOTE

WHAT WE'RE ABOUT TO READ

Naturally, it seems to me, any compiler of his or her critical essays hopes that they might explain as well as declare themselves; otherwise, a new set of essays would seem to be indicated. I will note, however, that the essays which follow were in all, save two instances, newly written: those dealing with comic strips I have treated before — mainly during the 1960s for magazines such as *El Corno Emplumado*, *Noose*, *World*, and *Caterpillar* — have been, in the main, reshaped, expanded, reconsidered. The two exceptions are the piece on Major Hoople, originally printed as you read it here by *Muoch* magazine, under the editorship of Harry Lewis, Basil King, and David Glotzer. All of the sentiments and most of the impressions which I express there about Gene Ahern's strip have remained intact. For James Swinnerton's *Little Jimmy*, I have added to the essay as originally printed by Henry Weinfield in *The Mysterious Barricades*, an addendum, in the form of a brief, scandalously overdue obituary essay, in which I have tried to say succinctly certain things about the overall character of Swinnerton's art which, I think, were displaced by my various visual impressions and rambling-rose prose rhythms in the earlier essay — which, however, I thought sufficiently expressive of many feelings, still valid, to retain.

The task which mainly occupied me through this project of the past five years, was the all-pressing one of defining and determining the kind of creative event which is the comic strip; and what, to me, are the peculiarly American definitions of style and form which the comic strip peculiarly embodies. I settled upon a selection of those comic strips which fascinated me throughout the 1930s, when I first encountered them as a child, and thereafter. By no means have I tried to give any comprehensive history of the American strip, any panorama of the most distinguished, most entertaining, or most otherwise momentous comic-strip productions of any given period or category. I have not, in truth, even included a total representation of my own likes or preferences: *Barney Google* and Billy DeBeck, for example, deserve full-length book if they deserve anything; as does Herriman, and *Krazy Kat* (a future Ph.D. candidate might, I hope, be guided by Herriman's shade to his astonishing pre-Krazy career as editorial and sports cartoonist, featuring the stunning cartoon commentary on the Johnson-Jeffries fight of 1910, before and after. Let us hope that the trophy-seekers of the present nostalgia press leave some flesh on those noble bones.

A governing aim of mine in writing and rewriting these essays was to free my writing from the respective follies of impressionism and of comprehensiveness. Impressionism as a critical technique (I'm thinking particularly of "popular arts" criticism) is to be practiced only with the sturdiest buttressing of experience and both well-evolved and formulated response to that experience. Too often, even when practiced with such authority, it can become a contraband route for pernicious kinds of ego-display and sentimental popping-off, all ratified by the writer's dexterity of craft. Comprehensiveness can be sheer critical quicksand, with neither shore nor saving hickory-limb in sight, for the writer on comic strips and films, unless managed with a clear and rigorously followed scholarly purpose. Films and comic strips are among the most parasitic of forms and of subjects; feeding themselves continually, voraciously, from contemporary social, artistic, political phenomena, usually from aspects and highlights. My earlier essays on comic strips were impressionistic "takes," done in a spirit of pleasurable reminiscence.

Without losing or causing others to lose the pleasure where well-founded, I have tried to concentrate on those most enigmatic and complex appeals that the comic strip makes to the imagination; to the mixture of the ambitiously creative and the scuttling, ad hoc artisanship that, in medley, make up the uniquely American form of the *serial* strip. It is probably no coincidence at all that I found the richest enigmas and creative sorties in the comic strips which flowered (though not necessarily originated) in the 1930s: *Thimble Theater*, J.R. Williams' *Out Our Way*; finding in these, too, with their vagrant transitions of mood and mode, nurtured so by the volatile transitions of the 1930s, the theater of the everyday to which I refer again and again. I must repeat, however, that I do not mean to suggest that all interesting, or rewarding creative developments in the comic strips were confined to one or two decades. The past two decades have seen at least one remarkable innovation in the comic strip chronicle, in *Doonesbury*; the reshaping influences of two major editorial cartoonists, Oliphant and one of his most gifted disciples, MacNelly; to say nothing of the richly procreative "underground comics" current, of which Art Spiegelman's brilliantly edited *Raw* presents some of the most interesting and encouraging examples, not to mention some of the most thoughtful projections of the comic strip's possibilities.

I have not, I am saying, worked here, in my view, as comic strip specialist, nor as comic strip expert; but rather as critic of some latitude and eclecticism, trying to articulate that which pleases and creatively perplexes me in my own samples of this phenomenon. I hope, and urge, that you read these at a non-compulsive pace. I do not preen myself on being obscure, nor am I, I think; and never would I knowingly, willingly, embog a lively subject; but I have tried to say as much, not as little, as I could find, in as apt a mode as presented itself; and certain occasions require slower reading than others.

May I make public here some unceasing private appreciation: To Martin T. Williams, of Smithsonian Institute Popular Culture Division, for unstinting nagging to begin, and encouragement to complete, this small project.

To Sheldon Mayer of Oxford University Press, for awesome patience, receptiveness, and good will.

To the facilities of the Newspaper Annex Library, West 43rd Street, for indispensable assistance, including searches for bound copies, and adjustment of microfilm apparatus.

To Bill Blackbeard for his critical and scholarly services, bountifully tendered; including daily access to the National Academy of Comic Art, San Francisco.

To Manny Farber and Patricia Patterson, for cherished guides and examples in a fledgling critical career.

And to a gallant, enterprising man of no small sympathetic perception and massive devotion; in memory of a certain Friday night on which I opened, perused, then read straight-on-through, his critical history, *The Comics*, Coulton Waugh.

Keep the change.

FOREWORD
BY FIELDING DAWSON

The comic strip — a feature perhaps overlooked in your daily paper — is a creation unique to American cultural life and has, for a century commented on the way we see and view ourselves as it has fulfilled its daily appointed task of amusement and distraction. From its "high culture" influence on Pop Art to its "low culture" appeal to children of all ages, this phenomenon has had a lasting hold on the imaginations of generations, and *Reading the Funnies* collects a wide range of noted writer Donald Phelps' ("...a phenomenon in contemporary American criticism... (a) critic of remarkable curiousity and perception," as Gilbert Sorrentino has written) ruminations on this often overlooked medium.

From essays on popular classics (such as Chester Gould's *Dick Tracy*, E.C. Segar's *Thimble Theatre*, and Frank King's *Gasoline Alley*) to the more obscure, Phelps' keen and discriminating eye discerns the sublime qualities of this most American of art forms with wit, candor, and an almost Baroque grace.

As Phelps tellingly notes in his introduction, he writes not "as comic strip specialist, nor as comic strip expert, but rather as critic of some latitude and eclecticism, trying to articulate that which pleases and creatively perplexes me in my own samples of this phenomenon."

For the curious and the well-versed in the history of American comic strips, *Reading the Funnies* offers an elegant and eloquent look into this fascinating slice of American popular culture.

SNAP OUT OF IT, WHITE . . . YOU'RE GOING NUTS.

FLAT FOOT FLOOGIE

CHESTER GOULD AND DICK TRACY

When comparing and contrasting Chester Gould's *Dick Tracy* with the faithful, admiring, generous-spirited, though not exceedingly courageous or enterprising adaptation of it by Gould's successors, Fletcher and Collins, always pay attention to the blackness. To, that is, the identity, the singular vitality, of the black, which figures in panel after panel of Gould's strips whether as represented in the overcoats of his gangsters, in the yawning alcoves (always as sinister in their implications as the doorways of *Little Orphan Annie*); or the dreadful, in their very ribbon-like shimmer, rivulets of blood; or the recurrent interjections of night sky, bracketed by city skyline. This blackness is not darkness — not the dimming or withdrawal of light — but the supplanting of light by a vigorous, surface-rending presence, which commands the design in its perverse, roughshod energy. The blackness of the "Gould-Fletcher-Collins" *Dick Tracy* is darkness. It is the formal, subdued representation of night-shadow, the savagery of the Gould design fearfully tethered, intimidated by design principles; without the Caliban-like defiance of, and remaking of, design, which went hand in hand with the ferocity — always barely confined, it seemed, yet inevitably confined, since it was self-engendered — of Gould's drawing. In other words, we are now presented with the most cordial, most amenable of lobotomies; accompanied, no doubt at all, by a more astute economy of plot development, a more purringly-geared efficiency, than Chester Gould's square-jawed Dick ever offered us. I say this, I might add, in full, if regretful, realization that *Dick Tracy* was probably as uncontinuable in spirit as any comic strip, even as far as any viable counterpart was concerned; for the extraordinary, seething ragout of extravagance and rage and amoral fervor which the closed-circuit system of Chester Gould's universe generated in episode after episode, until his final resignation to a kind of circled quaintness; and a self-burlesque not nearly as dispirited, or dispiriting, as most self-represented "camp," but — in term of the expressive absoluteness of which he became master during the '30s — almost as imaginatively shallow.

As a crime-detective-procedural strip (for his Defoe-like zest for procedure set forth the premise of his cosmos) to conjure, to codify, that flashy, percussive, danger-laden style in which all Gould's competition (Will Gould's *Red Barry*; Norman Marsh's *Dan Dunn*; Charles Schmidt's *Sergeant Pat of the Radio Patrol*; and its illustrious antecedent Dashiell Hammett and Alex Raymond's *Secret Agent X-9*) was, according to its diverse styles, investing. I mean, the mosaic of street naturalism and exotic-touched rodomontade, that sense of Odets and the WPA Theater, as marinated in a rancid sort of glamour, for which films like Joseph von Sternberg's *Underworld*, and the various successors of Keighley, Curtiz, and Wellman, had set the patterns, with some extra sociological piety supplied by the plays of Sidney Kingsley. *Dick Tracy* crystallized this style, over a period of some four decades, as a sheet of images that sometimes suggest the painter's eye of a Magritte or Bacon, entrapped on a studio set as art director (with Maxwell Grant/Walter Gibson, of *The Shadow*, as technical consultant) for one of those Edward G. Robinson-Barton McLane-Frank McHugh adagios. His imagery never had the chipper sportiness of Cagney, the spoilt gallantry of the earlier (*Quick Millions, 20,000 Years in Sing Sing*) Spencer Tracy, the eroded tragic stoicism of Bogart; but rather, the strait-jacketed near-hysteric bluster of Robinson, along with his borderline grotesquerie (Robinson's face did yeoman service for Gould as, among other duties, the visage of Junior Tracy's would-be corrupter, Dan Micelli, in 1932). Or the beefy, disaster-bound obdurateness of McLane, the scroungy feyness, of McHugh. Such figures, in Gould, are as shackled to the production, the solicitation, of a single emotion, or emotional mixture — loathing, scorn, and dread — as the work of one of his unmistakable progenitors, Edgar Allen Poe. He is non-deferential, in the cranky, idiomatic way of a Winchell or Pegler (in contrast to the urbane pieties of other syndicated columnists) in the way he rebuilt, handcrafting for himself, the available cops-and-robbers myths; for all the documentary *information* that *Dick Tracy* seems on occasion to have siphoned, one receives no sense of the strip ever being geared to the orthodoxies of journalistic style even during the early '30s, when Gould's drawing is more tentative, and illustration-locked (its decorous, light line suggesting, as a possible influence, the work of Frederic Dorr Steele — after whose Sherlock Holmes Gould is known to have modeled the crisp arabesque of the younger Tracy profile). The earlier work abounds with appreciative allusions to movies, and movie personalities: *Big Boy*, bottle-nosed and bullet jaded, incorporates George Bancroft and Bull Montana; Larceny Lu, with her picture hats, feather boas, and Sammy's Bowery Follies bangs, is Pert Kelton in sisterhood with a somewhat longer-fanged Sophie Tucker; while, under the platinum blonde 'ayrick 'ead of 'air sported by the ill-starred society beauty, Jean Penfield, is the scarcely-mistakable face of the youthful Claudette Colbert. Yet, while such forthright eclecticism contrasts, say, with the engaging boyish inventiveness of Will (no relation) Gould, in his *Red Barry* fandangos, one feels that the appropriations are being used, however gropingly, as such eclecticism can best be, but seldom is used: toward the methodical, self-willed carpentry of Gould's own imagery. They are constantly converted, even then, by the raw salients of Gould's design: the gawkish authority of the bodies, their ever-ready knees and elbows, the torsos, always about to challenge the pearly-prim elegance of the lines which Gould invests in his background of police lab, railroad depot, or movie theater.

He evolved a mode of narration which paid regular dues to the sketch-series tradition of Hogarth, Rowlandson, and Girlarny: especially, the distillation of demonic energy through the world of *things*, which throngs every study of aberrant, or professionally intense, personality as we follow the stages of a career flooded with circumstance. Things and the ways in which they are joined wield authority in *Dick Tracy*; that reassignment of priorities which embodies the artist's prerogatives, and his flourishing of them. Gould gave the term "mechanical," as applied to art, a value not to be found among his crime-chronicling peers. He is most Poe-like, perhaps in this, and in demonstrating the relativity of emotion/sentiment in many artworks, by erecting his own hierarchy of "feelings" in terms of what he reassembles from the world as value observed-imagined. There is meager sentiment only — and his tries at approximating it are fearfully stiff and ill-gauged, always marked by spasmodic tackings into burlesque: people, even those supposedly deserving of our empathy, display, in grief, symmetrical tear-coursed mouths in the familiar ricti of the freshly walloped Katzenjammer Kids. Or they will literally collapse with laughter, the hats of plainclothesmen flopping over their eyes, out-thrust hands protesting their happy abandon, at the tepid eccentricities of a wilting juvenile detective named Brighton Spotts. The one cardinal emotion I can recall receiving from Gould that ever struck me as authentic was frenzied willfulness: which anyone, daresay, can recall and not impossibly recreate, who can remember his or her own childhood. The other emotions and sentiments were constantly shading into burlesque, which is, itself, the jovial self-ridicule of the artist's will, mock-derisive of its own powers. This, in earlier work of Gould's we will contemplate further.

But the mode of tabloid fantasy which Gould forged, relied mainly on a universe of things, and the resourcefulness, combining a scavenger's ad hoc predatory alertness, and the design-geared, cold serenity of a Keaton, brought to bear upon this artifact-rich jungle by both police and the underworld. The inventiveness which both sides invoke is not the situation creating petit vision of Edison or Whitney, but the near-prankish energy that devised new roles and lines of action for the long-accustomed shape and function of mechanisms and utilities and common objects: alarm clocks, rolls of masking tape, garden hose. Gould confers a glamour on the carpentering, or, with Tracy in command, the quarrying of criminal plots, which now and then realized minor pornography. Craft itself takes on flesh:

the coaxing of lethal potential from a toy steam-engine; making a larder of venison and fish in an enforced forest hideaway; or, the bewitching demonstration by Tracy, during daily episodes of August 5-8 1937, wherein, using X-ray photographs, chalk-talks, and pantomime, he demonstrates that a number of hit-and-run "accident" insurance claimants are so many one-armed bandits. The '30s were marbled by American nostalgia for technology, and the skills to meet it and be fulfilled in it, of which the Romeo/Juliet romance, flourishing from the 1900's, had fallen under the Depression's sanctions. The longing, and sense of ambition, both craftsmanly and commercial, cruelly sidetracked into unlikely expedients, was honored by the hypnotic precision — precision itself rarely deserved the adjective — of his compositions and lines and blacks, and the passion of craft for which they merge to provide wave-length. The ascetic loveliness of his lines, the frost-magic of those metallic surfaces — drugstore counters, marble columns in hotel lobbies, the metal-work of wonderfully accurate elevator mechanisms and diesel locomotive structures — belong to a tradition of fairy tale illustration, fortified by the reek of 18th century rogueries and lusts, in which things are rediscovered and, as it were, reborn; far from the deodorized sleekness of *Flash Gordon*, but rather near the clunkish, human-scaled recasting of science fiction left us by H.G. Wells, Lang's *Metropolis*, or the Dick Calkins *Buck Rogers*. To contemplate Gould's cosmetics counters and switchboards and gasoline pumps is, moreover, to see the near-union of design and nature which might have triggered, in Robert Frost, a companion poem to his savage-chaste study in white on white: "Design."

And *Dick Tracy* itself was a comic strip self-nurtured on the theme of perverted and possessed art, sustained, not by the richly scaffolded clichés of characterization and situation, but by the images themselves. The best of his stories, like the epic pursuit of the Purple Cross Gang of mid-1936 through early 1937, amount to tapestries of vignette, action scenes, gimmicks, and eccentricities. The Purple Cross romance is as barren of mystery as any of Gould's yarns (the gang's hooded leader, Number One, all but wigwags his identity to the reader on his first appearance in *mufti*). Yet, the torrent of gritty and bizarre detail (the Maltese crosses tattooed on the gang's tongues, the short-wave device concealed in an office watercooler, the curious smudges on a small-time politico's cheeks); the genre-art-like ambience of the '30s in occasional panels, like that of Baldy Stark, the penitent member of the Gang, forlornly silhouetted against the alley entrance, watching the approach of his little blonde-haired daughter and grim, Sicilian-featured sister; and the intermittent views of the dingy politician, "Shirtsleeve" Kelton, with his small-town haircut and clipped mustache; the oriental-looking FBI agent, Jim Trailer; all add up to an excursion into melodrama-as-style nearly equaling, despite the balsa wood clichés of character, and jalopy-tempoed negotiations of "mystery," the visual richness of Feuillade's *Les Vampires.*

And all of it fired by the sense of an impounded, abandoned vivacity of caricature, which writhes and flutters inside the naturalistic, illustrational casing of the *Dick Tracy* settings, and craftsmanlike data. It is remarkable, the concentration, the concreteness, with which Gould's recurrent envy of caricature's freedom, of its absolute self-command, is felt over the years. I can remember being peculiarly infected by this feeling as a twelve-year-old; but also, by my own envy of how Gould's style had reconciled (a labor of Hercules it should have seemed to me, had I known more about Hercules) that upswelling audacity, and that cool command of the visible, familiar world. It filled me with an intuition, as I recall, of the drawing process as embodied in *Dick Tracy*, as realizing every definition of "magic" that professionalism can offer. And that *tethered* sense of caricature (of which the recurrent emblem is the writhing, convulsive activity of the bodies and faces) conveys, in itself, a firm apprehension of his own ground, and an accompanying ability to set the terms, the economy for, his imagination's action, which distinguishes Gould automatically from most of his contemporaries, smitten as they were — the "funny" strips included, under the double spur of *Thimble Theater* and *Barney Google* — with the challenging darkness of semi-exotic melodrama. During 1935, in the *New York Evening Journal*, even that most affable and frisky of comic strips, A. Carter's *Just Kids*, saw the Stebbins family, with Mush and his various associates, transported to urban China, for a variety of Shanghaijinks with a mysterious secret society and the opposing Tongs. But *Dick Tracy* alone — possibly excepting Roy Crane's *Wash Tubbs and Captain Easy* — treated melodrama as his own imaginative estate, and caricature as his agent. There was always felt in the drawing the imminence of something, not merely dramatically (that, too, in Gould's seldom-equaled erotic virtuosity with violence) but visually, outrageous: a monstrous absolute intruding itself, as in the 1937-8 apparition of the Blank, to threaten the drawing's silver-wired armature of plausibility. Even those who never heard or read of the (aborted, by fiat of publisher Joseph Patterson) episode, in which Gould attempted to draw his own hand rescuing Tracy from a mine cave-in, by abolishing the event, felt the sinuous enchantment of the drawing process, as they never did of Goulds' chief rivals of the '30s: *Dan Dunn*, *Radio Patrol*, *Secret Agent X-9*, *Red Barry*. Each of these offers its peculiar authenticity and animation; but also, its peculiar enslavement to the narrative conventions and locked-in moral premises, which the foreground crime buster myths of the day often decreed; with the resulting impression of the artist's imagination, whatever his skill and energy, held hostage to such convention. In *Secret Agent X-9*, the Dashiell Hammett prose (second-gear Hammett at best) seemed fatally upstaged by the opaque, monotonous elegance of Alex Raymonds's drawing, which highlighted the negative traits — cinchiness, vacuous hauteur — of the Hammett style; and, besides, was dedicated to showcasing a frigid clothes-horse, rather then the bustling, pragmatic Continenetal Op. *Dan Dunn* presented a chronic wintry aspect, with its arid, starved-looking drawing (reminiscent, in truth, of *Dick Tracy's* first year or so); the cavernous spaces surrounding the figures (I could imagine them giving off echoes); the huddled, stiff-jointed postures, and the general impression of crime, and crime-fighting still more, as lonely, under-financed, slightly inane businesses. Yet, Norman Marsh's dry, fatalistic, de-glamorized tone (even Dan Dunn's lady friend, Kay — unlike Dick's Tess Trueheart — *looked* like a fast-aging, attrition-haunted spinster) repeatedly managed to put across an image of no-fooling, Depression-bleak crook-hunting. Despite a regrettably graceless, ashen-literal drawing style, *Sergeant Pat of the Radio Patrol* exerted more genuine charm, through its general air of hardy, buoyant good sense, than either of the two above-described strips. It was also the only police-procedural strip of which I am aware, continually and distinctively to feature the *city* in which the police moved (that they were uniformed patrolmen, unlike the plain-clothes daredevils of

Charles Schmidt's fellows, probably played no small part), as a visual presence and autonomous source of occasion, and not a cursorily-invoked movie set. And in Pat's stammering, overweight sidekick, Sam, despite his drolly intended deficiencies (inherited, no doubt, like those of Porky Pig, From Clarence Buddington Kelland's Marcus Aurelius Tidd) Schmidt brought forth one of the few such sleuthing Sanchos (as set up against Tracy's Pat Patton, and Dunn's Irwin Higgs) who was competent, reasonably stable, and apparently not calculated solely to freeze our livers at the thought of such a man safeguarding our lives and properties.

Will Gould's sporty *Red Barry* was Hearst's entry, from 1933 in the *New York Evening Journal*, against Dick Tracy; and, as usual in the Hearst-Patterson bombardments, a high-spirited, inventive counterpart, done in a style of carbonated tumescence: a dashing, slashing black stroke that suggests James Montgomery Flagg with goat-gland injections: biceps that seemed to erupt like puffed wheat globules from the page; and dialogue balloons that fairly seethed and bubbled on the page. *Red Barry* was chipper and active, with none of the impacted morbidity of *Dick Tracy*; and, on more than one occasion, it veered towards farce, the farce of the theater, rather than of sheer circumstantial extremity, as in Gould's creation. Yet, stylistically, the very handsomeness and dispatch of Will Gould's drawing, brought into focus the contrast between his work and Chester's; the contrast between the smart undergraduate who takes the jetliner, and the Indiana dairy farmer who essays to duplicate the Wright Brothers in the angular accomplishment of his home-built contraption. Will Gould's vocabulary, dramatic and visual, was there, intact; as was his drawing vocabulary, which made no bones about the identification of style and overall attitude. And it abounded in appeals to the nostalgia of readers whose tastes in melodrama had been nursed by Sax Rohmer, Sir Arthur Conan Doyle, and John Buchan: the romantic (in the contemporary sense) imagination, pre-packaged, as it were, with a gleeful, coltish, and, at the same time, prodigally ingenious, homage to various movies; the engaging outlandishness of on-again-off-again Inspector Scott's Haroun-al-Raschid disguises; and a repertory of villains culled from *The Great Gabbo* (a mob leader who is a side-tracked ventriloquist) and London fellow-fog razzmatazz — the epic sequence, "the Song of the Flame," which featured oriental heavies, a hard-luck Cockney lawyer, and a mysterious old bird who favored Mandarin outfits and a patch over one eye). Such traditional echoes cohabited a little oddly with the breezy élan of Gould's style; yet, essentially, *Red Barry* was a boy's-book fantasy, attested by the central position held by Red's boy-satellite, Ouchy McGouchy, and his kid-vigilante unit, the "Terrible Three." Will Gould's very appreciable inventive power and capacity (let alone obvious intention) to charm prevented the elegant aircraft of his strip, though, from reaching firm ground as often as it should have. There is a kind of frivolity about it which is somewhat heady, even for a '30s strip, and which steers it too often into ditherish over-complications and tangents; the possible motto of which is that flying by the seat of one's pants too often can have negative consequences for pants and plane both.

In contrast with all of these works, in varying degrees, *Dick Tracy* proposed a *new* standard of precision, a rediscovery of precision, such as only those artists, major and minor, who are entitled to be taken with full seriousness, ever deal with. Like Aubrey Beardsley and Max Beerbom, he insists on presenting the terms and figures of darkness in the imagery of a superhuman, murderous daylight, the language of impeccable identification. No wonder his "stories," those doom-headed progressions, are, as Coulton Waugh perceived, weak in suspense. Did any comic strip artist ever evince less interest in ambiguity and nuance, the reverberant chord of suggestion? He is as explicit about mystery as Japanese theater. This is what brings him into such constant account, murderous cozening of the abstract. When he introduced the Invisible with the Blank, in 1938, the result resembled Maxwell Grant's *Shadow*, executed by Magritte (and was, indeed, a shy at Dick Tracy's most formidable competitors of the '30s, the masked avengers of the pulps). Gould's work is rich in references to other comic strips, as well as to the theater, apropos of which he loads his strip, on occasion, with loving-envious derision. Only one so affianced to the explicit could deal as he dealt with the new, minimal, cabaret style of comic strips like *Peanuts*, *B.C.*, and *Momma*, in the creations of Vera Alldid, Sparkle Plenty's cartoonist husband: *Sawdust*, and the *Invisible Tribe.* And by the same token, the most adroit jibes at *Dick Tracy* occurred in the early years of what was then the most acute parody of the strip among the multitude of such: Al Capp's Fearless Fosdick, when Fosdick is challenged by crooks like Anyface and the (murderous) Chippendale chair, who are inhumanly elusive. Capp's rapport with Gould — the gut-bond of the parodist and his subject — lay, I think, in their common aptitude, most manifest in their earliest work, for a desperate jugglery of melodrama and its burlesque opposite.

The image was his recurrent unit of continuity in *the Dick Tracy* 1933-9 strips (following which, the image began to assume a very different sort of priority). He was guided, in those days, by the knowledge, which he never outgrew but later became too old and/or tired to sustain, that design is actually the approximation of design, the *movement toward* its own completion. Therefore, in those early mid-'30s *Dick Tracy* strips, the reader is regaled with a succession of marvelous masks, eloquent in both their delicacy and their suggestive intensity, which is augmented in part by Gould's lingering ungainliness and stolidity in their portrayal. On their own terms, — terms which often seem all-but-immobilizing — the '30s faces are marvels of expressive execution, fortified by Gould's command of line and space, at once austere and lively, producing weddings of decorum and brutality that are more articulately grotesque than anything he came up with from the false-face '40s onward. The cold ferret-face of Bookie Joe; the razor-edge lips and diamond-drill eyes of Dan Micelli/Mizell (a name change, by the way, which occurred halfway through his appearance in 1932 — undoubtedly as the result of emphatic elbow-work by Italian-American lobbies, which had wedged a disclaimer into *Scarface*); the cruel carp-face of "Cut" Famon, the dissolute ex-politico's visage of "Whip" Chute, the jewel thief; the effete camp-Byron kisser of Karpse, the *sub rosa* poison gas manufacturer. Or the taunting Marlene Dietrich mask of Marro, Karpse's ex-mistress; the implacable hatchet-face of Black Pearl; the set, feral baboon countenance of Edward Numeroh's predatory mother. The very doubtful maneuverability of such features, their hint of the mask, only throws into sharpened relief the vein of authentic expression which Gould is able to work through them: faces as formalized as the masks of Noh drama, and with no less devout observance of consistent distance from their audience. And all assembled, as it were, from the scars and detritus of many a beginners' class in Design. The most rudimentary signals of "individuality" — sacs under the eyes, crow's feet and mouth-lines, liver-lips — all the apparently over-familiar ideographs of the human face and its emotions — were turned into imprimaturs of genuine, repeatedly fascinating expression, by Gould's own crass, mordant dexterous poetry of near-caricature; and the dark overtone which he realized from playing the aspects of naturalism to wit in a thin smiles' breadth of self-parody; milking this propinquity, not for cowardly laughter, but for the thrilling, giddying recognition of fantasy-as-potential in the very midst of fact. When you encounter a sudden, deliciously evocative image like the last panel of the November 18, 1937 strip — the hunchback Arthur Maylic, with his fragile, vicious, bespectacled face, bowler hat and fishhook-curved black overcoat, standing by his glistening car on a gray, night-time street — this, following a three-panel suite of silhouetting, black-and-white architectural blocking, lithe, warring postures — justifiably you may feel that it was just such style for which Fritz Lang was aiming in *M*, *Spies*, or *Hangmen also Die*. It is authentic conjuration.

I think that Gould recognized early on the importance of a well-bridled willfulness to his art; as well as the importance of formalism to his drawing, and the way in which, in its always somewhat mechanical aspect, this could be used, initially to control, and (later on, especially during the last decades) to ratify, his inclinations to outrageousness and manipulativeness. You can see these qualities in their disassembled state — gradually assembling, though, like the accelerating convention of metal filings under a magnet — in the largely awful "comic" forays which he performed during the mid-'20s, as comic-strip artist for Hearst's *Evening Journal* (and carried for a time, with slightly better success, since he was working within the stylized tough-professional milieu of *Dick Tracy*, in the Sunday *Daily News* bottom-page strip, *Cigarette Sadie*). Of the Heart strips, *The Radio Lanes* flowered during the short-wave fervor which overcame numerous households during the 1925-8 period, and was saluted by Segar's Mr. and Mrs. Sappo: a jejune gag strip which was puppy-fed an eye-dropper of "suspense" by father investing in an anti-static device.

Fillum Fables, the longer-running of his two strips for the *Evening Journal*, may, with a firm grip on one's patience and nose, be read with more interest. It had been assigned as a ringer for *Minute*

Movies, the long-running work of Ed Wheelan: a boisterous, unflaggingly amiable strip that plastered with its St. Bernard-like affections the silent films of Wheelan's doting, boyish fantasies. Their authentic fun came from the miniature glamour and bubbling energy with which Wheelan always seemed to be not so much parodying as adapting idiomatic extravaganzas and crisp imagery of his models. There is decorum to his puppetry which he shares with Harry Hershfield, of *Desperate Desmond*: a trimly-shaded prettiness, echoing the makeup and lighting of 1920's movies, which counterparts the romping, expostulating pep: heads aspray with perspiration-drops like fugitive dandelion-fuzz; dialogue balloons peppered with exclamation points; yet, never compromising the solidity of the little figures. I imagine Wheelan as looking like the dumpling-faced chief comedian Fuller Phunn (all roles were enacted, and specifically delegated via irised "introductory shots" to a repertory company that also featured Ralph McSneer, Archibald, Clubb, and the wonderfully-named portrayer of dangerous older women, Blanche Rouge).

I need not strain the imagination to believe that this consistently genial and effusive man experienced the most devastating anger of his life on viewing the replacement of his strip: not simply because it *had* been replaced, and with a laborious mimicry of his drawing style, at that; but, because of what must have impressed him as the perversion, the graceless and ungracious parody, of the love which he had accorded his *Minute Movies* as conveyances for his Pickwickian muse.

Fillum Fables seems now, as it must have then — to all not automatically and absolutely tickled by the prospect of men wearing eye makeup — singularly joyless, graceless, raspingly mechanical (its slapstick rhythm suggest the cranking of a Model T on a midnight winter road) assault upon, rather than parody or burlesque of, rather than any representation, informed by warm, if laughing empathy of, silent films and farce-melodrama in general. In a typical hilarity, from 1924, a couple visiting some desert real estate are attacked by bandits who knock out the husband's teeth with a rock flung from their airplane. As the fun accelerates, the wife, repelled by his gummy aspect, elopes with a neighboring sheik (of the hair, rather than tank-oil species) in the latter's automobile. In the thigh-slapping, chaw-swallowing climax, their automobile promptly slaughters a prized circus elephant. The elephantine damages for this disaster financially decimate the swain, of course, and send the wife back to her no-longer-toothy but still toothsomely-moneyed husband.

There is small point, however, in prolonged vituperative binges on what is already self-indicted as a ponderous and scabrous harlequinade. The immediately interesting factor, the complication and small but provocative enigma of it all is, that, to be sure, what I have just recounted is a possible, potential, *Dick Tracy* plot; with its heavy-knuckled manipulation, its impromptu-seeming, Jove-delivered disaster, its whimsically (when at all) motivated spasms of cupidity, sentiment, fear. Over the succeeding several years of *Fillum Fables'* career, we can see Gould accommodating himself, and his strip, more and more to a 60%-serious melodramatic concoction that virtually discards even the previous token shies at Wheelan's perky, decorative burlesque imagery. What I sense of the implicit attitude in those earliest Fillum flim flams is an ambivalence — "scornful wonder" may suit best — on Gould's part for not only burlesque but theater itself; which was carried on into the sometimes amusing, but monumentally misaimed parody of Vitamin Flintheart (a parody of one of the most knowing, and saddest, of self-parodists: the aging Barrymore), or, in the early '40s *Dick Tracy* tale of the twin brothers who are murderous stage rivals. There is a near-Gopher Prairie mixture of incredulity, fascination, and the deepest, envious possessiveness toward the stage's most brutal extravagances and contrivances, principally, I think, as demonstrated in his characters' haphazardly motivated, or non-motivated, sallies and frolic. He was a man of limited emotional range, and still more limited understanding of, or curiosity about (which would certainly have led to more plausible and interesting *inventions* of emotion), human feelings in general. I think further, that he valued burlesque not, as did Wheelan, as the Pegasus of his boyish forays, but as the plausible instrument of his own willfulness, and his full-hearted identification with the comic strip's resources of power. Alone among the creators of police-procedural strips, Gould yoked burlesque and near-fantasy ("near" at its best, that is: it was *Fillum Fables* all over again when he tried hauling in Junior's Moon Maid and her moon-calfish sci-fi retinue behind his chariot) to the proseyprobable, yet also erotically vivid style which was to become a famous if seldom openly acknowledged convention *in its own right*: therefore, a vehicle and agent of numerous other styles and conventions. I don't know of many comic strips of which the manifest imagination is so tightly defined, so firmly *anchored*, as in *Dick Tracy*. And this sense of his imagination's own terms enabled Gould, as it had Conan Doyle, his preceptor, to conduct Tracy, and us, through the varying "locales" of other genre conventions. Gould, with an instinct for the *spectacle* aspects of the comic strip, always permits us to feel that, through his deft, hard-headed, engineer's or architect's explicitness, we are actually discovering these genres for the first time, even when what he does is not so very successful, so imaginatively bracing or persuasive. Science fiction, as in the moonshine episode referred to above; the western, in Tracy's pursuit, with the Indian sleuth Yellow Pony, of Cutie Diamond and Boris Arson; a return to the *Fillum Fables* Lon Chaney razzle-dazzle, done "straight" this time, in the opus of Jerome Trohs, the midget racketeer, and his towering, page-boy blonde Big Momma (a couple aimed, I always thought, by the indefatigable Editor of the Universe, to be reconciled in a series of skits by Stiller and Meara); and once, at least, Gothic: in that 1939 midsummer fugue when Tess Trueheart, after an 8-years' bender of true-heartedness designed to make Little Annie Rooney kick Zero, gave the seismograph of Tracy's life a few salutary wobbles by eloping with the aging ex-ballplayer-millionaire, Edward Nuremoh (whose name, yes, is to be read backwards). In the course of her antic haymaking, Tess met Nuremoh's mama, her face set as though in constant watch for scurrying small game; his hatchet-chinned, flinty-benign aunt: and his nitwit cousin, who was approximately four feet tall, giggled a great deal, and sported an immense Ascot tie stolen from either of the Katzenjammer Kids. The tour of Brönte Heights was conducted in a splurge of that kind of flash-powder-and-glycerin handsomeness once associated with what were called "women's magazine" illustrations; and, appreciably less engaging, a household staff, bowing to the beat, and in full, dusty uniform, of missing-will-chicanery clichés.

Gould's comic strip was *about* art in the form of mulish, eccentric enterprise, the informing force and, as it were, demon of

Dick Tracy. Whereas the readers of *Radio Patrol* and *Dan Dunn* were expected to be wowed by the authoritative competence of the police mechanism, they were allured, in *Dick Tracy*, by the pragmatic craft, combined with loner's resourcefulness, of detective and crook — or, in truth, crook leaders — alike. The *skilled* amateur, his various skills ignited by a passion not so distant from the imperious lusts and furies of Jacobean melodrama. I can remember few police strips — make that, none — with less sense of the police department as a corporate unit. It was merely the machine of which Tracy, the true priest of justice, availed himself: and Tracy was an avowed avenger from September 22, 1931, when he took an oath of retribution against Big Boy, who had murdered his prospective father-in-law, temporarily deranged Mrs. Trueheart, and kidnapped — and, implicitly, raped — Tess. Tracy's world swarmed ever since with go-it-aloners: individuals willing, lusting to take into their own hands not only the law — which was the least of it — but, all the available power and experience of the world. The gang bosses themselves were overreaching, capricious spirits. They are like the rebellious sons of a family that the gang embodies, and which they wind up abolishing: Karpse, in 1938, by exterminating his clamoring, greedy associates with the poison gas in the manufacture of which they collaborated; Number One, of the Purple Cross Gang, with sub-machine gun in an abandoned garage, February 3, 1937; in a gruesomely concise rendition of St. Valentine's Day, some years before. They are also, on occasion, capricious farceurs, whose flaring whimsies Gould observes through the methodical - — almost drawling, at times, in the manner of Mark Twains' "How to Tell a Ghost Story" — tempo, which highlights their zaniest excursions: the midget assassin escaping on the back of his Great Dane, silhouetted on a totally inactive city street; Little Face Finney, setting afire a dangerous, tell-tale monogrammed pocket handkerchief, still in the pocket of its bumbling owner; the Black Pearl playfully raking Tracy's face with an oriental metal cat-claw. All such gestures, gratuitous and isolated — for the loose, chronicle-paced rigging of Gould's plots allowed for numerous such vignettes — receive a kind of romantic swelling from Gould's close-reined, sober sides focusing on wildcat personalities, or at least, the capricious drives which are often the major fuel-sources of personality. Again, it is the allure of caricature, showing itself — at Gould's best — as a kind of privileged, i.e. by his character's irrationality— *imitation* of comic strip behavior.

The cliché attending such fantastical-plausible work as Gould's is, as a rule, that he "created his own world." A phrase I think particularly subject to stringent modification in *Dick Tracy's* case; in which the world usually portrayed was spectacularly molecular, unstable, and subject to moment-to-moment upheaval. Where is the public that supposedly embodies the issue of priority in Tracy's vendetta with the underworld? You never feel even that the city has an autonomous existence outside of its function as a perennial sitting duck for the bank robbers, kidnappers, narcotics dealers, and counterfeiters. Gould's usual feebleness at establishing any personality not demonic, his bent for caricature and that near-grotesquerie, and his corresponding impatience with, and inaptitude for, any very shaded characterization, lends a common vapid primness to his "normal" characters speech and bearing; except when, like Tracy, they vengefully, or with pious zeal, take up arms against the crooks themselves. There is, in truth, very meager feeling indeed for the law as an agency of justice, or even much in the way of order. Tracy, as a result, seeming like a loner, even amidst the ever-more-sophisticated police apparatus; Pat Patton being little more than an avatar, a two-legged Sandy, at best, and a pants-dropping Panza at worst. The "personalities," especially the subordinates, in *Dick Tracy* are transparent vessels waiting for the boiling wine of Gould's energy to lend them scarlet vividness (the counterpoint of this inertia, and the arresting razzmarazz of plotting, fingering, exchanging fire, again brings to mind the Japanese theater, in which such contrast is accepted, and — as with Gould — implicit in the ritual nature of the dram). The recurrent heroes in *Dick Tracy* include the engineers who, in 1938, hand over their diesel locomotive, in order to accomplish the bringing to bay of pop-eyed, unshaven, grimacing JoJo Nidle. Or the intern who bops a charging Purple Cross member, intent on delivering *coup de grace* to the battered Jim Trailer. Or the white-haired mother of the Scotland Yard inspector, paralyzed by a bullet of Steve the Tramp and /or Larceny Lu; who tracks them down, her son's service revolver poised, or some Dickens-raising mayhem which costs Steve a leg and an eye.

What Chester Gould's minimally detailed, non-entity-peopled world manages to convey is an image of crime as a scourge against nature itself, rather than any set of laws or any local principalities. There is in Gould's work through some four decades, an utter minimum of dialogue between evil and good, or any personalities to make such an exchange volatile and persuasive. He is image-oriented first to last, and rehabilitation, for instance, is realized by a corresponding change in image. "Lips" Manlis shaves his mustache and sideburns, showers, and emerges as patrolman (Tracy as sponsor) Bob Honor. On the other hand, the renegade son of a decent old cop carries a birthmark (it's extraordinary to note how vivid this seems, as against the wax work oddities of the later decades' figures) which may be an "acquired-hereditary" trait from Cain. Gould's image-processions convey a moral anarchy very different indeed from that of Harold Gray — a man embodying, whatever his abrasive eccentricities of authentic morality and, as the progression of *Little Orphan Annie* informs me, moral courage. But the will to retain order, to cling to something, however fast-expiring and barely discernible, of civilization, which makes so much of *Little Orphan Annie* quietly poignant and quietly chilling, has no place amid the sanguinary gusto of *Dick Tracy*, the flash-fires of greed and treachery and vengeance. The pestilent atmosphere, acrawl with erratic undertakings, with skills tuned awry, which Chester Gould's perverse craft midwifes, is a lineal heir of Webster and Ford, as is the spasmodic, half-blundering rhythms of the actions, the sense of stumbling through a miasma, which even his masterminds, cop and crook, exhibit. What would in any neutral context, be excruciating beyond reclaim, is in fact gratifying and reassuring: basically because the humor is that of the battlefield or the plague-smitten community, its very crudity and funkiness is a relief. Second, because of our instinct of gratitude to Gould for merely recognizing the need for such humor: for doing his duty, and at the same time realizing (as an escapade from his ceremonial cops-robbers limitation) a return to his *Fillum Fables* burlesque formula. And the routine appearances of the Plentys reassured the readers, I should surmise, on another score: that of the limitations of a formula (Gould's drawing) which was capable of providing such horrors within its usual boundaries. The drawing medium was, for these fandangos, definitive; as it could not have been in the case of any of Gould's rivals, even the effervescent Will, whose tone was that of a *wit,* to which Chester never aspired; so that the humor was smoothly incorporated under the aegis of the style, in a way (literary, basically) that it never was in Chester's case.

The apparatus of the Plentys' unhygienic fripperies is, to be sure, the formula, in this ongoing spectacle of nature reversed and violated, of nature avenging herself, of nature becoming the attacker of her attackers, whether though the retaliations of former allies and henchmen, or through more direct agencies. Gould, in fact, invoked natural setting in contrast with criminal apparatuses set up within them in numerous episodes. One of the earliest during August of 1932, when Tracy, on vacation, exposed the scheming fiancé (drug dealer and would-be killer) of Tess's friend; the wildcat-cordoned rustic hideaway of Cute Diamond; and, the poison gas plant of Karpse, amid the mountain greenery. All such, fairly certain, according to the recommendations of Sherlock Holmes, about the likelihood of rural quiet as a cover for criminality.

Yet, generally, the violation and perversion of nature which the crooks in *Dick Tracy* embody, is to be found in the drawing: the repression of the rigid patterning, the tightly braced bodies; the compulsive passion of the contorted faces, the angular, spasmodic gestures. The design itself, in other words, represents an affront to nature that she is demonstrated as avenging again and again; either through the retaliation of the associates (the midget's Amazon consort scalding him to death; Krome, the toy-maker, executing his doublecrossing mistress under a hairdryer) or, through some of the most ferociously attenuated death sequences, the most broodingly exact depictions of decay and death agony depicted in any comic strip. Gould's competitors, expert at slam-bang violence as they might have been, had nothing on him for the portrayal of stage-by-stage agony and shred-by shred relinquishing of that compact imagery which their drawing accorded them. Little Face losing his ears to frostbite, and the blackened flesh of his neck mocking its grotesque expanse; the lethal toy-maker, Krome, dying in a doorway, huddled, the *risus sardonicus* which had imprinted his acts during his life, fringed with dainty icicles as it forms on his lips. Laffy, his ribald, freckled face sunken to prisoner-of-war abjectness through the results of lockjaw. A savage mockery of his own design is here, in the decorative magic which Chester accords the violation of his own emblematic patterns, the sacrifice as it were of his gift to the retributive demand of nature. And the most terrible aspect of his studies in attrition, the graphic violence — that is, the erotic fandangos which he would compose from such violence — was, the service to which Gould put his decoration: the Hogarthian minuteness plus the elegance of an unfrocked fashion designer, and the absence of any compassion are, in fact, the essential ingredients of that awe that his graphic force thrusts upon us. And yet, does this suggest that such emotional attributes are irrelevant, in all drawing, to the step-by-step *autonomous* creation of emotion, the erection of feeling, that Goya, as well as Gould, knew could be evoked through "ruthless" caricature?

Style seems to have carried the day during the later metamorphoses of *Dick Tracy* (late '50s through '60s); during which, while his contemporaries corseted their drawing with ever-more-drastic bids for illustration-like literal felicity, Chester Gould steered his drawing into ever more radically expressionistic, more flagrantly decorative exhibitions. He reverts also, of course, to decoration in his characters. The criminal all-stars, which have in the interim receded from at least demonic personalities, to names around which a figure — not even, with the occasional (rare) exception of someone like Flattoo's brother, Blowtop, a "personality" but an emblem, a comic tag, the final alienation of criminals into "freaks" with which the normal can regale themselves. Yet, not quite, perhaps — for these figures have still some of the now near-grotesque impressiveness of the old Herod and Pilate masks, in the medieval mystery plays. And Gould's viewpoint, which might be called medieval-by-way-of-Jacobean, is almost unique even among his fellows, in his capacity for *assuming* so much about the nature of evil; that as with all mythologies, once the assumptions had cooled, he was fully equipped to people his space with lesser (devil) deities. Alfred Andriola, of *Kerry Drake* (Gould's most fervid, and sadistic, competitor—coolly sadistic, in contrast with Gould's stormy blow-offs of violence) lagged sadly behind Gould. Andriola seems to be constantly striving for a style, for Gould's secret. Whereas, Gould, for those with short memories, seems to have "had" his style, as was remarked by Henry James, congenitally. He was, in any case, the most gallant artist, well-seconded by Dick Moores of *Gasoline Alley*, for defiantly maintaining the vitality of style — if not, past a certain point, content — and compositional elegance, against the garret-like space accorded them with increasing, absurdly both frivolous and leaching contempt, by distributors and retailers proffering themselves as "editors." Nothing — a "good detective strip" — can follow. To regard the "continuation" of *Dick Tracy* as one with *Dick Tracy* is merely — easily, to be sure — to confuse the genre with a brilliant, well-nigh unique, off-branch.

THAT'S THE FELLOW, ALL RIGHT- HE HELD ME UP IN MY STORE
YEP, THAT'S THE BIRD THAT STUCK UP MY FILLING STATION.
HE'S THE MAN, ALL RIGHT THAT HI-JACKED MY DRUG STORE FOR FIFTY DOLLARS
THAT'S THE BIRD.
1-18
AND HERE'S THE MONEY, GENTLEMEN THAT WAS RECOVERED FROM THE "25" GANG. SUPPOSE WE PRO-RATE IT ACCORDING TO EACH OF YOUR LOSSES?
GREAT!
FINE.
ACCORDING TO MY FIGURING THIS WILL RETURN TO EACH OF YOU ABOUT 98% OF YOUR MONEY
THAT'S RIGHT.
Copyright, 1934, by News Syndicate Co., Inc., Reg. U. S. Pat. Off
GENTLEMEN, I SUGGEST THAT WE TAKE JUST 90% -AND CONTRIBUTE THE REMAINING 8% EACH TOWARD BUYING THIS YOUNG TEN-YEAR-OLD-WELL.. SAY A NEW BICYCLE, EH?
GREAT.
WONDERFUL
CHESTER GOULD
YOUR MOUTHPIECE, SPALDONI, IS HERE TO SEE YOU, JIMMY.
COME ON IN, SPALDONI.
1-19
WELL, DETECTIVE, WHAT ARE YOU WAITING FOR? WE WANT TO BE ALONE.
NOT A CHANCE, SPALDONI! I NEVER TRUSTED A SHYSTER LAWYER AND A CROOK TO-GETHER IN MY LIFE. SIT DOWN!
JIM-YOUR FATHER HAS REFUSED TO FINANCE YOUR LEGAL FIGHT. HE HAS DISCLAIMED ANY INTEREST IN YOUR CASE AND WILL HAVE NOTHING TO DO WITH YOU.
WELL-WHAT OF IT? WHAT DOES THAT MEAN?
Copyright, 1934, by News Syndicate Co., Inc., Reg. U. S. Pat. Off
I'LL TELL YOU WHAT IT MEANS! IT MEANS THIS SHYSTER ISN'T GOING TO MAKE ANY DOUGH OUT OF THIS CASE AND IT MEANS YOU'RE GOING TO THE PEN FOR TWENTY YEARS! ADD THAT UP, WISE GUYS.
CHESTER GOULD
TRACY-I'VE GOT NEWS-BIG NEWS!
YEAH?
1-20
THERE WAS A GOODLOOKING GAL OUT THERE IN THE HALL ASKING IF JIMMY WHITE WAS HERE. I SAID YES AND SHE ASKED TO SEE THE CHIEF. MUST BE ONE OF JIMMY WHITE'S SWEETHEARTS.
LET'S SEE.
LOOK! THERE SHE IS NOW.. IN THE CHIEF'S OFFICE!
MUST BE WHITE'S MOLL ALL RIGHT.
Copyright, 1934, by News Syndicate Co., Inc., Reg. U. S. Pat. Off
WHY, CHIEF BRANDON-DON'T YOU KNOW ME?
ER... ...UM.. ..ER..A..
CHESTER GOULD
WHO IS THIS GIRL?

DICK TRACY
by CHESTER GOULD
WHY, JEAN PENFIELD! I HAVEN'T SEEN YOU SINCE THE NIGHT YOUR FATHER PUT MY NAME UP FOR CHIEF OF POLICE.
IT HAS BEEN A LONG TIME - HASN'T IT? MY, YOU'RE LOOKING FINE, CHIEF.
YES, JEAN, YOUR FATHER AND I WERE THE BEST OF FRIENDS IN OUR BOYHOOD DAYS AND... THE BITTEREST OF RIVALS TOO, WHEN WE WERE ON THE FOOTBALL TEAM AT YALE. I HAVEN'T SEEN HIM FOR A LONG TIME, BUT ANYTHING I CAN DO FOR HIS CHARMING DAUGHTER.. I WILL.
THAT'S VERY SWEET OF YOU, MR. BRANDON.. YOU SEE I'M WRITING A BOOK AND..
..AND YOU WANT TO MAKE A CLOSE-UP STUDY OF US COPPERS SO YOUR CHARACTERS WILL BE AUTHENTIC?
NO, YOU'RE WRONG.. I'M NOT STUDYING COPPERS TODAY, THANK YOU.. I'M STUDYING CRIMINALS AND I'D LIKE VERY MUCH TO TALK TO THIS JIMMY WHITE, THE HEAD OF THE "25" GANG THAT YOUR EXCELLENT POLICE FORCE RECENTLY CRUSHED.
OH.. SO THAT'S IT?
AND HERE IS JUST THE GENTLEMAN TO ESCORT YOU TO MR. WHITE'S PRIVATE SUITE. TRACY, I WANT YOU TO MEET MISS JEAN PENFIELD, DAUGHTER OF AN OLD FRIEND OF MINE WHO IS ABOUT TO BECOME A PROUD AUTHOR.
I CAN IMAGINE HOW BORING IT MUST BE TO ESCORT A BUDDING YOUNG AUTHORESS ABOUT YOUR JAILHOUSE, MR. TRACY, BUT I...
DO I REALLY LOOK AS SAD AS THAT? LISTEN, MISS PENFIELD, THIS WOODEN FACE ACT GETS TO BE A HABIT WITH US DETECTIVES. DON'T LET IT FOOL YOU. WELL, HERE WE ARE.
OH, HELLO, SPALDONI - I DIDN'T KNOW YOU WERE HERE. MISS PENFIELD, THIS IS MR SPALDONI, JIMMY WHITE'S LAWYER.
HOW DO YOU DO.
BUT YOU SURELY CAN'T HAVE ANY OBJECTION TO MISS PENFIELD TALKING WITH JIMMY.
SHE MAY TALK TO HIM ONLY IN MY PRESENCE. SHE MIGHT ASK HIM QUESTIONS I WOULDN'T WANT HIM TO ANSWER.
JIM - THIS IS MISS PENFIELD, A WRITER. SHE WANTS TO TALK TO YOU.
OH, SHE DOES, EH.. WHO IS... OH—
WHY YOU LITTLE DOUBLE-CROSSING @#!! I REMEMBER YOU... YOU'RE —
HEY-STOP IT!
I'M NOT HURT.
I WAS IN A NIGHT CLUB WITH BIG BOY ONE NIGHT WHEN THIS DAME INTERVIEWED HIM AND NEXT DAY THE COPS RAIDED HIS DUMP... YOU'RE A SQUEALER, THAT'S WHAT YOU ARE... A STOOL PIGEON.. GET OUT OF HERE!
TAKE IT EASY, WHITE.
YES, I DID INTERVIEW BIG BOY ONCE... A FRIEND OF MINE ARRANGED THE MEETING.. I WANTED FIRST HAND INFORMATION FOR MY BOOK... AND IT SO HAPPENED HIS APARTMENT WAS RAIDED NEXT DAY - BUT IT WASN'T MY FAULT.. I'M NOT SQUEALING ON ANYONE... I SWEAR IT.
IT'S O.K. MISS PENFIELD, I'M SORRY THIS HAPPENED.
SPALDONI, AS COUNSEL FOR WHITE, YOU'D BETTER TELL HIM TO KEEP HIS HANDS WHERE THEY BELONG OR I'LL PERSONALLY TAKE A HAND IN BREAKING HIS PIPE-STEM NECK.
AND AS FOR YOU, DETECTIVE - I FEAR THAT SOME DAY YOUR MOST DELIGHTFUL LADY FRIENDS WILL GET YOU INTO A VERY GREAT AMOUNT OF TROUBLE.
Copyright, 1934, by News Syndicate Co., Inc. Reg. U. S. Pat. Off.

SO YOU DIDN'T RECOGNIZE ME WHEN I CAME IN, CHIEF BRANDON?
JEAN PENFIELD - I CAN STILL HARDLY BELIEVE IT'S YOU.
1-22
I WAS BEST MAN AT YOUR FATHER'S WEDDING MANY YEARS AGO. AND YOU MUST REMEMBER THAT I HAVEN'T SEEN YOU SINCE YOU WERE JUST A CHILD.
WELL, I LIKE THAT! AS IF IT HAD BEEN YEARS AND YEARS.
MISS PENFIELD, THIS IS PAT PATTON, MY ASSISTANT. PAT, MEET MISS JEAN PENFIELD, BUDDING YOUNG AUTHOR OF UNDERWORLD BOOKS.
PLEASED TO MEET YOU.
Copyright, 1934, by News Syndicate Co., Inc., Reg. U. S. Pat. Off.
GEE, MISS PENFIELD, DO YOU REALLY WRITE UNDERWORLD BOOKS?
DETECTIVE TRACY IS MUCH TOO COMPLIMENTARY. YOU SEE, I'M JUST WRITING MY FIRST BOOK AND I MAY NEED SOME HELP BEFORE I'M THROUGH.
CHESTER GOULD
YOU SEE, MR. TRACY, THE BOOK I'M WRITING IS AN EXPOSE OF THE UNDERWORLD POLITICO COMBINE AND IF IT IS TO BE AUTHENTIC I SIMPLY MUST GET MY INFORMATION FIRST HAND.
BUT I TELL YOU, MISS PENFIELD - JIMMY WHITE WON'T TALK TO YOU
1-23
WON'T YOU PLEASE TAKE ME BACK TO HIS CELL ONCE MORE? I'M SURE I CAN GET HIM TO TALK TO ME.. PUL-EESE!
OKAY. BUT YOU MUST WATCH OUT FOR THAT FELLOW..HE'S A BAD NUMBER.
WHAT! ARE YOU HERE AGAIN?
NOW JIMMY - DON'T BE LIKE THAT.
SEE - WHAT DID I TELL YOU?
Copyright, 1934, by News Syndicate Co., Inc., Reg. U. S. Pat. Off.
PLEASE DO ME ONE FAVOR, DETECTIVE. GO AWAY AND LET ME TALK TO HIM... I'LL BE RESPONSIBLE FOR THE CONSEQUENCES.
OKAY, BUT KEEP YOUR EYES OPEN.
CHESTER GOULD
WHY SHOULD I TALK TO YOU - AND GIVE YOU ANY INFORMATION FOR A BOOK? I NEVER TRUSTED A DAME IN MY LIFE.
BUT JIMMY - YOU'D BE DOING ME SUCH A BIG FAVOR.
1-24
HA! DOING YOU A BIG FAVOR? THAT'S RICH! WHY SHOULD I DO YOU ANY FAVORS?
AH - JIMMEE!
WHAT COULD YOU EVER DO FOR ME, EH? WHAT COULD YOU DO FOR ME?
WHAT COULD I DO FOR YOU? I'LL TELL YOU- ...LISTEN... SH...
Copyright, 1934, by News Syndicate Co., Inc., Reg. U. S. Pat. Off.
CHIEF - I THINK WE'RE LETTING A CUTE SKIRT PUT SOMETHING OVER ON US. I DON'T QUITE LIKE THE IDEA OF THIS PENFIELD GIRL CHINNING WITH WHITE.
TRACY, THAT GIRL'S ABSOLUTELY O.K. WHY, I'VE KNOWN HER FATHER FOR YEARS.
CHESTER GOULD

YES, MISS PENFIELD- WHAT CAN I DO FOR YOU?
I TALKED WITH JIMMY WHITE YESTERDAY, MR. SPALDONI, AND YOU, BEING HIS ATTORNEY, HE ADVISED ME TO COME AND SEE YOU.
YES?
I UNDERSTAND SINCE JIMMY'S TROUBLE HIS FATHER HAS DISOWNED HIM AND HAS EVEN REFUSED TO PUT UP ANY BAIL MONEY FOR HIS RELEASE.
THAT'S CORRECT. HIS BOND WAS SET AT TWENTY THOUSAND DOLLARS. AND SO FAR IT HAS NOT BEEN PROCURED.
STRANGELY ENOUGH TOO, I HAVE TWENTY THOUSAND DOLLARS THAT I WOULD..ER. BE DELIGHTED TO LEND AS BAIL MONEY IN EXCHANGE FOR..ER.
1-25
Copyright, 1934, by News Syndicate Co., Inc., Reg. U.S. Pat. Off.
IN EXCHANGE FOR WHAT?
THAT'S BETWEEN MYSELF AND JIMMY- MR. SPALDONI, ISN'T IT ENOUGH THAT I'M WILLING TO PUT UP THE MONEY?
CHESTER GOULD
OH, HELLO SPALDONI- YOU'RE DOWN BRIGHT AND EARLY FOR A CONFERENCE WITH YOUR CLIENT, I SEE.
YOUR POWERS OF DEDUCTION ARE TREMENDOUS, DETECTIVE.
1-26
LISTEN KID - I'VE GOT GREAT NEWS FOR YOU! THIS PENFIELD WOMAN HAS AGREED TO PUT UP A TWENTY GRAND BOND FOR YOUR RELEASE. SHE'S GETTING SOFT IN THE HEAD, I GUESS.
OH YEAH? LISTEN, YOU'RE THE ONE THAT'S GETTING SOFT IN THE HEAD, SPALDONI! IN THE FIRST PLACE WHY WOULD SHE BE THAT INTERESTED IN ME AND WHERE WOULD A DAME LIKE SHE GET TWENTY GRAND?
HELLO-THE BANK? OH, IS THIS YOU GEORGE? LISTEN, DRAW TWENTY THOUSAND DOLLARS OUT OF MY ACCOUNT AND HAVE IT READY FOR ME IN ABOUT AN HOUR. I'LL DROP BY.
JEAN PENFIELD- AUTHOR! I FEAR, DEAR LADY, YOUR AMBITIONS ARE GOING TO TAKE YOU TOO FAR!
1-27
WELL, YOU'RE RIGHT ON TIME.
THIS ENVELOPE CONTAINS EXACTLY TWENTY THOUSAND DOLLARS-THE AMOUNT NECESSARY FOR JIMMY'S BOND. ALL I ASK IS A RECEIPT.
WHERE SHALL WE COME AFTER HIS RELEASE?
COME TO THE COFFEE SHOP OF THE STAR HOTEL. I'LL BE THERE AT TWELVE-THIRTY HAVING LUNCH.
TWENTY THOUSAND DOLLARS SHE RISKS JUST FOR A CHANCE TO INTERVIEW BIG BAD JIMMY WHITE! SHE DOESN'T KNOW THAT I KNOW THAT'S WHAT SHE WANTS TO DO -BUT I DO. AND, OH BOY! WHAT AN INTERVIEW SHE'S GOING TO GET!
CHESTER GOULD
Copyright, 1934, by News Syndicate Co., Inc., Reg. U.S. Pat. Off.

DICK TRACY
By Chester Gould
YEAH- YOU'RE BAILED OUT
GEE, SPALDONI, I CAN'T BELIEVE IT!
YEP - I'M GETTING OUT ON BOND, DETECTIVE. GUESS AFTER MY OLD MAN THREW ME OVER- YOU FIGURED I'D BE IN THIS DUMP FOR- EVER, EH?
NOT EXACTLY, WHITE, BUT OUT- SIDE OF YOUR FATHER, I CAN'T FIGURE WHO'S INTERESTED ENOUGH IN YOUR HIDE TO PUT UP TWENTY GRAND TO BAIL YOU OUT.
WHERE WERE WE TO MEET THIS PENFIELD DAME ANYWAY, SPALDONI?
IN THE COFFEE SHOP OF THE STAR HOTEL.
AND REMEMBER IT'S A STRICTLY BUSINESS PROPOSITION- I PUT UP YOUR BAIL MONEY, AND IN RETURN, NOW, YOU'RE TO GIVE ME INFORMATION FOR THE BOOK I'M WRITING.
GEE, I'M SORRY I MADE A PASS AT YOU LAST WEEK, MISS PENFIELD- I DIDN'T KNOW YOU WERE SO SWELL.
NOW, MMY, TELL LL...DON'T OLD ANY- THING BACK.
WELL, WHAT DO YOU WANT TO KNOW FIRST...? HOW WE SNATCH CARS- AND THEN DISMANTLE THEM-OR.....
HOLD ON! WAIT A MINUTE! SO THAT'S THE SECRET AGREEMENT BETWEEN YOU TWO, EH?...AS JIMMY'S LAWYER I REFUSE TO LET HIM TALK...FOR AN AUTHOR...OR ANYBODY ELSE!
NOW, SPALDONI- DON'T BE LIKE THAT! SHE ISN'T GOING TO MENTION ANY NAMES.
ALL RIGHT-BUT I MUST READ EVERY LINE OF YOUR MANUSCRIPT- AND PUT MY O.K. ON IT BEFORE I'LL CONSENT.
WITH PLEASURE, MR. SPALDONI, WITH PLEASURE.
THAT NIGHT
THIS IS TRACY- OH YES, MISS PENFIELD HOW'S THE AUTHOR?,
YOU SEE, I'VE FINISHED THE INTRODUCTORY CHAPTER TO MY BOOK, AND I'D LIKE FOR YOU TO COME UP AND TELL ME WHAT YOU THINK OF IT.
I'M AWFULLY ANXIOUS TO SEE YOU-I'LL EXPECT YOU IN AN HOUR.
MMY!
YES! SPALDONI CHANGED HIS MIND! HE AIN'T LETTING ME TALK FOR ANY AUTHOR- I WANT THAT MANUSCRIPT!
BUT...THAT'S PART OF MY BOOK. AND YOU PROMISED ME!...YOU CAN'T HAVE IT!
OH, I CAN'T, EH? GIVE ME THAT MANUSCRIPT, OR.....
45 MINUTES LATER.

HELLO - CHIEF OF POLICE?
THIS IS THE PENFIELD'S BUTLER, JILES! DETECTIVE TRACY AWSKED ME TO CALL YOU AND TELL YOU TO COME HERE RIGHT AWAY!
1-29

ALL I KNOW, PAT, IS THAT IT WAS THE BUTLER AND HE SAID TRACY WAS THERE AND WANTED US TO GET THERE AS SOON AS POSSIBLE.
I BET A PICKLE THE GIRL AUTHOR'S IN TROUBLE.
POLICE

COME ON JILES - GIVE ME A HAND.
TRACY - WHAT'S IT ALL ABOUT?
YES SIR.

ALL I KNOW, CHIEF, IS THAT JEAN PENFIELD CALLED ME AND ASKED ME TO COME OVER HERE TO HER HOUSE. WHEN I ARRIVED THE BUTLER AND I FOUND HER LYING ON THE FLOOR UNCONSCIOUS.
WAS SHE ROBBED?
CHESTER GOULD

SHE'S COMING AROUND. SHE'LL BE ALL RIGHT.
THAT'S A NASTY BUMP ON HER HEAD. ROBBERY WAS EVIDENTLY THE MOTIVE BUT WHO WOULD HAVE WANTED TO ROB HER?
1-30

PAT, WHILE I'M EXAMINING THE WINDOW SILL GO DOWN STAIRS AND LOOK FOR FOOTPRINTS BENEATH THIS WINDOW.

IT'S A DIRTY TRICK, SPALDONI! AFTER THAT DAME PUT UP BOND MONEY TO BAIL ME OUT, YOU MAKE ME GO STEAL HER MANUSCRIPT! I DONT LIKE IT!

BESIDES, I PROMISED I'D GIVE HER INFORMATION FOR HER BOOK!
WELL, YOU DID THAT. BUT YOU DIDN'T PROMISE NOT TO STEAL HER MANUSCRIPT AFTERWARD, DID YOU? --HM-- LET'S SEE WHAT IT SAYS...
CHESTER GOULD

MY MANUSCRIPT! MY MANUSCRIPT! IT'S GONE - HE TOOK IT!
1-31

AH YES, MISS PENFIELD! WHAT'S THAT? YOU'VE BEEN DOUBLE-CROSSED? WHY MY DEAR GIRL, I DON'T KNOW WHAT YOU MEAN!
2-1

YOU KNOW WHAT I MEAN YOU DOUBLE-CROSSER! AFTER JIMMY GAVE ME INFORMATION FOR MY BOOK IN RETURN FOR PUTTING UP BOND MONEY, YOU MADE HIM STEAL MY MANUSCRIPT! IT'S NOT FAIR!

MY DEAR LADY - ANYTHING IS FAIR IF YOU CAN GET AWAY WITH IT! NOW IF YOU WANT IT PUBLICLY GOSSIPED AROUND THAT YOU FURNISHED BAIL FOR THE NOTORIOUS JIMMY WHITE - WHY JUST START SOMETHING!
Copyright, 1934, by News Syndicate Co., Inc., Reg. U. S. Pat. Off.

MEANWHILE, PERCHED HIGH UP AT A TELEPHONE TERMINAL BOX BEHIND THE PENFIELD HOME!

BOY! THAT GIRL REALLY GOT A DIRTY DEAL, TRACY!
YEAH, AND THAT'S NOT ALL SHE'LL GET IF SHE FOOLS AROUND WITH SPALDONI.
CHESTER GOULD

DOUBLE-CROSSED ME! THAT'S WHAT THEY'VE DONE! I'VE BEEN TAKEN FOR A RIDE TO THE TUNE OF TWENTY GRAND!
2-2

DOES THAT JIMMY WHITE AND HIS SHYSTER LAWYER THINK THEY CAN GET OUT OF A BARGAIN WITH ME? -PROMISED TO GIVE ME INFORMATION FOR MY BOOK -AND INSTEAD THEY STEAL MY MANUSCRIPT!

A SAP - THAT'S ME! I THOUGHT I WAS SMART —BUT INSTEAD I'M A PATSY! A PATSY!
PARDON, MISS, BUT IS THERE SOMETHING I CAN DO?

H'I SAY!
Copyright, 1934, by News Syndicate Co., Inc., Reg. U. S. Pat. Off.
CHESTER GOULD

IT'S A GOOD THING WE GOT AHOLD OF THIS MANUSCRIPT, KID! THIS STUFF'S DYNAMITE! THAT GIRL HAS THE REAL McCOY!
YEAH?
2-3

LISTEN TO THIS :— "BIG BOY, KING OF THE UNDERWORLD HAS ON HIS PAYROLL TWO ALDERMEN, ONE STATE REPRESENTATIVE, ONE OF THE WORLD'S CROOKEDEST LAWYERS AND TWO JUDGES."...

..."THEIR NAMES ARE..." -HOLY MACKEREL! THIS STUFF IS EVEN HOTTER THAN I THOUGHT. HAND ME THAT PHONE!
WHO ARE YOU GOING TO CALL?
Copyright, 1934, by News Syndicate Co., Inc., Reg. U. S. Pat. Off.

YEAH — THIS IS BIG BOY — OH — IT'S YOU SPALDONI? WHAT? YOU'RE COMING OVER? OKAY.
CHESTER GOULD

DICK TRACY
by Chester Gould
SAY, THIS IS THE NIGHT TRACY AND YOU AND I ARE GOING OUT, ISN'T IT?
YES, JUNIOR - I'M GOING TO CALL DICK RIGHT NOW.
BUT DICK, WE WERE GOING OUT TO DINNER TO-NIGHT.. SURELY YOU HAVEN'T FORGOTTEN OUR DATE?
NO, I HADN'T FORGOTTEN, TESS, BUT I JUST CAN'T MAKE IT, DEAR.. SOME IMPORTANT WORK HAS COME UP AND I'VE GOT TO ATTEND TO SOME THINGS THAT JUST CAN'T WAIT. I'LL SEE YOU TOMORROW, HONEY.
THIRTY MINUTES LATER...THE HOME OF JEAN PENFIELD.
THAT WILL BE ALL, JESSIE - YOU MAY GO.
YES'M - I THINK THAT'S THE FRONT DO'BELL NOW, MA'M.
WELL, HAS THE YOUNG AUTHOR FINALLY RECOVERED FROM THE CLOUT ON THE HEAD ADMINISTERED BY THE MYSTERIOUS INTRUDER LAST WEEK?
OH, YES INDEED, DETECTIVE - PRACTICALLY AS GOOD AS NEW.
AND YOU STILL MAINTAIN YOU DON'T KNOW WHO THE PARTY WAS THAT KNOCKED YOU OUT AND STOLE YOUR MANUSCRIPT?
WHY SHOULD I LIE TO YOU? I TOLD YOU ONCE I DON'T KNOW.
JEAN, ER..MISS PENFIELD.. I HAVE PROOF THAT YOU ARE THE ONE WHO PUT UP THE TWENTY THOUSAND DOLLAR BOND THAT FREED JIMMY WHITE! WHY DID YOU DO THAT - MAY I ASK?
WHAT?
YES, IT'S TRUE. I MAY AS WELL TELL YOU THAT I DID PUT UP BAIL FOR WHITE, IN EXCHANGE FOR WHICH HE WAS TO GIVE ME INFORMATION FOR MY BOOK. WELL, HE AND HIS LAWYER DID GIVE ME INFORMATION ALL RIGHT - BUT THAT NIGHT JIMMY WHITE CAME TO MY ROOM AND TOOK MY MANUSCRIPT!
EXACTLY AS I THOUGHT. THIS GUY, WHITE, DOUBLE-CROSSED YOU.
ABSOLUTELY! OH..(SOB..SOB)...I'VE MADE A TERRIBLE MESS OF THINGS.. I'VE.....
THERE, THERE - DON'T TAKE IT SO HARD! EVERYTHING'LL WORK OUT.
AND, MEANWHILE - IN THE SECRET HIDEAWAY OF BIG BOY, THE FUGITIVE GANG LEADER.
AND LISTEN TO HOW SHE CLOSES THE FIRST CHAPTER: - BIG BOY'S GAMBLING RIGHTS ARE BOUGHT THROUGH ALDERMAN KERNEL VIA HIS LAWYER, SPALDONI, AND HIS STOLEN CAR RACKET IS CONDUCTED UNDER THE PROTECTING EYES OF A STATE REPRESENTATIVE - OSCAR MILREY."
WHY, BOSS - IF THIS GIRL'S BOOK IS ALLOWED TO GET INTO PRINT... YOUR GOOSE IS COOKED! AND TO THINK - THIS REPRESENTS ONLY THE FIRST TWO CHAPTERS.
ONLY THE FIRST TWO CHAPTERS? WELL, WHERE'S THE REST OF IT? WHY DIDN'T YOU NAB IT ALL?
JIMMY, HERE, MADE THE GRAB, AND THIS IS ALL THE MANUSCRIPT THE GIRL HAD IN HER ROOM.
WELL, GO BACK AND GET THE REST OF THE BOOK - OR ELSE! GET THE GIRL - THAT IS, KEEP HER FROM WRITING, UNDERSTAND?
YES, BIG BOY, WE UNDERSTAND.

NEVER MIND HOW I FOUND OUT ABOUT YOUR PUTTING UP MONEY FOR JIMMY WHITE'S BOND! THE POINT IS THIS - IF YOUR BOOK WRITING AMBITION IS GOING TO GET YOU MIXED UP WITH GANGSTERS, MY ADVICE IS TO DROP IT NOW!
2-5
I HAVE A BETTER PLAN- SUPPOSE I CONTINUE WRITING MY BOOK EXPOSING GANGLAND- AND YOU BECOME MY PERSONAL BODYGUARD, HU'M ?
YEAH?
MEANWHILE
I KNEW YOU'D WANT TO SEE THESE FIRST TWO CHAPTERS, BIG BOY... AND WE'LL DO AS YOU SAY.
OKAY! SEE THAT YOU DO.
WELL, JIM - YOU HEARD HIS ORDERS - **YOU'VE GOT TO GET THE REST OF THE MANUSCRIPT!**
CHESTER GOULD
YOU SAY JIMMY WHITE GOT ONLY THE FIRST TWO CHAPTERS OF YOUR BOOK... LET ME SEE THE REST OF THE MANUSCRIPT.
OKAY- IT'S LOCKED IN MY DESK.
2-6
HM-M... YOUNG LADY- IF THIS GETS INTO PRINT, YOUR LIFE WON'T BE WORTH A PLUGGED PENNY.
WHY, DICK.. YOU FLATTER ME. IS IT REALLY THAT GOOD?
BUT LET ME HAVE THE MANUSCRIPT- I WANT TO LOCK IT BACK UP IN MY DESK.
I HAVE A HUNCH YOUR MANU-SCRIPT WILL BE A LOT SAFER.. IF I CARRY IT IN MY POCKET- AT LEAST FOR THE TIME BEING.
MEANWHILE, ON A STREET CORNER NOT FAR AWAY...
YOU'RE JILES, THE PENFIELD'S BUTLER, AREN'T YOU?
WHY..ER- YES SIR, BUT WHAT'S IT TO YOU- MAY I AWSK?
CHESTER GOULD
YES, IT'S TRUE- I'M THE PENFIELD'S BUTLER.. BUT WHAT IS IT YOU WANT OF ME, STOPPING ME HERE ON THE STREET CORNER THIS WAY.
WELL- YOU SEE MY NAME'S SMITH - I'M AN OLD SCHOOL CHUM OF JEAN PENFIELD.
2-7
LISTEN - I HAVE INFORMATION THAT HER LIFE IS IN GREAT DANGER.. SHE MAY BE KILLED ANY MINUTE.... STEP IN THIS DOORWAY A MOMENT. IT'S IMPORTANT THAT YOU KNOW.
MY WORD!
WELL?
NOW, COME ON, FLUNKY... HAND OVER THE KEY TO PENFIELD'S BACK DOOR.. AND SCOOT UP THIS STAIRWAY!
I'LL BE SEEING YOU!
CHESTER GOULD

HA! IT WAS A GREAT IDEA OF MINE- WAYLAYING THAT BUTLER AND SNATCHING HIS KEY TO THE PENFIELD HOUSE.
2-8

NOW TO FIND OUT WHERE THAT DAME'S GOT THE REST OF HER MANUSCRIPT.

AHA! WHAT'S THIS..SOMETHING ALL ROLLED UP! LOOKS LIKE IT MIGHT BE...IT!

AND AT THE HEAD OF THE STAIRS-
CHESTER GOULD

WHO'S THERE?
2-9

IT'S YOUR LITTLE FRIEND, JIMMY WHITE- SWEETHEART... I JUST CALLED TO GET THE REST OF YOUR MANUSCRIPT- AND I'VE GOT IT.

WELL.. I'LL BE RUNNING ALONG- GIVE MY REGARDS TO THAT DICK.

CRACK
CHESTER GOULD

YEAH - SHE KNICKED ME IN THE ARM - I DIDN'T KNOW SHE HAD A ROD.
2-10

BUT ANYWAY- I GOT THE REST OF THE MANUSCRIPT! LOOK IT OVER! YOU AND BIG BOY CAN'T SAY I DON'T GET WHAT I GO AFTER.

WHY, YOU DUMB-HEAD! THIS IS BLANK PAPER-YOU'VE BEEN FRAMED!
I'VE WHAT?

YOU SEE, JEAN, I PLANTED THAT BLANK PAPER ON YOUR DESK-AND PUT A THIN FILM OF PARAFINE OVER THE DESK TOP AND LAMP BASE SO THAT ANYBODY PILFERING THE DESK WOULD LEAVE THEIR FINGER PRINTS IN THE PARAFINE. WE NOW HAVE A PERFECT CASE OF ROBBERY AGAINST JIMMY WHITE.
CHESTER GOULD

DICK TRACY
by CHESTER GOULD
AND I PREDICT, CHIEF, THAT IF THIS PENFIELD WOMAN PUBLISHES THIS BOOK SHE'S WRITING EXPOSING GANGLAND, SHE WON'T LIVE TO COLLECT THE ROYALTIES
WELL, HERE IT IS — A WEEK GONE BY-AND WE AVEN'T RUBBED OUT THAT ENFIELD DAME YET! BIG BOY'LL PUT ME ON THE SPOT- TO SAY NOTHING ABOUT WHAT HE'LL DO TO YOU.
JIMMY, I'VE GOT AN IDEA! IT CAN'T FAIL.
SNAP
YOU STILL HAVE THAT EXPENSIVE ROASTER YOUR FATHER GAVE YOU FOR A BIRTHDAY PRESENT LAST YEAR, HAVEN'T YOU?
YEAH, I HAVE, SPALDONI — BUT WHAT'S THAT GOT TO DO WITH GETTING RID OF THE GIRL?
ONE HOUR LATER..
BUT, MR. SPALDONI, I DON'T UNDERSTAND. YOU SAY JIMMY WANTS TO GIVE ME HIS CAR?
EXACTLY, MISS PENFIELD.
SINCE YOU PUT UP THE TWENTY THOUSAND DOLLARS BAIL FOR HIM HE NATURALLY FEELS OBLIGATED TO YOU AND HAS ASKED ME TO PRESENT YOU WITH HIS CAR AS PARTIAL SECURITY FOR THE LOAN OF THE MONEY. IT'S A DUESENROLLS CAR AND IN PERFECT CONDITION.
THEN HE'S CHANGED HIS MIND ABOUT ME — EH?
YES, MISS PENFIELD... THIS IS TRACY. WHAT'S THAT? O.K. I'LL BE RIGHT OUT!
-BUT I THOUGHT YOU WERE IN TROUBLE. YOU'VE GOT YOUR NERVE CALLING ME OUT HERE JUST TO SHOW ME A NEW CAR..... WHAT'S THE GAG?
THE GAG?
JIMMY WHITE EVIDENTLY HAS HAD A TURN OF HEART. HE'S REPENTED FOR WHAT HE'S DONE AND HAS GIVEN ME HIS CAR AS PARTIAL SECURITY FOR THAT BOND I PUT UP FOR HIS RELEASE. SPALDONI, JIMMY'S LAWYER, JUST DELIVERED THE CAR.
I DON'T QUITE GET IT. IT DOESN'T SOUND RIGHT. THERE'S A CATCH SOMEWHERE.
GET IN... I'LL START THE MOTOR AND WE'LL DRIVE AROUND THE BLOCK.
WHAT ARE YOU DOING?
GET OUT OF THAT CAR!
BANG
IT WAS JUST ANOTHER ATTEMPT OF THE UNDERWORLD TO PREVENT YOUR BOOK BEING PUBLISHED. THERE WAS A POWERFUL BOMB ATTACHED TO THE IGNITION UNDERNEATH THE CAR-BUT DUE TO FAULTY WIRING IT FAILED TO EXPLODE THE INSTANT YOU STEPPED ON THE STARTER. I SAW SPARKS FLY AND KNEW WHAT WAS UP..
THE UNDERWORLD IS AFTER YOU!
Copyright, 1934, by News Syndicate Co., Inc., Reg. U. S. Pat. Off.

FOR THE LAST TIME, JEAN, IF YOU VALUE YOUR LIFE - LAY OFF THIS BOOK! IF YOU PERSIST IN WRITING THIS EXPOSE OF THE UNDERWORLD, I PREDICT YOU WON'T BE ALIVE FORTY-EIGHT HOURS FROM NOW.
2-12
THANKS FOR THE LUNCH AND THE WARNING, DICK, BUT I THINK YOU'RE UNDULY ALARMED.. LITTLE JEAN CAN TAKE CARE OF HERSELF.
STEPPING INTO A TELEPHONE BOOTH FOR PRIVACY - SHE HASTILY OPENS HER PURSE..
I'LL JUST MAKE SURE THIS LITTLE PEARL-HANDLED BODY-GUARD OF MINE IS IN PROPER WORKING ORDER AND WELL-LOADED.
BUT WHILE JEAN PENFIELD EXAMINES HER GUN - A FAMILIAR FIGURE STEPS BRISKLY UP AND ENTERS THE ADJOINING PHONE BOOTH...
IT'S LAWYER SPALDONI! I WONDER WHO HE'S GOING TO CALL?
CHESTER GOULD
STEPPING INTO A TELEPHONE BOOTH TO CHECK UP ON HER REVOLVER, JEAN PENFIELD IS DUMFOUNDED TO SEE LAWYER SPALDONI ENTER THE ADJOINING BOOTH...
BIG BOY, THIS IS SPALDONI. "ALDERMAN" ZELD WANTS TO SEE YOU, MYSELF, MILREY AND WHITE RIGHT AWAY! VERY IMPORTANT.
2-13
WE'RE MEETING IN ONE HOUR AT THE WORTHINGTON HOTEL - ROOM 710. DO YOU GET IT? OKAY!
WHILE I'M HERE, I'LL CALL JIM WHITE AND REPRESENTATIVE MILREY, TOO.
WHAT A BREAK! NOW TO LAY LOW UNTIL HE'S GONE - THEN I'LL NOTIFY TRACY.
CHESTER GOULD
WHILE JEAN PENFIELD LISTENS IN ON LAWYER SPALDONI'S CONVERSATION FROM THE ADJOINING PHONE BOOTH, A PORTLY PATRON RAPS ON THE DOOR..
YOUNG LADY - ARE YOU THROUGH USING THAT PHONE?
2-14
TELEPHONE BOOTHS ARE FOR PEOPLE WHO WANT TO PHONE. YOU'RE NOT SUPPOSED TO SLEEP IN THEM!
AS JEAN PENFIELD HASTENS FROM THE BOOTH, SPALDONI'S EYE CATCHES A REFLECTION IN THE SODA FOUNTAIN MIRROR.
WHAT!
IT'S THAT DOUBLE-CROSSING GIRL AUTHOR! SHE'S BEEN LISTENING TO EVERYTHING I'VE SAID - I MUST CALL BIG BOY - THE MEETING IS OFF!
DRUGS
CHESTER GOULD

HELLO - JIMMY - THE MEETING IS OFF! THIS PENFIELD DAME WAS LISTENING IN AND SHE'LL TELL THE COPS - BUT I CAN'T GET IN TOUCH WITH BIG BOY!
2-15

WHAT? YOU CALLED BIG BOY BACK TO TELL HIM THE MEETING WAS OFF AND YOU GOT NO ANSWER?

YEAH - BIG BOY AND HIS MEN MUST HAVE LEFT THE HOUSE RIGHT AFTER I MADE THE FIRST CALL - THEY'RE WALKING INTO A TRAP! WE MUST STOP THEM!
CHESTER GOULD

JEAN, THIS IS THE GREATEST TIP-OFF SINCE I'VE BEEN ON THE FORCE - THAT IS, IF YOU HAVE THE RIGHT DOPE.
BUT I TELL YOU IT IS THE RIGHT DOPE. I HEARD SPALDONI WITH MY OWN EARS.
Copyright, 1934, by News Syndicate Co., Inc., Reg. U. S. Pat. Off.

HOPING THAT JIMMY WHITE WILL BE ABLE TO INTERCEPT BIG BOY BEFORE THE GANGSTER WALKS INTO THE HOTEL TRAP, SPALDONI PACES THE FLOOR IN TERROR . .
BIG BOY WILL THINK YOU FRAMED HIM, SPALDONI!
BUT I DID ALL I COULD TO STOP HIM.. I . .
2-16

IT'S NO USE! THEY REACHED THE HOTEL BEFORE THEY COULD BE SPOTTED. I GOT THERE JUST AFTER BIG BOY WENT IN. HIS CAR WAS OUT IN FRONT
Copyright, 1934, by News Syndicate Co., Inc., Reg. U. S. Pat. Off.

MEANWHILE
WHAT WAS THAT ROOM NUMBER, JAKE?
SEVEN TEN, BOSS.
UP
CHESTER GOULD

HERE WE ARE HOW DO THINGS LOOK, JAKE?
I DON'T LIKE IT, BOSS. I HAVEN'T SEEN A FAMILIAR FACE SINCE WE ENTERED THE DUMP. WELL, LET'S KNOCK!
710
BEYOND THAT DOOR LIES-WHAT?

THERE'S NO ANSWER.. MUST NOT BE ANYBODY IN THERE.
710
2-17

LOOK- THE DOOR'S UNLOCKED.
PUSH IT OPEN, JAKE.
710
Copyright, 1934, by News Syndicate Co., Inc., Reg. U. S. Pat. Off.

NOBODY HERE.
CHESTER GOULD

STICK 'EM UP HIGH, BOYS!
WHAT IN—
WE'RE FRAMED!

REAL PEOPLE, REAL THEATER

E.C. SEGAR AND POPEYE

A sailor's life is supposed to be
A hell of a lot of fun.
— Cole Porter, *Anything Goes*

From its inception in the mid-1910s, Elzie Crisler Segar's *Thimble Theatre* kept in mind that it was a theater indeed; and the outstanding result, and wondrous paradox, of this belief was that even the original cast — Olive Oyl; her ferrety brother Castor; her staid, forbearing parents Nana Oyl and Cole Oyl; and her fiercely disconsolate suitor Ham Gravy — occupied the foreground of the strip in physical presences, and, *a fortiori*, as it continued, and their proper demons entered them, their personalities. In the manner of the one-night-stand theaters after which they were patterned — with who knows what rich reinforcement from Segar's memories of his boyhood in Chester, IL where he worked at the opera house — they seemed to have acquired their background on-the-run, from the leavings of previous troupes and stage houses — the Oyls' meagerly furnished little house, with the tiny end-tables draped in floor-length, black-bordered cloth; a Segar Furnishings touch, which he may have appropriated from the comparable décor of his revered neighbor in the *New York Journal*, George (*Krazy Kat*) Herriman; the barrenness of the open countryside, which is obviously present only to usher them toward their adventures; all these set off the ever-more-foxy, willful, casually cruel, explosively gallant presences; which never have any apology to offer for their seediness, nor will yield an inch of their right to parade their funny, barnstorming wares.

Theirs was, from the first, an overbearing earnestness which was unlike any comparable parody (so *Thimble Theatre* initially professed to be) among Segar's fellows that can easily be recalled. Not the ponderously inventive lampoons of Kahles's *Hairbreadth Harry*; nor the spluttery, jovial, boyish *Minute Movies* of Ed Wheelan; nor the scornful, bleakly mechanical *Fillum Fables* of the pre-*Dick Tracy* Chester Gould; nor Harry Hershfield's haphazardly whimsical, decorously drawn escapades of *Dauntless Durham of the U.S.A.*, or his more wanton, and more popular, *Desperate Desmond*; none of those display the sort of identification with play-acting, the farcical-melodramatic imagination taking hold and assuming sway as an *élan vital*, rather than as the tatty merchandise of parody. I think that Segar never had the taste for parody, any more than his close-by colleague and cousin germane of the '20s and '30s, Billy DeBeck; who initiated *Bunky*, the superannuated baby, as a parody of *Little Orphan Annie*; but whose own anarchic theatrical zest soon became impatient with the downscaling, the confinement, the cunning self-subordination which parody tends to involve; and delivered instead a wayward epic as volatile and shaggy and boisterous as *Barney Google* itself. There figured originally in *Thimble Theatre* a certain Willie Wormwood, a stage villain of the high-silk-hatted, mustachio-twirling variety; but he was dispensed with within the first year suggesting, perhaps, that Segar felt the villain-stereotype to be bolting into a place too securely the burlesque formula, already a cliché in itself; and, too, selling too cheaply his secret (then) infatuation with villainy.

Segar was affected, not with parody, but with camp as a viable comic tone. Involved in this feeling was his awareness of farce and melodrama, not as "effects" to be siphoned as lubricants into the hiccoughing mechanism of some formula, but as vigorous imaginative currents, as the natural prerogatives and powers of the comic-strip medium, which meant its terrain, to be expanded, exploited, and gloried in; and, also, the comic strip's points of contact with the actual world; even as believed some of the most redoubtable of the silent-film makers: D.W. Griffith, Abel Gance, Erich von Stroheim, Thomas Ince. Above all, Segar perceived melodrama and farce, I believe, as the *properties* of an artist like himself, to be transcribed into his own terms and rediscovered in his own graphic language. This was shown in the vocabulary of his cast, which bestrode the landscapes of theater and actuality — meaning, here, imaginative validity and authority. In following this perception, he was to create new standards of actuality, which is the sovereign concern of all art. His only respectably close competitors, and collaborators, in this achievement of whom I know, were Sidney Smith of *Old Doc Yak* and *The Gumps*; Roy Crane of *Captain Easy*; and Billy DeBeck, especially in *Barney Google* of the mid-'30s. Of course, on January 17, 1929, the great catalytic wind blew off the ocean, blowing down, with twister-sock impact, not a few accustomed attitudes toward the comics-strip.

From the mid-1910s until the beginning of the '20s, the drawing remains hesitant and gawkish; timidly arranging and directing the doodle-ruled forms of the characters, who seem always on the threshold of reverting to the linked jellybeans, or semi-collapsed balloons, of their basic shape. Even during and after 1920, by which time the drawing's execution has become much more crisp and assured, the sense never comes across of a *summarizing* style which makes all else cohere, and infuses posture and composition with sparkling, or somber, or flashy energumen. Such style as can be seen coalescing in the earliest *Bringing Up Father* strips, or *Little Jimmy* — the declaration of vision as authority — does not show in so much as an occasional stroke, or odd felicity of gesture. It is extraordinary to reflect that in this comic strip, which calls to mind Gilbert Seldes's dour reflection on *The Katzenjammer Kids* — they looked the way people who never read comic strips thought they all looked — what appear to be drawing conventions, and the most rudimentary at that, turn out, on close and serial scrutiny, not to be conventions in the generally acknowledged sense at all; nor the "style" to be any acknowledgeable style, even a bad one; least of all, the sense of any authority, any fanfaring of the strip's personality, its worthiness and beaming future intentions, in terms of a visual plumage, such as the daft elegance of *Bringing Up Father*, the jaunty scurry of *Jerry on the Job*, and the slapstick swank of *Polly and Her Pals* alike convey.

What *Thimble Theatre* yields up, through most of its stages, is a feeling of fugitive desperation, of these figures fighting their way, determinedly and recurrently, out of some abstract limbo, like spooks trying to regain — or retain — their hold on the real. Such space — their space, as allotted them in panel after panel — often seems opaque, even tangible, and underscores their appearance of listlessness when standing at ease; underscores, too, the power of stillness, of passivity within the non-reality of the drawing, which Segar worked with startling evocative power in numerous of his pantomime sequences, like the first entrances of the monsters, Toar and Limbo; or, a beautifully weighted little gesture, like Popeye slipping a pillow behind the head of the recumbent, supposedly dead Sea Hag.

When standing, they resemble crane-assembled golem; they give animation, by contrast, to the wharves and shanties down along the seaside, when Popeye and Popeye's own ambience finally assume command. At other times, they seem to convey an all-but-inexpressible frustration, which propels a manic obdurateness: the frustration of laboring with the jagged, unpliable, pitiably raw fragments of an alphabet inherited from long, long before. The unarguable life, the histrionic vigor, jubilant or wrathful, which engineers the jokes and the *frissons* of its extravaganzas and its dark, rumbling fairy tales in years to come, will seem the more wondrous and mysterious because of the stolid, dissolution-threatened look of the drawing from which it arises; the style not as the inscription of imagination, but as imagination's vehicle, the conductor of its convulsion. The vivacious litheness of Floyd Gottfredson's line, the seething busyness of his action, gave every gesture of the newspaper *Mickey Mouse* the inventive verve and the downright expressiveness of a single frame from the most magically explicit silent films. Segar's characters express anger or joy with the heavy limbs of the Midwest. Anger means fist swinging and teeth bared, with "Grrr!" popping from all sides of the figure, as from concealed vents. "Goin' 'Grrr!' ain't no good," Popeye admonishes a prostrate opponent, late in 1934; to no avail, of course, since this belated student comes from the same Actor's Studio as Popeye's other contenders.

Yet, in examples like this, it is the imagination and the will urging each other on which achieves much of the comedy and power of the best *Popeye* sequences: the rudimentary drawing turned away, at the last moment, from abstraction. The "actors" continue to act with the remnants of their burlesque tradition juggling and flopping around them; but they also retain, in heady force, that awareness of the artist's own power, and rejoicing in it, which furnish the *éclat* of burlesque Segar is constantly invoking, especially under the mystery-touched reign of Popeye.

One by-product of Segar's contention with space is that the sense of time is more alert and suggestively right than in most of his "serious" contemporaries. He evidently acquired early on in the Popeye sequences not only the grand operatic gravity which he imparted to the lovely little businesses, like the one with the pillow described above, or Olive Oyl's kittenish-wistful tilting of Popeye's sailor hat in the Skullyville adventure; but of Segar's apprehension and general deployment (at once "primitive," i.e., in its literalness, and sophisticated beyond most of his contemporaries) of "actual" time-space, his use of both attenuation (the *longueurs*, the off-stage sequences of action, chronicled in the characters' reactions); the use of pause and double-take (in which I do not believe he was matched until the advent of intimate-toned comic strips like Johnny Hart's *B.C.*, Charles Schulz's *Peanuts*, and Mell Lazarus's *Miss Peach*, and later, *Momma*); and, on the other hand, the excited jamming of conversations, interjected comments, hasty summaries of relevant information, or the conveyance of which he advanced the use of dialogue balloons in alternating tier or stair-steps. Techniques which are backed by, and counter-pointed with, the lingering, dominating near-abstraction of Segar's work. "Near-abstraction" is, of course, of cardinal importance, because the holding back from abstraction *in toto*, the skin of probability and mobility, is what supplies the extraordinary energy to *Thimble Theatre*, and its magical mutability. Being so far infatuated by space, Segar was a wary enough artist to be extra mindful of its laws.

Once Popeye takes charge, Segar's *pas de deux* with abstraction serves increasingly the boyish cruelty — the playful wantonness as of young children with modeling clay, or some of their most "cherished" toys — which he visits upon his actors' anatomies, going in for grotesquely manipulative sport, which he uses both the skin of physical probability, and the core of abstraction; grading the freedom play of the drawings' doodle-principle against the, as they must have been in the early '30s, still-fresh memories of Mack Sennett, and the cartoon-like travails of Laurel and Hardy. These are always laced with cruelty, often with figures of castration (Segar feverishly intent, as it seems, on divesting his figures of their makeshift-looking plausibility, reducing them to what they were; but in terms of their physical "humanity"). Wimpy, in a 1933 adventure (and one of Segar's most horrendous *buffo* episodes) tears out handfuls of the oblivious George W. Geezil's whiskers, in order to fashion himself a Goon disguise, complete with a wilderness of phony pubic hair. Olive Oyl snatches a female adversary, a Mata Hari from the Brutonian Empire, literally bald-headed during a no-hold-barred skirmish over Popeye. Segar's self-deriding sport with the limitation of his drawing constantly gives him latitude for the most savage sport with sheer human perishability. Have maimed people ever figured more prominently, or recurrently, in a comic strip — from the legless man who is Castor Oyl's "test customer" when he applies for a job as a shoe salesman, to Popeye himself, whose missing eye nowadays is transcribed as a winsome wink, but which was depicted as a persuasively puckered and wrinkled socket? Segar's wry awareness of his drawing's own limitations, maintained to be sure over nearly two decades, and his frustrated scoffing at them, and the furious élan of being able to do "whatever he wants," or the next thing to it, with this assemblage of sticks and modeling clay, result, as he harnesses these emotions and plays them against each other, in some of the most insidiously dream-like appeals that cruelty and megalomania can be seen exercising in a comic-strip, apart from Chester Gould's too easily mis-docketed *Dick Tracy*.

Two cardinal images, both of them recurrently exciting and liberating to Segar's style, appear, like twin masts, over the remote horizon of his strip's actual-plus-imaginative space. There is the image of whipping, volatile transformation, the familiar figure swirling "before our very eyes" into a series of others, the shimmering, shuttling works of the sorcerer/witch, or quick-change artist, holding the stage, as we feel ourselves brought breathlessly close to the invocatory magic of the drawing act itself. The Sea Hag, in three incomparable panels of December 1936, magicking herself, with the aid of her witch's-flute, into a hitching post, then into a Grecian maiden (always retaining a fascinating residue: the suggestion of her customary black garments, her hideous and impenetrable austerity of face); or Merlock Jones, bodyguard to King Blozo, successively transforming himself into zany, darting replicas of Popeye, Olive, the ship's Chinese cook, the grinning, bucktoothed Oscar, and the white-whiskered (and, surely, beside himself, at the best of times) King Blozo himself. One feels in these sequences as though the theater projected in *Thimble Theatre* has become the prototype of our most ancient, most solicitously buried dreams of the theater as we would like to see it, with illusion perpetuating itself beyond what everyone's awareness of stagecraft now informs one is "plausible" and "reasonable."

The other sort of image recharging Segar's poky-looking style is that of the lacerating, clothes-shredding, pummeling battles, usually between Popeye and opponents like Toar, or Slag the Slugger, or in the episode of the "Eighth Sea," a redoubtable Bluto indeed — Mack Swain crossed with a threshing machine. Or, one might recall the squalling, snarling bout between the Sea Hag and her sister, in the peeling course of which both sisters are revealed wearing identical flowered lingerie ("Amusing, is it not?" murmured Mr. Wimpy, that connoisseur's connoisseur, to the chortling ogre, Toar). In these two kinds of primary events, the gaucherie and somnolent-seeming inanition of Segar's drawing rallies itself to a champing, ground-pawing momentum, and seems to take revenge for its long doze.

These two sets of images, dream-like transformation and bloody melée, share a common importance to *Thimble Theatre*: the twin source of that gravity which converts humor into comedy, by investing it with the undertow of the world, and what Kafka called the weight of our own bodies. They represent that habitation within the world-at-large which, in the most notable comedy, and much other art, the imagination makes of itself. And their extremity, winging toward the poles of legerdemain and the savage sculpture of fight-to-the-finish, set off, by contrast, the marvelous kind of seriousness, the sense of reality being hard-by, which informs *Thimble Theatre* through its thirty-six short seasons under Elzie Crysler Segar. Without my memories of such scenes, I could almost believe in the successful film adaptation.

The double source I speak of represents the two aspects of survival: the salvaging of ego, of soul, of what one has no choice but to claim, in its remaining tatters, throughout and after so many long walks, so much hunger, so many, not often evenly matched batterings. One performs the salvaging action through adaptability, through Mercury-footed change, by surrendering the vanity of one's "own" shape to the kaleidoscope of shapes that this life comprises. And/or, one surrenders one's self (while returning to the remainder counter any transcendental "wisdom" picked up on the way) to the paring, peeling efficacy of all those scufflings and lashing and batterings; not to mention the ego-buffetings lustily administered by the characters to one another from the Olive-Ham phase of *Thimble Theatre* on, and imparted a certain formal class by Popeye's entrance.

The eccentric dignity which this attention to survival takes on, the authority which Segar grants it, provides the rock-buttress-like raw outcroppings on which the funny pictures are inscribed, for the burlesque, and the later, mobile and mood-rich comedy of *Thimble Theatre*. There is provided a counterpoint of earnestness, and a looming shadow of dignity, by Segar's inability to disallow the world; coupled with his obvious faith that his comic style, as a style, can accommodate the world's truths as he knows them. His is not a laughing-away laughter, but an accommodating laughter; which results in the extraordinary range of truth — funky, brutal, poignant, grotesque — which *Thimble Theatre* is able to view about the bedrock facts of sheer getting-on. He has been quoted a number of times as saying that he believed Popeye to have had considerable sorrow in his background (typical of Segar that he did not profess to know that background!) and that this sorrow enriched comedy generally. The comment, cliché though it be, is refreshed, as clichés can be, by the actuality of Segar's own practice and the way it strains out sentimentality.

And the sense of the actual is carried over into the remarkable way that Segar's style showcases the mulish egomania, offhand savagery which his characters regularly exhibit, indeed like a theatrical troupe stranded and frustrated almost beyond human sanity by the trashy inadequacies of their stage and appurtenances. His figures are vessels of their own wills and imaginations, projections of Segar's though these be; and no less in the recurrent gallantry and *noblesse oblige* which were Popeye's contribution. Even love-slighted Ham Gravy's repeatedly muffed attempts at courtship and occasionally suicide have the ferocious propriety of performance and the dedication of a Noh player engaging in a Tony-aimed hari-kari ceremony. On one milestone Christmas Eve 1920, he delivered himself to Olive in an enormous Christmas stocking (which she dispatched to the nearest snowdrift). The chronic testiness of Mr. Kilph, millionaire promoter, is kindled to homicidal, perhaps suicidal, fury by Popeye's losing the bout with Kid Jolt, due to the sailor's heterodox notions of ring procedure. "Now — SLEEP!" cries the inflamed sportsman, as though parlaying hypnotism with fisticuffs, as he aims a blow at that precipice-chin; but, thanks to Popeye's smiling tolerance ("He's layin' me amongst the swee'peas"), the only casualties from the confrontation are Mr. Kilph's skinned knuckles and his more deeply lacerated vanity. But, like an Elizabethan *dramatis personae*, the *Thimble Theatre* cast's invention is escalated by frustration; and Mr. Kilph's attempted recoup by matching Popeye against a robot, whom the sailor — with the imperturbable obduracy which is the other aspect of Segar's people — demolished.

The magical literalness with which Segar accepted the nature of his characters and was able to portray it, the weight and fullness which their presences acquire, as you watch the creative zeal at its assembling work with the rag-tag vocabulary of the theater, is what gives *Thimble Theatre*, even in pre-Popeye days, its basic hypnotic persuasion; this, coupled with the haunting recurrent sense, as conveyed through that master-conveyance of his style and the increasing tumescent conviction which he brought to it, that the people themselves are aware of their limitations as *cartoon characters*, and the feisty defiance with which they pick up that challenge. That and the awareness, shared by them and their creator, that style is no more and no less than any inhabitant of this life is condemned and privileged to make do with; and that one of the chief prerogatives of style is to defy its own limitations. It might not be too much to infer, although dangerous to critical commonsense to dwell in, that Segar regarded many of the world's appearances as no less than masks, and no more than vehicles or vessels, for the human imagination and will at their giddying, rambunctious full tilt; and that, in consequence, style is at once a conspicuous vanity, and one of the indispensables of this life; the resolution to the riddle being that style reveals itself and enriches its subject only through its changes — the protean movements, the abrasions and lacerations which it undergoes in the world.

The chief bearer of this news in the earlier *Thimble Theatre* adventures was Castor Oyl, Olive's eccentric, turbine-driven brother, who combined the naïveté of a disenfranchised Parsifal with a stud weasel's tenacity and resource. Castor was aptly named, for his ability to charge like a dose of salts to the profit-issue of any situation, and to invest his seekings with the unmoored idealism of a perpetual near-loser. We find him in 1924, tending a fighting-cock named Blizzard. With complacent reasonableness, Blizzard is devoted to jumping the diet Castor has assigned it. His common-sense survival principles anticipated those of J. Wellington Wimpy some seven years later. Blizzard was succeeded by a considerably less sanguine human counterpart in 1925, when Castor, as fledgling fight manager, espoused a tiny, shovel-jawed slugger named Batt McGnat (according to whose face, the nickname might have represented either "Battling" or "Battered") who safety-pinned the tatters of his professional dignity with the plaintive catch-phrase, "Did I ever tell you what I did to Wildcat O'Connor?" Castor's engagement with these clunkish, improbably resourceful champions (the fighting cock, Blizzard, won the title by devouring his opponent, Ham Gravy's Tasmanian wood-pecker) suggests that in such misfitted Horatio Alger enterprises, represented as much as anything for the battle of wills in which he could free-wheelingly engage, a preparation for his marathon partnership, in years to come, with Popeye. He was a tryer-on of hats, a fancier of public roles, *Thimble Theatre*'s virtuoso entrepreneur of the '20s, and as such a soured, zany offhandedly vicious (one of Castor Oyl's merry japes, in his footloose youth, was to drop a retractable quarter into a blind man's cup) version of Harold Lloyd. He embodies that crazy chiaroscuro of knightliness and jabbing willfulness which the younger Popeye was to embody for all time, later on; and, too, the scapegrace, parodistic aspect of role-changing, and status-seeking, in the '20s, the darker side of both Lloyd and (in a maestro's finesse, the glistening silent style) of Charlie Chaplin. The way that Castor transmutes Chaplin's masterly urbanity into a darting, wayward, and ad hoc ungainliness — which also manages to win — is Segar's homage to, and translation of, one of his icons. In late 1928, one year before the excursion to Dice Island and Popeye's fateful entrance, Castor is found sporting a black Stetson hat, editing a newspaper, and trying, with his usual convulsions of frustration and (appalling) inspiration, to find a libel-proof way of calling the mayor a crook.

Castor's careening sorties into career after career, his skylarking bids for lightning prosperity, could not survive into the '30s (it is notable that, on the Depression's threshold, Castor's last pre-Popeye career-try was in a profession). The wind-blown, single-sail craft of his personality required towing by a more rugged vessel; and, a year after Popeye's appearance, a more weary, more pragmatic, somewhat gentled-down Castor is found squiring the sailor, becoming his grousing, Sancho-like foil (in anticipation of the Joe Palooka-Knobby Walsh teaming of the '30s); and, in the last major role Castor was to play for a while, steering the sailor-man into a partnership in Castor's detective agency: the ultimate vocation for his ferrety, Quixote-Panza personality, in which his wayward traits found an authentic channel; and in which, on at least one occasion — the Susan Brown adventure of mid-1937 — he was able to play a genuine *deus ex machina*, upstaging, with the sailor's generous acquiescence, even Popeye himself.

Castor was the outstanding, by no means only, personification of Segar's own bone-deep affection for theater and improvisatory, something-from-nothing pervasiveness of theater in the flattest and scantiest-looking circumstances of everyday. There is a loving curiosity about his people's own presences, and their bearing in their world, in the mosaic of vignettes, usually presented as gags, with which Segar shows theater and theatricality receding into scrungy actuality, and emerging again. Fantasy is buoyed by the near-melancholy slumpishenss of the "normal." King Blozo, Popeye's sponsor in 1931 (and, two years later, regal rival, when Popeye ascended the throne of his self-founded nation, Spinachova) was harassed to near-dementia by his royal anxieties, with which he performed a frenzied saraband, racing in circles, his white whiskers (they were dark on his first appearance; then, by 1933, had whitened; a tribute, perhaps, not only to Popeye's considerable rivalry, but to the multitude of Blozos, his progeny, whom Europe was fostering) trailing on the floor: while "Worry! Worry! Worry!" explodes around him in dialogue balloons, like half-crazed distress signals from some forsaken tower. His consolations included reading comic strips (the recurrent partnership of comic strips and melancholia diverted Segar increasingly, during the assured self-consciousness of the Popeye years); and by attempting to promote the eternally plummeting national currency of his kingdom, Nazilia: the pezoozie ("Take care of the pezoozies, and the pezoozies will take care of themselves.") The constantly-imperiled (even by his obsequious bellhop-in-waiting, Oscar, who usurped his throne in 1934) tatters of fantasy in which he clothes himself (as did so many subsequent Blozoids of the '30s) are, however, a sort of comic grace to the monarch whose throne rivals a therapeutic exercise-horse. Segar's rhythmic emphasis is on fantasy pieced out of the glummest, most daunting of circumstance; and, in fact, elusive of anyone's direct control; recalled, like a benign ghost, again and again, even as he called it, from that abstraction of his constant flirtations.

It was peculiarly apposite that Popeye made a successful radio show in the late '30s, on Saturday nights, sponsored by Wheatena: a complicating factor that Popeye might snort with laughter over, since, of course, Wheatena replaced spinach as the old tar's regalvanizing food. (Entailing small charley-horse, even in that elastic imagination normally encouraged by radio; since boxes of the breakfast cereal, pressure-cookers for heating it, milk, and/or a diner to supply all of these was required to be repeatedly on hand. I can imagine Popeye ingesting his Wheatena raw, or, for that matter, sprinkling it onto his spinach —Wheatena florentina? But I can recall no advantage being taken of these possibilities by those in charge of this well-produced, engagingly fanciful show.) The program's long suit, apart from the considerable care and affection invested in it by whoever was responsible, was, of course, that radio itself provided a perfect counterpart to the murmurous void from which Segar's characters, and Segar himself, rallied their fantasies. And too, the emphasis on the voice; which provided the equivalent, in its bounty of suggestion, and the off-again on-again vitality of the characters, of the ventriloquial sense, of being microphones or megaphones for their own demons, which the *Thimble Theatre* cast members repeatedly get across.

Segar's own perceptive, richly grounded regard for theater, its interplay with people's daily lives, bears comparison and contrast, of course, with the assured vaudeville hand which his confrère, DeBeck, applied to the daily gags of *Barney Google.* DeBeck was preoccupied with the exotic swank and velvet-curtain opulence of theater; and, with the working of the stage as a wondrous aperture between Barney and that outside world which represents, among other things, Barney's audience; which DeBeck repeatedly depicts as somewhere just beyond the edges of the strip, in its actual presence; but with that presence always reflected, as in the sequences like those of Barney going thorough his "fan mail." DeBeck saw theater much more consistently in terms of an élan which transformed the world itself than did Segar; and, unlike Segar, DeBeck did not postulate a fantastical-appearing world, but rather, a world which was actual enough-looking (and plentiful borrowings from John Sloan, Bellows, and Dickens illustrators Leach and Cruikshank went into making it so) in both its grime and its glamour; counterposing to that world a figure so diminutive and inconsequential-looking that he could only expand on any and all of his contacts with it, the world becoming Barney's theater. DeBeck's recurrent images are of Barney being suspended along; on a hod-carrier's ladder, gaining illicit attendance at a ball-game; as a flagpole sitter, etc. His procedure apropos Barney is to try and create a theater within the world, which will be of the world, yet, somehow, in control and, in spirit at least, impervious to it: a community of good fellows, like the Secret and Mysterious Order of the Brotherhood of Billy Goat (reconstructed by Barney from what started out as a small-town Ku Klux Klan). DeBeck is more gregarious than Segar: Popeye had no "audience" beyond his little somewhat Johnsonian household (Swee'pea, Toar, Alice the Goon as Swee'pea's nursemaid and occasional seafaring acquaintances); you never get the sense of him playing to an admiring throng; and, other than seaman, his between-voyage occupations, apart from the prizefighting, are those of loners: cowboy, detective, even king.

DeBeck was allowing theater of participation to go too far: he was playing a never-ending game of touch-tag with fantasy, or the more drastic reaches of melodrama and plausible actuality. In his *Bunky* of the mid-'30s, occasionally promising fables are called to halt so preemptively that I wonder about editorial intervention. But this apparently was not the case, for DeBeck seemed to enjoy free decision over his stories. Bunky's and Fagin's encounter with a witch, who magicks them all into animals and abandons Bunky, as a poke-bonneted duck, on the highway at night, was unceremoniously disclosed as a dream before anything further could happen; so, too, what appeared to be a prospective espionage adventure, in *Barney*

Google, featuring Barney and his wrestler protégé, Sully. My own speculation is that DeBeck was looking at this time, and attempting by these discarded means to project, a fantasy landscape; which, since the traffic of the fantastic and actual was more dynamic and more expansive than in Segar, involved, in the universe of the '30s, some arduous decision. Fairy-tales tempted him, but he had problems in sustaining, or arriving at, the proper tone, incorrigible farceur that he was. Unlike Segar, who never experienced such complications in concocting his myths (without benefit of the Golden Bough), DeBeck required a world of fantasy which was in this world but not of it. The arrival of Barney in the Ozarks, in 1934, gratified his author's quest for the remainder of his life.

Segar also presents an interesting vis-à-vis to his revered neighbor in the comic supplement of the *Journal*, George Herriman's *Krazy Kat*, and, before that, the nourishing hive for many of *Krazy Kat's* motifs and comic veering, the *Dingbat Family* (intermittently titled after the Dingbats' domestic *bêtes-noires*, the *Family Upstairs*.) In Herriman's work, too, theater was a benign specter invoked from squalor, like the higgledy-piggledy, rummage-sale décor of the border town, which is *Krazy Kat's* transient, illusion-filtered setting. Herriman's theater is the home and the distributing warehouse of improvised royalty, the oompah-pah of a hippodrome orchestra backed up with scrub recruits from Luchow's and any touring talent en route to Mexico at the moment. His people are irrepressibly self-aggrandizing (except for Krazy, who has no occasion for, no interest in, no need for, proclaiming him/herself as anything beyond the endowments of Nature); insistent on their rights and powers (as was Mr. Dingbat, early on before the *Family Upstairs* tipped its mysterious hand, watering-can in grasp) and engaged in a constant love-hate tango with all that is unknowable and undomesticable — yes, and unnamable — in Nature. Herriman's theater thus lay somewhere between that of Segar and that of DeBeck, with considerable program-space allowed for the formula in which he delighted. (He might have been a "kat's whisker" away from becoming a remarkable mathematician, delighting as he did in the rhythmic permutations and multiplications of gags and comic events, semantic play, etc.) The formula augmented the scrappy luxuriance, the rag-tail pomp, of his little personages; branching, as they did from the common trunk of the supreme Krazy-Ignatz-Offissa Pupp formula, which set the tone and the mock-classical theater rhythms, plus the entire fable sequence of identity and its balkishness toward theorists and moralists — which defined *Krazy Kat* all during its existence. Herriman evidently delighted in the play of puppetry that the little figures, and their rag-and-bone stage, afforded him; and, in a way totally different from Segar — one of the most non-manipulative of artists, with an awareness of the theater as an avenue to freedom on the imagination's own terms — Herriman loved the "kat's play" with formula, as he did with language — stroking it, tossing it this and that way, letting it turn a course. He loved to stage-manage, to be present as stage-manager, as does Segar, who, however, is earnest about his make-believe in a different way from Herriman. Herriman's mock-grandiose, jovially unctuous (a favorite word of his, by the way) introductions to *Krazy Kat's* episodes seem to call for the voice of Sergeant Bilko at his colonel-diddling smarmiest. Segar is more boyish and excitable; he wants his theater, burlesque or not, to be literally present before his readers: and he never abandoned the announcements of tomorrow's episodes, in the title-space above each daily strip; or, the proclamations of coming adventures, delivered from the cigar-butt with which he signed his name; which suggests, in turn, the stogie jutting from a theater-manager's mouth-corner — possibly that of Walter Shuchert, his well-loved boss at the Chester Opera House. Constant renewal, in the form of novelty, of the differing aspects of persons and things, provided him with constant excitement, and so they apparently did for Herriman; to whom, however, this was an old story, and a perplexing (though of course amusing even in its confusion) and sometimes alarming one.

Like Segar, Herriman was affianced to the notion of richness: not of conventional luxury but of what can be subscribed to the aspect of luxury, those artifacts and that décor which are precious in their relevance and, perhaps, in their appearance as well: a moon which alternately resembles a demobilized tortilla, a six-months-employed saddle, and a vagrant Band-Aid; flower-pots outside a long-abandoned hacienda; and within it tinted photographs and bordered tablecloths — richness as tangible possession, and as possession rendered through language, of which Herriman enjoyed a something-near-Shakespearean appreciation.

But Segar's concept of richness lay entirely with the giddying abundance of space, the luxury of the imagination, to which Popeye delivered Olive Oyl and, with his commercial-acquisitive aspirations, Castor Oyl. Money never played any considerable role in Segar's imagery of genuine wealth, any more than it did in Herriman's: since 1931, when he cheerfully squandered his take from the Tinearao bout on pressing concerns such as pocket adding machines (for kids who shared Popeye's perplexities at addition), and an afternoon's hamburger feast for Wimpy (who devoured them all in his sleep). Segar's principal concern with money is to devise various ways for Popeye to dish it out; I recall no other major comic strip in which prosperity is so patently unreal. Nor do rhetoric, or visual imagery, offer any counterpart to the worldly luxury, which we may find lacking. He is uniquely dedicated to faith in the untilled void that outlives the comic strip.

Imagination was, in his altogether just and surpassingly creative view, the perennial tenant of actuality, even in its crudest, least negotiable aspects. It is fallen-arched, though very gutsy, Castor Oyl as Icarus, marching up from ledge to ledge of the mountain from which he must make his test flight, depending on the wind, and on the state of his digestion.

The purest rendition of Segar's imagination, his evaluation of the imagination, is the comic strip the *Five Fifteen*, which, in 1921, he was conscripted to draw by an editor, a signal disciple of William Randolph Hearst's field-labor approach to his staff artist; to wit, that ideal time equals ideal space equals a softball court in the devil's playground (all such formulation directed at Segar, when he was discovered making fishing expeditions with Walter [*Smitty*] Berndt). The *Five Fifteen* was obviously designed as another entry in the marital-horror wing of the Hearst Comic Zoo, in the company of *Let the Wedding Bells Ring Out!*, *Bringing Up Father*, and the fledgling *Toots and Casper*; and, as such, was the yoking to a formula, and one of the most implacably determined, of a man to whom formula in general were anathema: a stereotyped acceptance of basic human relationships by an artist whose vital comic concern had been the fluidity and re-adaptablility of such ties.

His only recourse was to seek whatever cracks for his imagination the stucco surface of John and Myrtle Sappo's life together might yield, some little hairline flaw of anarchy which he could avail himself of in this pre-Cheever tablet of suburban existence (the very title the *Five Fifteen*, later supplanted by the hero's name, Sappo, referred to the suburbanite's morning timetable). It had been easier, in a sense, for DeBeck, for whom the anarchic animus existed in Barney, his family life as collapsible and reversible as a kid's cut-out doll's house, from the strip's inception in 1919. Segar's escape route, from early on, was to introduce a zany volatility into the Sappos' flower-potted marital life: streaks of mania in both John and Myrtle. John became, during the mid-'20s and the fever pitch of short-wave mania, a radio devotee even beyond the home-threatening fanatacism of Chester Gould's *The Radio Lanes*, or Harrison Cady's *Peter Rabbit.* Myrtle acquired, possibly in consolation for the narrowness of the little household, a no-mutts-barred, voracious hospitality toward stray dogs. John, like Barney, became a periodic fugitive from Sappo flowers — although without Barney's cowbird insouciance: the wild vagrancy of John's occasional life is a feature, a factor, in their relationship, not an escape from, or denial of it. "He's probably in Paradise now," sniffles Myrtle at one point; then, with typical Segar corrective matter-of-factness: "Thankful, no doubt, to be free of my rolling-pins."

The true liberation of John, Myrtle, and their creator arrived, however, during the early '30s. In the course of the Sunday strips, Segar converted John into an illusionist, an amateur inventor (hence, master of new appearances and unfamiliar aspects) who, with the assistance of a magician friend, devised a system of escape-ways from the Sappo home. As amateur inventor in his own right, he undermines, in effect, his home, and subverts the formula, which was incorporated in its plumbing and roof-beams, converting the entire strip into a fugue. At last, in the episode of May 14, 1932, the triumphant conqueror, the demon-self of Sappo's fantasy life, enters the tumbled Sappo fortress of conventionality: Professor O.G. Wotasnozzle, the mad inventors' mad inventor; white whiskers reaching, bib-like, the length of his black frock coat, eyes suspiciously a-glaze below or above his perpetually misaligned glasses, mouth even more suspiciously grinning and cackling, to announce the hatching of some fresh illusion-egg. The patriarch of illusion: Santa Claus, Father Time, the Old Man of the Mountain, had entered Sappoland.

When Wotasnozzle cackled his way into their family circle, the Sappos were delivered over to a fantasy more giddy-spirited, more loosely playful, than any of the impersonations or sorceries under Popeye's reign; without the contrapuntal darkness, and even the cruelty reduced to knockabout, the hoopla of circus clowns, with their detonating slapsticks and water-spraying shotguns. "You can't kid me — you've lost your arms!" snorts Sappo, with that delicacy which, together with his height (he was a mustached runt; Myrtle, in Barney/Lizzie proportions, about three times his size), suggest a kinship with Castor Oyl: Wotasnozzle has been demonstrating the effects of an invisibility ray, in which he will presently urge that Sappo expose his head. The troll-like savagery with which Segar played on anatomical distortion in *Thimble Theatre* becomes open-faced fun, once old Wotasnozzle has demonstrated that human shape, to be sure, is displaceable and replaceable. Wotasnozzle was, in effect, the genius of the cartoonist, of Segar himself, in an ideal vision of deliverance, in which he can turn physical vulnerability into innocent shape-stretching (a series of episodes in the mid-'30s involved Sappo's nose, exposed to some Wotasnozzle growth-promoting salve, lengthening and lengthening, like a daft vine, until the panels of the strip themselves had to be removed). Sappoland had been transformed into a cartoonist's Cloud-Cuckoo-Land. And the crowning acknowledgment of this shadow-free nation, the other side of Popeye's own lunar landscape, came when Popeye installed himself in a neighboring panel, next to Sappo: offering advice on manners and attitudes, and cartoon lessons, to his juvenile readers. It was the world adjoining Popeye's; it was also the world that only Popeye's corrective darkness, Popeye's captaincy of the fantastic within the real, could have made possible.

PART TWO

Neither Segar nor anyone else, it seems to me, ever quite got used to Popeye as a hero; how could they? Even after Kingmaker Hearst, in the early '30s, had forwarded the laurel crown, with the most unambiguous instructions about fitting it to Popeye's skipper's cap; even after Popeye acceded, free-and-easy as always, to the guidelines of exemplar for the Kids, he did it in too jocular, too gruffly workmanlike a way, to be slid into the warm, receiving niche of respectability; for there was no self-delusion on Popeye's part that myth was just another role such as he had already, by 1933, a good apprenticeship in playing. The laurel crown! What difference between it and many another hat? He, who was to engage himself as prizefighter, as detective (with Castor Oyl, in his newly launched agency), as gold prospector; as Chaplin-like squire for Susan Brown, ousted from her home and inheritance by her newly and suspiciously eccentric father. As slippery as the ocean god himself, and inseparable from that barb-pronged fork, Popeye, who was mysterious at his core, only became more rich a mystery with the addition of bromides about always eating "yer" spinach, and being careful of swings. He set his heels life-long (meaning, of course, Segar's life) against being dragooned into an institutionalized respectability, such as had embraced Steve Canyon, in dispiriting degree both Wash Tubbs *and* Captain Easy (both in his own person, *and* his transubstantiation into My-T-Fine pudding, during World War II, as Buz Sawyer, a single-note buzz-saw, who made little sawdust fly indeed): institutional fantasy at its near-worst.

Even when occupying stage center, Popeye never let us forget that he had drifted in at the very outset of the Depression, from the scraggly ranks of that scrub team which Depression comedy was to identify as the home team: those feckless, footloose, often discountenanced (which didn't matter a hair, since their countenances were more elastic than they appeared) small entrepreneurs and willing factotums who numbered Laurel and Hardy, W.C. Fields (whom, I suspect, Segar regarded very nearly as highly as his revered Chaplin); all tryers-on of hats, though always returning to their original derbies, their Atlantic City straws, or, as in Popeye's case, captain's official. They introduced to their audiences a crusty fatalism, a sassy resiliency, and a strain of makeshift, momentary fantasy and illusion which, in a sense, Chaplin, as a great theatrical intelligence had anticipated, but with crucial differences. For, among the comedians to whom I allude, you couldn't so much as profess to prevail over the world, through, say, style and guile. Style and fantasy, when the occasion permitted, were ways of defying and countering what was least sufferable in the world; but to have, and eat, the cake of reality, to upstage the world, even W.C. Fields's capacious gorge would have refused.

And Popeye's, I submit, for Popeye, as one of those eccentric, slop-heeled, available-for-any-work-or-role perennial recruits, introduced the '30s to *Thimble Theatre*, and vice versa; and, to keep both sides from each other's throats, he introduced myth and legend to a strip which tossed some fugitive kisses to the latter, in the instance of Castor Oyl and the fabulous *fioretti* of Castor's improbable success. But Popeye, who was at once one of the most mulish of realists, and a seeker, a wooer, of space, delivered to *Thimble Theatre* the indispensable counterpoint of myth: out-sized enterprises couched in gravelly particularity, the sense of the eternal everyday.

Like Wotasnozzle some three years later, he made his entrance, on January 17, 1929, as a wrinkled, improbable old man; as common-looking as a sun-shrivelled skate a on a pier (for he had to take command before his age could reach its own level, the forty-ish plateau of his later life). In the always-mobile repertory world of *Thimble Theatre*, Popeye's wrinkles were as straightforward a guarantee as his sailor's whites (the regulation navy-blue shirt and orange pants, too, were yet to come) that he could move in any direction he pleased. His earliest movements, however, were those of a typical '30s foil-as-hero, a shaft of ill-met, cantankerous driftwood, insouciantly wayward as W.C. Fields. "I yam what I yam an' that's all I yam," in the early-'30s phase of Popeye's life, was not merely stoic humility, but a warning volley of defiance: he was not only tough, but tough in an authentically anarchic, chartless way, trading Olive Oyl badmouth-for-badmouth ("Ya long piece of bad luck!") some time after they became recognized sweeties. He is as unabashed a bully, on occasion, as are the swaggering hulks like Bluto and Limbo: pasting a hapless passerby for "Walkin' too close to me" (space, we are always being reminded in those days, is Popeye's kingdom, beyond the Spinachova limits), and then pursuing the intervening policeman all the way back to the station house ("When I'm sore, I socks a cop, the same as anybody else."). He is as wholehearted a boor as McGill of the *Hallroom Boys*, or Gus Mager of *Nervo the Monk*, could have dreamed up: his 1933 career as a newspaperman, under Editor Works, reaches one of its numerous trough stages when Popeye is discovered seated on a curb, sharing chortles with Wimpy over the correspondence in a breach-of-promise suit he is covering. To cap that, he exhibits a sailor's wandering eye for Olive Oyl substitutes like the glamorous Mary Smith (more than a fellow cow-puncher to Popeye, even when his perceptions are muddled by Bonkus of the Konkus) and poor Olive's most persistent Popeye-eyer, June Van Ripple. To cap all *that*, long before Popeye the holdout championship against comic-strip matrimony, over competition such as *Li'l Abner* and *Dick Tracy*, he brought his own tough flourish to the role of Inconsiderate Husband: pulverizing a meal at Olive's home with Roughhouse, a boulder-like dinner guest; demolishing a visit to the vaudeville show with gratuitous assistance to the players.

A foil, in fact, from first to last, in the very manner of Fields, whom Gregory LaCava reportedly called a perfect straight man. A begetter of occasions, that is, and an obdurate, abrasive prop for his relatively more genteel and world-polished fellow players. A catalyst of the imagination, which — as a continuing foil, even after he has attained star billing — continued its expansion, in dark ripples, conveying a mood to *Thimble Theatre* which was of the Depression, to be sure, in its melancholia, in its nervous juggling of skittishness and no-playing-around defiance, in the most fabulous and somber resources of folklore — but, always, a folklore reshaped, revisualized, repopulated, by Segar's own myth-making imagination. Popeye, a walking imagination in his own right, managed to project a whole procession of dream-images onto *Thimble Theatre*'s two-a-day stage, which — be they induced by the times, or some conclave of the popular subconscious which contributed to the style of those times — took their place, as easily as the Civil War frames that James Agee cites from the *Birth of a Nation*, among my own seven- and eight-year-old emblem images of the 1930s.

Not only did Popeye donate his own melancholia (which showed up as "melankonkus," at various points in his saga — notably, when Eugene the Jeep predicts Popeye losing the championship match to James J. Jab), but, he ushered in a slog-footed caravan (its pennant-bearer, of course, the collapse-prone, yet unsinkable, King Blozo, who re-appeared, a shaky-kneed specter of the '30s, from 1931 when Popeye served as his Field Commander, until the last episode drawn by Segar: "Hamburger Sharks and Sea Spinach," in 1938). This grousing, maundering, head shaking procession, features, to be sure, certifiable depressives, foremost among them Segar's projections of cartoonists: Mr. B. Looney Bulloney, that pearl of humorous talents acquired by Popeye during a 1933 stint as editor of the moribund small town journal, the *Puddleburg Splash*. Mr. Bulloney — who actually seems a visualization of Segar's increasingly cheery, expansively self-deprecating view of himself as artist — traipses into Editor Popeye's office, trailing labels, which are appended to his briefcase ("Briefcase"), shoes ("Shoes"), etc. He is the most joyless enactment conceivable of the cartoonist-as-hack, the bête-noire of Segar's life-long self-tussles. When surprised, this disconsolate zombie spirals into the air, feet in propeller-blade formation, and descends again with the patient explanation that this is a cartoon convention. And, extending outward from the celebrated Bulloney, are the ranks of dour, harassed, weasel-tempered professionals whom Popeye's crag-like patience, orneriness, and impenetrability summon to the *Thimble Theatre* troupe. The doctors who cluster around Popeye's 300 degree-fevered body, animatedly debating the best trout-fishing spot; the fourth-dimension expert, a remainder-counter Einstein with bushy white whiskers (from Drawer A of Segar's Makeup Department) who, faced with the thicket of wires he has enlisted in his explanation of Jeephood, exclaims: "Aw, gnats! I wish I'd become a clam-digger!" The hammily hectoring prosecuting attorneys, who seem to view the world as Exhibit A. Amidst these weed-strewn waters can occasionally be seen the flashing lilies, humane, pragmatic, no-nonsense professions: self-effacing walk-ons, as it were, who counter the peevish, self-advancing hams and hacks in the company. Private Schultz of the Spinachovan army, a true-blue martial spirit despite his barely three-foot height (which was so cruelly scored by King Popeye that Wimpy — the Commanding General, and only other member of the Spinachovan troops — felt called on to remonstrate); or, Bill Barnacle, Popeye's capable, reasonably greedy, reasonably fearful old shipmate; or, as *Thimble Theatre*'s most distinctly liable minor figure, the portly, imperturbable knowing judge who presides over Popeye's vagrancy trial when the sailor is acting as Susan Brown's hobo-protector. Indeed, the judge was recalled by Segar later in 1937, to act as defense for Poopdeck Pappy, charged with over-exercising paternal privileges on his son's finances.

Apart from this Hogarthian parade, Popeye's presence in the strip, as a poetic image in his own right — lively and enigmatic at once; monolithic, yet always displaying new side-glints of hue and light — introduced his theater to an imagery of mass and darkness and stillness, such as I am hard put to recall duplicated in any of *Thimble Theatre*'s neighbors (possibly excepting *Krazy Kat* in which an occasional figure — like the great, black ship manned entirely by owls, whose eyes prick out the blackness of *Doña Gata*, Blanca's tale of her drowned children — offers something comparable in its weird elegance and dusky pomp). The melodramatics of *Barney Google*, especially such escapades as Barney's pursuit of, and by, Eli Hawker and his Magpie gang and the Madame LaMousse murder case, are indentured to the memories of Charles Dickens and Sax Rohmer, who furnished Barney's own midget-Belasco stage with that outsized swank beloved of DeBeck. But the peculiar atmospheric wavelength, wavering between melodrama and the beefiest, medieval-descended farce, which Segar propagated, in the earlier episodes of the Sea Hag, in the 1933 "Plunder Island" adventure, or the 1932 "Eighth Sea" yarn, a mist-drenched, lockstep-paced waltz of explosive and murky, static images aboard a former coolie-smuggling ship called the *Blue Squid*, actually embodies the conjuring of interlaced moods and tones from a graphic vocabulary carpentered by Segar, and the marveling, intermittent bafflement, occasional anger, recurrent incredulous amusement, which the act of drawing was capable of kindling in him until the very last. This is what I feel from those static, extraordinary absorbing, panels of Popeye and detective Merlock Jones sitting in Popeye's cabin: the claustrophobic air of the place nicely depicted by the scratchy pale shadow, a persuasive spook from German Expressionist films, on the wall between them, as Jones mopes about the ominous appearance of the mist-filtered moonlight. It is what I feel from another tightly-cabined sequence, during the first week of February 1935; when Popeye, Olive and Castor, with their strangely-terrified hostess, the Sea Hag, are huddled together in a succession of black-encased panels, while Toar, in one of the most impressive of those delayed entrances in which Segar became virtuoso, is heard howling and stomping off-panel. The melodramatic razzmatazz in such episodes — the chloroformings, mysterious voices below-decks, shatter-and-splatter bouts between Popeye and any number of towering pushovers — all amount, it seems to me, to no more than the most occasional apparatus for Segar's presentation and as a rule, short-breathed sustenance of, poetry-tinctured views of looming bulks, architecture, night, and the enchanting suggestion which seems to emanate from certain combinations of these elements: that unexpected shapes *may beget themselves* in such a womb of apprehension and illusion.

I believe that Segar would be the first to reject the palm of "master storyteller" which has been tendered him from time to time. What he and his sailor discovered, or restored for many of us, through these medleys of moods, was the oppressive, shamble-gaited night of the '30s, and the cozy jitters of immemorial storytelling situation: huddled around the light of a bed-lamp, or the knotted newspapers in a coal stove. The deepening, or attenuation, which conventional good narrative involves, was deep-sixed by Segar's sometimes brutal manipulativeness, which often came within rum-bumping distance of grotesquerie, and might have turned freezingly grotesque (I hardly dare suppose the reactions of parents who expostulated to Segar's editors over his relatively low-keyed use of the Goon's terrific image) if carried on with something of the intensity which went into the original imagining. Two of the key nightmares which Popeye squired onto *Thimble Theatre*'s boards, the Sea Hag and the Goon, embody the apprehensiveness about women, their "irrational" energy and manipulativeness — which emerges in Olive's manic, havoc-wreaking moods. The gentle, poised, adoring women whom Popeye encounters along his ports of call — Mary Smith, Susan Brown, June Van Ripple — are as palled, and desultorily imagined as their names. But the Hag, with her sexless, black bonnet and dress and the frigid spitefulness of her set face and slitted eyes, can evoke even now, not exactly the same fear I felt as a child of six, of her and of her anger; but, a keen sense of unease at the act of *denial* she represents. "Unease" a doorknob's turn away from awe, I should suppose. Implicitly, the Hag (which steepens my admiration at the spendthrift use of her by Segar) is a great figure of horror: a woman given the clothes and demeanor of an evil celibacy, into whose character Segar poured the cruelty and puppeteer's arrogance which he elsewhere exhibited in the deployment of his characters.

The Goon is terrible in her debut, in the *Sunday Journal* of December 1933, in a way that lies beyond horror: the children knew well what they feared in her, because the Goon is a walking abstraction, the penultimate stage of Segar's never-completed mating dance with the literally unthinkable stillness of abstraction which he carries on throughout his work. With her hairless head, its breath-catching mask, as of a Cocteau drawing for one of the Eumenides, and the gross thatches of hair on her forearms and shins, and swaddling her loins, the Goon is both the near-abstract reduction of female aggression, and the comparable reduction of the puppet-like, "tractable" woman — a hideous coupling. Yet, it stops, essentially, with the mask of these beings, the mood engendered by Segar; and the rich assurance of terrors to come (whether from editorial instance, or the slackening and fence-bolting of his own imagination, I can't say; but, on internal evidence alone, would suspect the latter, in major part, at least) is disavowed by the cursory, skittery fate to which Segar subjects his sinister sisterhood. It's at this point, in fact, when he does undertake storytelling — a loose-knotted rigging of burlesque specialty acts, including Wimpy's Goon impersonation, noted above, and Popeye's disguise as his own severed head — that Segar's story begins to run out of steam, the Hag and the Goon lapsing into mere costumed players, or even less: cavorting marionettes. Yet, in the 1935 episode the "Pool of Never Die" (Segar's construction of the Fountain of Youth; which was revived, inexpertly, by his successors under its own name in a 1939 episode) there is a much more accomplished knitting of somber fairy tale and slapstick; thanks in great part to the singular personality of Toar — featured player straight from Jack the Giant Killer's roster of pushovers — who fused the sinister and the knockabout. The "Mystery Melody" episode of 1936-37, however, which involves the Hag's unique breach-of-promise suit against Poopdeck Pappy, poops out as adventure, into clattery farce, after the enchanting early imagery of the Hag summoning Pappy with her magic flute — a black veil over her face — and is redeemed only in another arresting image at the end, when the Hag, apparently done in by Eugene the Jeep, dwindles into a frail old woman — her womanhood returned.

The element of passivity in episodes like these cannot be

carelessly regarded; because it, as much as the bellicose chatter and skirmish that make up Segar's surfaces in such stories, is summed up in the character of Popeye. Not only the stoic patience of various actors, in syncopated relief to their own convulsive transports, but in the ruminating, clunky rhythm of those panels which examine a mania or infatuation, like Olive's spasmodic jealousy, Wimpy's hamburgerphilia, or the misogyny of Mr. Sphinx (promoter of Popeye's Ark, in 1935): the sedate pace at which all are allowed to utter, for themselves, variations on Popeye's for-a-time classic "I yam what I yam, an' that's all I yam!" None of the others reach this pure equanimity, but all testify to its example, through the deliberate pace, the blocky, Giotto-like compositions (which can dice up even the most volcanic action sequence of Segar's presentation: an accord of violence and staidness which recalls the introduction of L. Frank Baum's Oz citizenry, poignantly recalled in the monstrous Slag the Slugger's line: "That's the kind of guy I am!"). Such fusion of ingenuousness and wantonness is Popeye's bequest to *Thimble Theatre*, the statement of its nature, by its Natural Man.

The most bilious irony to descend upon this sailor, as Bill Blackbeard has pointed out in his infectiously spirited and keen-sighted "The Greatest (Arf! Arf!) Superhero of Them All," in *All in Color for a Dime*, was to stereotype him as a rocking-socking, spinach-gulping demolisher of a black-whiskered geezer called Bluto (originally, as Blackbeard notes, a considerably more redoubtable and mordant comic figure: a fanatic gold-hunter, capable of knocking out some poor bit-player's teeth, to soothe his infatuation; and a one-time-only performer in the "Eighth Sea"). The stereotype, in great part, is the legacy of Max Fleischer's animated cartoons, which, while in their earlier years at least, creating an often funny, cheerfully hammy myth-imagery, also achieved the perverse miracle of creating a formula, a hypnotically consistent and persuasive one, from a character, and nature within that character, which were desperately entrenched against formula, even in the better sense of the term. We may recall with rueful wonder that Fleischer was engineer of the jazz-tempoed, hoydenish Betty Boop, KoKo the Clown, Bimbo the Dog — Cab Calloway roof-raisers of the early '30s — and wonder how things might have turned out had Fleischer, along, perhaps, with some renegade from Disney Studios, tried using an occasional slowing, or even stopping of tempo; occasional water color backgrounds, and /or their most likely India ink counterparts, for spooky, brooding effects; widened their range of *dramatis personae* to include some of Segar's panoramic lampoons; and attempted, in general, to build the project more around Segar's piecemeal, mysterious intimations of personality, and less around the crassest reduction of Segar's puppetry. My own guess is that, had Fleischer been willing to invest in such an enterprise anything like the cost and care that found their way into the sweet-natured, visually tepid Nice Try, *Gulliver's Travels*, the Disney Studios, during their crucial early '40s period, might have found themselves with a competitor and mentor who could have occasioned a redefinition of the animated cartoon vocabulary. Yet, even the arguable best of the Popeye cartoons, and the only "full-length" (about half and hour) try that I know of — *Ali Baba and the Forty Thieves*, with its amusing allusion to Fields's *Never Give a Sucker an Even Break*, as Olive tried to peddle her screenplay — was very much the same old spinach, with never a breast of chicken, or flounder, underneath.

Popeye, on the well-tempered fiddle-string of his personality, captured all the vibrations — touching, ferocious, awesome, grotesque — of Segar's double vision of survival, even as every authentic hero of myth and legend: the protean plasticity which fascinated Segar, and the battered, pared-down staying power which, deeper than fascination, he *recognized*, was stirred and guided by. Time after time, during the climactic "main events" of his adventures, contortions were visited upon the belabored sailor which make it the more extraordinary that Popeye could resume, afterward, his jagged humanity, and cause us to care about it. The contortions, which might inspire an envious jig on the part of Lon Chaney, Sr., actually come across the equivalent of fabulous sufferings, translated into burlesquese; and armatured by the awful boyish seriousness of Segar's shape-kneading pen. Unlike the mortifications of Li'l Abner, in which are manifest Al Capp's own jeering patronage of his characters, Popeye's ordeals, I can still recall, inspired me not only with excitement but something as akin to awe as anything in any near-comparable comic strip which I can now recollect. When a wrestler deploys him like a hunk of pretzel dough; or Toar literally breaks his neck in a neat, elbow-joint formation (impelling the Sea Hag to moan: "He was a brave little man!"); or when Bluto, like a crazed interior decorator confronted with an extra yard of sateen, wraps Popeye, Christmas-ribbon style, around the mainmast; drapes him ballroom-decoration style, over the yardarm; and finally decides on the classical simplicity of stretching his neck from the top-gallant-mast; or when in a drag scene which should then and there have discouraged all Jerry Lewises and Jack Lemmons of future generations, Popeye, posing as a dance-hall hostess in a demon-ridden western town, delivers a parody of ballet which equals a tight-rope walk, consummately cool, many miles above the rapids of mere grotesquerie. We can actually see the most fugitive reaches of caricature, defined by Segar's own dogged, narrow awareness of shape, coming around to meet, and match, humanity in the very images Lon Chaney and Laurel and Hardy have presented it to us. As with these artists, it is Segar's amalgam of poise and crust, along with the bowel-deep apprehension about reality itself, which makes us laugh with a resonance of wonder at how far he can afford, and dare, to beat the strange plausibility which he himself has created.

Popeye, apart from his considerable self, projected an authentic and irreducible image of nature, which lies basically in his serenity, of a nature both in its sweetness and its awfulness; which proceeds from the profoundly funny foil which he was at the launching of his career; and which is refracted, as is his violence, in the menagerie of figures which he summoned to him after his ascent to star and impresario. "Menagerie" I use advisedly for the dumpy, unshakable presences of the various small, miraculous animals which, in both senses, charmed their way into Popeye's ever-expanding, ever-more-amorphous household, and — in the case of Castor's Cockpit Kid, Blizzard, and Bernice, the Whiffle Hen (whereby Popeye was introduced through the Dice Island expedition) — anticipated the sailor, their own patron saint.

The thing to remember in referring to Popeye's own serenity is that Segar did not disavow violence out of hand (he was a faithful prizefight fan by account of his long-time assistant Forrest "Bud" Sagendorf); but that he saw through, and minced neither words nor images about the kind of monomaniacal, pile-driver violence, and the fantasy of such violence as any possible ultimate resolution, which *pace* Max Fleischer fans, is popularly assumed to be, "What 'Popeye' (*Thimble Theatre*) was about." *That* notion of violence was recognized, and regularly portrayed, by Segar as preposterous, frustration-headed rodomontade: the property, and fallacy, of Popeye's tooth-gnashing, biceps-brandishing opposition. But, on the other hand, Segar had an all-but-unrivaled eye for, and matching sympathy with, Popeye's sort of violence, dating back to his days as a weather-warped *enfant terrible*: the kind of violence, I mean, which is involved in getting out from under, in making, and assuring, space for one's self. And a hint, such as Segar's art never missed, or failed to deliver again — of the desperate sense of shapelessness in a displaced man, such as DeBeck discovered in *Snuffy Smith*, and marched into the world fully armed five years after Popeye's first appearance. I am referring to the hemstitch which Segar's comic journalism traced between quiet, stoic-seeming equanimity, and the potentiality — and willingness — to trip the time-bomb mechanism in others.

Reflecting on the Whiffle Hen, Oolong the Chinese parrot, Eugene the Jeep — on that self-content, affable little assemblage, all as presentable to company as the plaster animal figures in the window of a Blarney Stone saloon — all of whom shared a common capacity for splintering all attempts to monopolize or destroy them — one is tempted to strike comparisons with Bugs Bunny, the impresario of daft charlatanry used as non-stop counterfighting. But Bernice, Eugene and Oolong — even Castor's uncoachable hedonist, Blizzard — all have a deeper, more beguiling, more impishly deadpan that Bugs, who is a harum-scarum virtuoso, impersonating both rabbit and zany (on the television Warner Bros. Cartoon Show, Bugs is regularly seen in his dressing-room, performing as M.C., etc.). But there is something unsentimentally opaque, a blankness about Segar's little animals (who, although they are all fabulous, and Spark Plug is not, observe the same restraint about exceeding their animal identities as Barney's horse-partner). Segar, one of the least whimsical of men, given his medium and style, and one of the least sentimental, recognized playing-for-keeps when he saw it. The uncertainty he sustains about where the limitations of their wisdom might lie is a feather-stroke to one's mystical sense, however atrophied, in these tiny beasts, who are weirdly expert at not being under the meaty, grasping hands that would stow them in some safety deposit vault. The secret of their personality, in each instance — its absence — is bound up with the impenetrability that they and Popeye share: the frontier of what-nature-is-about, where Segar firmly and discreetly draws his line. Bernice, the Whiffle Hen, is an escape artist in the tradition of John Sappo, and Eugene is something more: a smiling, mute commentator on the cartoonist's art, even as his unsilenceable counterpart, Wotasnozzle. Eugene is shown materializing at one point — he is a child of the fourth dimension — in a charming pattern of little dots: a "dot drawing" from kids' puzzle pages. His gentle, mercurial presence goads his master-pursuer, Mr. Chizzleflint, into essaying a drawing of him. (It looks somewhat like a DeKooning version of a cheetah — which provokes his thug audience to exclaim: "There ain't no such animal!" "Now I know why cartoonists make so much money," the chastened amateur moans.) But all such creatures are sensibly motivated by a clean-lined, chess-expert's route to their own survival, the salvaging of their own space, Oolong's bearing in this respect is positively aristocratic (he is the gift of Popeye's ancient Mandarin friend, Woo Fong); and, as the only such animal with speech (therefore, the only one susceptible to human weakness) he makes the tactical error of snooting Popeye's English ("What's a 'shicken'?") and is half-throttled by the wounded sailor man.

Apart from Popeye himself, the animals' human prototypes — smiling guardians of their own duration, who can topple towers of efficient brutality and craft — include Batt McGnat's sparring partner, a diminutive black man called Asphalt, who runs some additional furrows of frustration into Batt's well-eroded face by his polite indifference to Batt's every proffered haymaker. Asphalt is like a Bartleby of the arena: he prefers not to fall down. In fact, he is Segar's transmutation of an ancient racist jibe at the density of the black man's skull; which, however, Segar, in his proclivity for both recasting and rehabilitating myth, deftly converted into a symbol of Asphalt's dry, astute, and pragmatically hard-headed personality (compare and contrast with that well-heeled St. Francis of '30s and '40s liberalism, Ham Fisher; who made laughs in a 1937 *Joe Palooka* episode, at two black contenders butting their heads together). The small-scale beauty of Asphalt is that, as with Nature, Segar will not declare or counterfeit what he does not know, what he is unqualified to know, about black people; but neither does this inhibit him (as it continues to inhibit how many popular artist today, apart from the authors of *Beetle Bailey*?) from paying his comic respects.

Of course, the Immovable Object in exaltation is J. Wellington Wimpy, who also best knows, and most directly and devoutly serves, his own appetites, in obedience to his nature. He defers not only to his appetite, but to the world at large; with few lapses, he is the most signally and consistently affable of *Thimble Theatre*'s cast. He looks like a down-at-the-heels Buddha, with the closed eyes, the mouth (unless seen in action on some hamburger) similarly invisible under his mustache, his hands invisible behind his back. Wimpy seems to be attempting a return to the condition of an oyster, a barnacle, or even an amoeba. He refereed, of course, Popeye's major bout against Tinearo in 1930; where, booed with fervent impartiality by both sides, Wimpy replied: "Thank you, thank you"; not masochistically, nor with coy reproach — Wimpy's gentleness was totally un-Christian — but with the bum's granite-like appreciation of being recognized *at all*, the faintest smudge of hope for a future grubstake; the realization that this, having one's identity acknowledged, is the grits to all of life's available gravies.

It is a little alarming, in those early '30s days, to see Wimpy in his shirtsleeves, in his native orbit and home of his great adversary: the Café de Roughhouse. He looks unhoused without the Wimpy carapace, that black coat hung eternally open (without buttons, perhaps). The coat thus represented that paper-thin, yet enduring, shell of decorum which was Wimpy's personal style; hence, his right to occupy his own space, before our eyes. It marked his unbuttoned self-presentation to he world — without ambition or romantic aspiration, alone among the *Thimble Theatre* stars. Physically, Wimpy suggested W.C. Fields; and I notice that yet another Fields imitation has been conferred as his animated cartoon voice; but Wimpy was impeccably, candidly, himself; whereas Fields's outstanding comedies, like *Never Give a Sucker an Even Break* and *It's a Gift*, were motivated by his projected realization, saturnine beyond bitterness, of his own uniqueness in a world of underachievers and fragmented drudges and hacks. The roles of barber, pharmacist, grocer, which he performed in his shorter films, conveyed the air of expedience, adopted, with proper condescension, just to tide him over. Wimpy was never more, nor less, than Wimpy, and the style which was Fields's discreet badge of superiority — that murmured, unctuous deference, relieved by beaming courtliness — was wonderfully distilled, in Wimpy's case, to the purest self-deprecation, the gentleman bum's bone — bred meliorism. Not a flake of irony; for, unlike Fields, Wimpy's goals in life are always modest and attainable, tomorrow if not today. His little felicities — "I'll gladly pay you on Tuesday for a hamburger today;" "Let's you an' him fight" (left over no doubt from his referee period); and the all-purpose cop-out, "Jones is my name. I'm one of the Jones boys" — were more than a con artist's push-buttons; they were little pearl buttons on his selfhood. And, quite apart from his motives, they were tokens of a gentle, patient ceremony amidst the rather steady cacophony of brays and buffets which distinguished Segar's universe.

His instinct for ceremony enabled Wimpy to prevail, more often than not, at least, over his two heartiest adversaries, and two spectacular boors. Roughhouse, who I suspect to have given up a career in the ring, or retired from one, to become Popeye's and Wimpy's favorite restaurateur, was baffled to screaming desperation, not merely by Wimpy's utterly predictable behavior, but by Wimpy's mere, utterly self-sufficient, gratuitous existence; and baffled to within a meat-cleaver's edge of sanity by Wimpy's ability to beguile Roughhouse, day after day, into Wimpy's formula, his ceremony; in the solid intuitive knowledge, of course, that Roughhouse was a man of action already, through his work, subservient, against his nature, to routine.

George W. Geezil, Wimpy's other would-be boisterously self-proclaimed nemesis, was another story. Geezil, an East Side Jew in frock-coat (disclosing striped pants, salvaged, perhaps, from some long-ago wedding), derby, and steel-wool whiskers, was undone, apropos Wimpy, by his own theatricality, his stage style a legacy, additional decibels courtesy of Geezil himself, of Maurice Schwartz and Jacob Adler. (He was one of the rare ethnic characters Segar used, apart from a very infrequent Negro and an occasional Chinese cook; his caricature aspect converted, even as was Asphalt's, by Segar's deference to the cyclonic energy of Geezil's self-esteem and self-fantasizing: an eccentric in a community of eccentrics, and the most sheerly spirited portrayal of a Jew in comic strips, apart from the jubilantly frenzied choreographers of Milt Gross). Geezil's mode of response to Wimpy was a frenzied saraband (his own Hassidic translation of King Bozo's worry-walk) while mutterings of menace, disdain, and self-commiseration detonated on all sides, in dialogue-balloons like volleys from a die-hard fortress. But Geezil, in such moods, was easily guided, as weightless as an underwater swimmer, amenable to the gentlest tug or stroke from Wimpy, who was *intime* with every button on the Geezilmeter. "Ah, he's a fine boy, that Wimpy boy! I, George W. Geezil, say so! Yes, ain't it so? Yes. Yes!" The Chagall-like euphoria would, of course evaporate with Wimpy's next polite, and unfinanced, request, and Geezil, would be delivered back to the melodrama of stricken faith: "Bah! Bah! Bummer! Low-life! You are flies in mine zoop!" and his second-act curtain line, the Geezil signature: "Pooey from me to you!"

Wimpy was neither Popeye's partner, nor yet his foil; for, while far from useless (acting as intermediary, from time to time, between his friends and the dark agencies of the Sea Hag, or mundane criminals like Mr. Chizzleflint; he was wonderfully usable. Popeye, I think recognized and, for all his well-earned spasms of exasperation and rejections, appreciated Wimpy's entirety from early on: an embodiment of nature, wholly gratuitous and self-sustaining and a mask which was exactly itself. So, he was totally admissible to the orbit of Popeye's own mystery; this, although Wimpy was recurrently a doubtful friend (he accepted Olive's commission to disingratiate Popeye from Mr. Van Ripple, father of Olive's budding rival; and, during one of the sailor man's dimmest periods, after Olive had jilted him, Wimpy delicately proposed aiding his pal in a suicide attempt, in return for Wimpy's inclusion in the will). But Popeye surely knew the world as turbulent and self-willed; and the hypnotic innocence of Wimpy's bearing must have come as a relief. As for friendship, why, leave him his own terms. Popeye was used to that, also. In the transports of weakness, Wimpy might double-cross Popeye, but he would never dethrone him.

Wimpy had nothing to gain directly from Popeye's personality: he was an alter-type. Olive, however, blossomed from Popeye's blistering bounty, from the scrawny though resilient, mullen-stalk of the Ham Gravy days, to the bodacious cactus flower of the '30s: a portable encyclopedia of womanhood as viewed by E.C. Segar, and in this a corrective. Segar's best (the second best is certainly Mr. Sphink, the misogynist sponsor — "No women!" — of Popeye's Spinachova project) to any woman-sour impressions left by the Sea Hag and the Goon. Whatever were Segar's fears of women's energy and instinctuality, Olive provided range for their lust and generous complements, within the coloratura stage, which her salty new stage-manager had elicited from her. As against the Tweety-voiced simp of the animated cartoons (done with such lethal skill that the stereotype persists), I wish Olive had been projected with the no-nonsense contralto plangency of Cass Daley or Virginia O'Brien, or the gritty plaint, always curbed from whining, of Joan Davis. A one-woman gallery of Lillian Gish, Louise Fazenda, Mazeppa, Colleen Moore, Olive linked, and made somehow intelligible, our most disparate-seeming reactions of apprehension, hostility, affection and admiration, all steepened by semi-understanding to something like awe. She could emerge from a rip-snorting slapstick routine, like the dance she performs as a saloon entertainer in the western pock-mark of Scullyville: legs Charlestoning at Sennett-like velocity, and (at the behest of her economy-disposed boss, Mr. Holster: a possible delayed valentine to that editor who boarded him with the Sappos?): and hand us a very seed-pearl of pantomime, when she quietly walks up behind her estranged Popeye and tilts his sailor-hat with one finger. The purity of this tiny event could only come from what is so often lost to us in the overbearing vaudeville, isolating and magnifying each stage of comedy or sentiment, of comedians like Chaplin or Lloyd: the *continuity* of moods and traits, their unity as aspects of each other, *not* successive commander of a Victorian universe, which Segar impeccably understood, and which Olive personified for him. Just as Popeye, she could play coquette with grotesquerie without becoming grotesque — all thanks to the fluency, the freedom, of her nature and the style which conducted it.

Somewhere on the outskirts of Popeye's little constellation, place must be recognized (like his fellows in the *Thimble Theatre* Company, he had already made it) for Oscar, whose cartridge-belt of perennially grinning buck teeth, and golf-club nose, likely prompted, or helped decide, the bucolic mask of Edgar Bergen's Mortimer Snerd. Oscar's was as sheerly and patently a mask, and a very old one at that, of anyone in the cast; and, at the same time, that mask represented the thinnest ice separating Oscar, and us, from daunting drenchings of bathos and sloppy farce. For Oscar, who first entered as orderly to the Napoleon-affected General Bonzo during Popeye's 1931 Naziliz adventure, was the Popeye fan at his most erratic, fervently (but never abjectly) admiring, and at times terrifyingly imitative. Popeye was an exemplar for Oscar, with his praying-mantis build, his macaroni-like arms, and Oscar, in turn, became Segar's audacious, gently (not over-gently) distorting mirror for the importunities and embarrassment of, say, the Kids, that well of posterity which the old, anarchic example of the earlier Popeye threatened, in editorial eyes, to poison. Oscar is the undiscouraged torch-bearer for this pugnacious, freely-elbowing image, and Segar, as much as with any of his characters, allowed full tilt for his capacities of defiant fantasy, often suicidal in their presumption: sticking his head inside Toar's mouth, bullyragging tough seamen (who have been tipped off by the forbearing idol himself). Full space for all such, and for the scariest realization of Oscar's ambitions and the dizzy *esprit* that they expressed: when, in 1934, Oscar actually usurped the throne of his much-beset patron, King Blozo. Otherwise, however, Segar yielded not an inch of pavement-space for the dismal comedians' shell game of self-pity. Try and imagine anything left of the cheeky, unstaunchably chipper Oscar, after ninety minutes in the custody of Jerry Lewis. But Oscar's ego and energies are guaranteed, not compromised or denied, by his mask. When Segar remarks to us, in 1932 (as Oscar eavesdrops on a mutiny); "The poor kid's trying to look serious, but his face won't let him," he is offering us not sentimental taffy, for a cud of projected self-pity, but a deeply touching, literal statement, of Segar's own belief, both in his character, and in the actual physicality as frontier — no more. A coda for *Thimble Theatre*.

Popeye's authentic progress, through the appalling brevity of his career's nine-year course under his first skipper, carried him from foil in the narrow, though rich sense of his earliest stardom to a catalyst and patriarch of *Thimble Theatre*'s haphazard freedom and vagrant democracy. For as he disassembles and disorients (creatively) the rhythms and conventions of the original *Theatre*, he is seen rallying, magnetic force that he is, a totally extempore, free-traffic household. The little pillar of his "fambly," Swee'pea was delivered parcel post in a crate, which Popeye (with a delirious approximation of a "new father's" fidgets) dithered about opening, for fear of some wild animal leaping out and "Bitin' me neck off." Only the warm toughness and elastic invention of Segar's art could have engaged a baby as character in a burlesque adventure without dropping the entire story-line into the Cream of Wheat sooner or later; but his style, and equally elastic faith in that style's capacity to accommodate almost anything of nature, maintained. After some mildly engaging, mercifully unstressed interludes of Popeye's distractions as a "mother," discussing how to hold a baby with Wimpy (who opted for the mother-cat approach, dangling the kid by the scruff of the neck), Swee'pea was launched into his own story (he was the Crown Prince of Demonia, and had been posted to Popeye by his mother, in flight from the intrigue-shaken Demonian government). So, the jagged improvisational rhythms of the *Theatre* resumed, with another yarn for the old salt; and Swee'pea, who kayoed a bellicose jack-rabbit for lunch during their flight through the desert, adopted the sailor's hard-knuckles address and resourcefulness, although retaining his own "Glop!"-restricted vocabulary until, after Segar's death, Tom Sims and Bela Zaboly gave Swee'pea a cram course in remedial English. The name, however, stuck (in fact, "Me lil'l Swee'pea" had been Popeye's standard endearment for Olive, and the name "Schooner" was originally tried out on the youngster) as a seal for Swee'pea's own standing and repertory mask, and the insurance of Popeye's own establishment as off-center center of the assemblage. His crated arrival was Segar's funny, loving tribute to the puppet aspects of his stage (in the same company, Castor Oyl was inspired to adopt a similar entry, during one of his detective escapes; while, on the opposite shore, in the *Daily News*, Moon Mulins had previously gotten himself boxed and delivered to Jack Dempsey's training camp, for the launching, in 1925, of Frank Willard's puppet troupe). More, it represented the opening step, as might the delivery of tools and timber, in Popeye's doughty, makeshift carpentering of his own Peaceable Kingdom, without the egregious benefit of any Sphink's patronage. A wacky, surreal kingdom, it was as volatile as Popeye himself; a preserve, the lightest of domestications for the wild things that Popeye had gathered around him, not subservient to any confining norms, but free as ever in their new, adopted styles. Alice the Goon, whose baptismal package had included a permanent outfit: flowered blouse, skirt, and Minnie Mouse hat. Toar, with his turret-tank physique and mushroom-cap head, sliced by a smiling fanged mouth; a 20,000-year-old "prehistoric man," rescued by Popeye from the toils of the Sea Hag's sister (he had figured as a kind of relief-monster for the retired Alice); and now, Popeye's overgrown, auxiliary Swee'pea, Popeye's would-be protector and often-importunate buddy; all of which added up to a new, wonderfully nervy parody-relationship on an allegedly "untouchable" model: George and Lennie. Poopdeck Pappy himself, of course, Popeye's father, was abducted by Popeye from a little orbit of old-time sea-dog's fantasy: his private island, attended by Rockette-trained mermaids (who, when Popeye carted Pappy off, tearfully marched up the beach, in farewell chorus, on their hands); a man-devouring octopus as shore patrol; and a trained-for-close-combat gorilla named Clarence. Pappy's first appearance to his son, on shipboard, trailed smokes of legend: disguised as a white-sheeted spook, supported by two co-haunters: Clarence, and a tiny, bewhiskered sidekick, Pooky Jones, who doubled as a disembodied head. Pappy was an alter-Popeye, the straight-on course into fantasy and myth that lay open to the sailor, without his enthronement as *Thimble Theatre*'s, and his universe's, ruling imagination.

The Peaceable Kingdom, with its cheerful shapelessness, and its haphazard, amiable concessions to convention, was a perfect replica of Popeye's relation to his world and the ripples of a presence almost beyond imagination's own compass, which, in the very way of myth, have continued to circulate years after Popeye's creator's death: the myth now bereft of the rhythm, the principle of growth, which made it private, and dream-nurturing, and crazily vital, as well as public, and simply fun. Elzie Crysler Segar articulated something about so-called "popular art" which obtains today, infrequently as influence, much more often as tacit reproach; the occasional capacity for the most seemingly forbidding, stolid-looking "primitive" art to engage, to honor, to refract numerous levels of the imagination at once, with neither the commitment nor the restriction of form.

THIMBLE THEATER

NOW SHOWING—THE "HEEL" AND A HEALER.

Tomorrow—He Who Gets Slapped.

THIMBLE THEATER
NOW SHOWING—HE WHO GETS SLAPPED.
Tomorrow—The Shimmy Queen.

THIMBLE THEATER

NOW SHOWING—THE SHIMMY QUEEN.

Tomorrow—Do a "Hole" Job.

THIMBLE THEATER

NOW SHOWING—DO A "HOLE" JOB.

Tomorrow—Shell-Shocked Castor.

THIMBLE THEATER

NOW SHOWING—SHELL-SHOCKED CASTOR.

Tomorrow—The Exterminator.

THIMBLE THEATER

NOW SHOWING—THE EXTERMINATOR.

Monday—Protecting a Lady's Molars.

H-A-L-P!

COME ON, CASTOR - DON'T STALL AROUND LIKE THAT- GIVE HIM THE WORKS

SAY, HAM! MAYBE YOU'D BETTER SHOOT HIM

HALP!

NO - IT'S YOUR GUN I NEVER USE OTHER PEOPLE'S GUNS!

O.K. HERE GOES

HURRY UP. CASTOR, BEFORE HE SHAKES HER TEETH OUT

I THINK I'D BETTER SNEAK UP ON HIM - I WANT TO MAKE A "GOOD CLEAN JOB" OF THIS

HALP!

6-1 SEGAR

THIMBLE THEATER

NOW SHOWING—PROTECTING A LADY'S MOLARS.

Tomorrow—The Empty Barrel.

THIMBLE THEATER

NOW SHOWING—THE EMPTY BARREL.

Tomorrow—Blank Cartridges.

THIMBLE THEATER

NOW SHOWING—BLANK CARTRIDGES.

Tomorrow—Blows and Shots.

THIMBLE THEATER

NOW SHOWING—BLOWS AND SHOTS.

Tomorrow—The Smoke Screen.

THIMBLE THEATER

NOW SHOWING—THE SMOKE SCREEN.

Tomorrow—Out of Range.

THIMBLE THEATER

NOW SHOWING—OUT OF RANGE.
Monday—Bullet-Proof.

THIMBLE THEATER

NOW SHOWING—BULLET-PROOF

Tomorrow—Popeye Gives Till It Hurts.

THIMBLE THEATER

NOW SHOWING—POPEYE GIVES TILL IT HURTS.
Tomorrow—A Disabled Accomplice.

THIMBLE THEATER
NOW SHOWING—A DISABLED ACCOMPLICE.
Tomorrow—Snork, the Ship Wreck.

THIMBLE THEATER

NOW SHOWING—SNORK, THE SHIPWRECK.

Tomorrow—The Bigger They Come, the Harder They Fall.

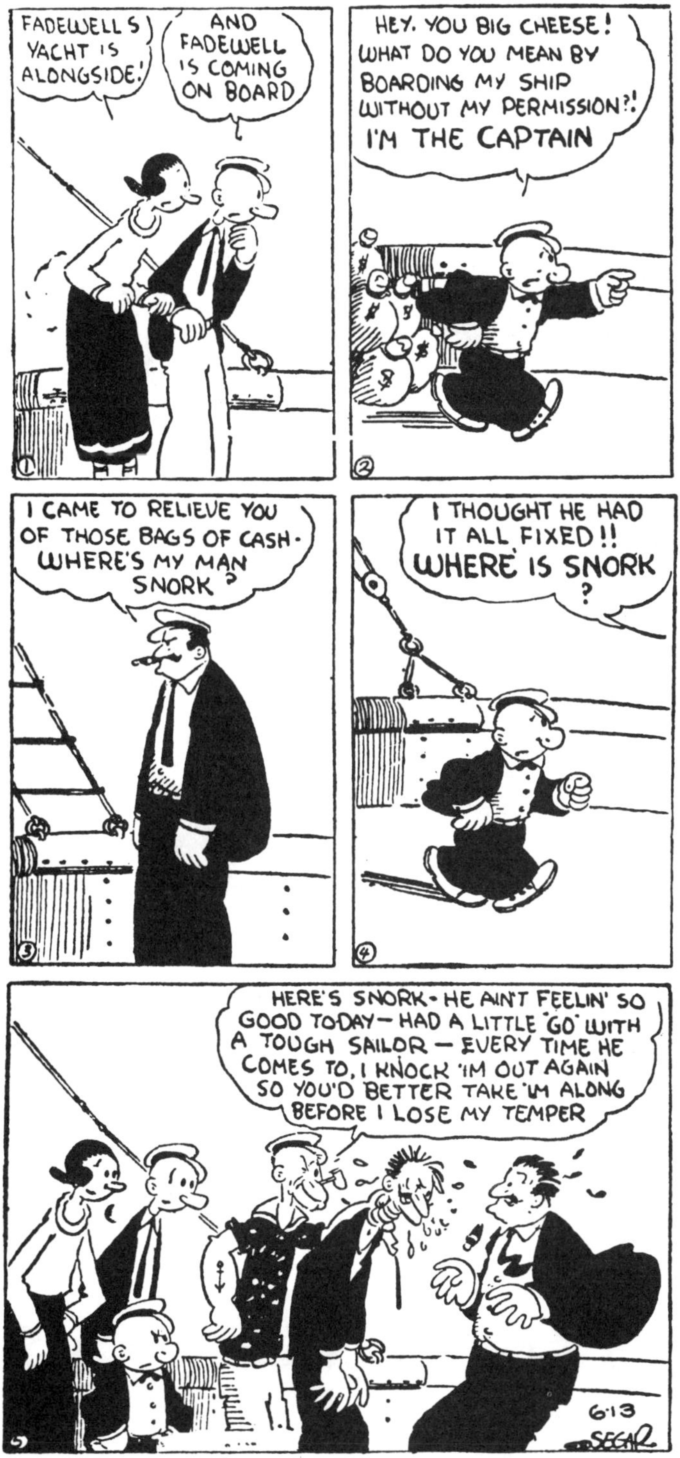

FADEWELL'S YACHT IS ALONGSIDE!
AND FADEWELL IS COMING ON BOARD

HEY. YOU BIG CHEESE! WHAT DO YOU MEAN BY BOARDING MY SHIP WITHOUT MY PERMISSION?! I'M THE CAPTAIN

I CAME TO RELIEVE YOU OF THOSE BAGS OF CASH- WHERE'S MY MAN SNORK?

I THOUGHT HE HAD IT ALL FIXED!! WHERE IS SNORK?

CADY DID

HARRISON CADY AND PETER RABBIT

The creation of folklore is not the fabrication of Wagnerian generalities, nor the muscular attitudinizing of patriotic murals, nor the pseudo-Biblical orotundities of an Archibald MacLeish. Rather, the making of folklore involves the minting of popular imagination's small coin: phrases, anecdotes, vignettes, fleeting images, all of which convey the sense of identity being infinitely extended, without ever being totally realized. Harrison Cady, if never a major innovator or enlarger of American graphic art became, I think, one of our authentic folklorists in the torrent of specifics which his drawings, over more than half a century, lovingly identified and inventoried, often in terms of the American landscape's most inconsiderable-looking components: crickets, grasshoppers, June bugs, grubs, and those cherished virtuosi of Cady's repertory company: the centipedes and Daddy Long Legs. He was, moreover, one of the most accomplished and consistently dedicated stylists that American popular art has seen. "Stylist," in its most exact, and highest, and most vigorous sense: i.e., an artist who has evolved from texture and rhythm and selection of data, a record of his continuing history: to wit, his appetite, prejudice, irritation — which itself, this record or style, becomes the integument of his art and of his personality. And, as though all this were not enough, Cady, in his comic strip of nearly three decades' duration — *Peter Rabbit* — managed something really quite as extraordinary as innovation might have been. From a name and figure already long beloved and traditional — Beatrix Potter's cabbage-ravishing scamp — and from his trans-atlantic cousin, the Massachusetts philosopher of the same name created by Cady's long-time collaborator, the naturalist and children's author Thornton W. Burgess — from these two imposing Petercessors, Harrison Cady conjugated, so to speak, a third Peter Rabbit: the rotund layabout, sportsman, shortwave radio buff and indefatigable hedonist of the 1920s; later, the smoking-jacketed burgher — more domestic, but no less self-esteeming or venture-some — of the 1930s; in a comic strip which, for considerable though, alas, not nearly all of its twenty-eight-year career, was as rambunctious, head-knocking, and skeptical of popular pieties as the original *Barney Google*; and hauled its hero's cotton-tail into nearly as many and as drastic (though never, of course, permanent) states of disrepair as his pre-puberty audience might have visited on his plush-coated nursery counterparts. Cady created the anti-hero (and, one is tempted to say, anti-rabbit) with the most remarkable effect, that Cady's Peter Rabbit never overwhelms, never threatens to absorb, his antecedents; but augments the sense of a continuous identity which Potter introduced, and Burgess helped to perpetuate. And this success surely proceeded from Harrison Cady's transmission of his own voracious inquisitiveness about the landscape in which Peter Rabbit dwelled; and, matching such curiosity, his appetite for immersing himself in that world.

In considering the work of an artist at once as omnivorously roving and as tautly insular as Cady, the handful of facts one can adduce may prove quite enough — even, perhaps, too much. For, whereas the work of the consummate originator may portray the evolution of personality, the work of a first-rate virtuoso-craftsman like Cady more often holds intact, career-long, like a brilliant aspic, certain basic traits, proclivities, and paradoxes of his nature. Thus, even the fragmentary biography may slip too facilely between thumb and forefinger as an index or "guide," which "aids" us only at hypostasizing the precious variables of the work itself; tempting us away from that task which is the best any biographical information may achieve; helping us articulate the vital uncertainties in the process of the work.

Yet, in Cady's case, a minimal biography provides, I think, a kind of controlling metaphor for what otherwise might seem simply a diffusely scintillating plethora of skills. Walter Harrison Cady (I have never encountered his first name signed to any of his work) was born in Garner, Massachusetts, June 17, 1877 (a portrait of Cady in *Life*, October 27, 1910 [reprinted in Number One of Jim Ivey's *cARToon Magazine*] lists the year as 1878; but this is contradicted by every other source I have consulted). According to the same *Life* article, and a feature-length (by E.W. Watson) interview portrait in the April, 1945 issue of the magazine *American Artist*, his father was a general storekeeper, a notable bibliophile (*American Artist* reports Cady's claim that over 1500 books lined the store's back rooms) and a spare-time naturalist.

Cady's work was noted by the visiting naturalist-explorer, Paul Du Chaillu, whom Cady had drawn, with an entourage of animals, on a sheet of brown wrapping paper. Leaving for New York at 18, he shortly thereafter sold some of his earliest work to *Harper's Young People* and a short-lived rival of *Life* called *Truth*; and was a staff artist on the *Brooklyn Daily Eagle*, until his crucial addition to *Life's* staff.

However, many question marks must be rubber stamped on the simplest assertions in this elementary account. (How much of a scholar was Cady's father? If, as claimed to *Life*'s interviewer, he had no formal artistic training, were there no informal studies, no influences, direct or otherwise, to be accounted for?) The central image of which I spoke remains as valid as it is persuasive: that of a distinctly gifted provincial, in the greatest and some of the lesser senses of that word; retaining, throughout a career of repeatedly astonishing volume and variety, the brilliant provincial's fiercely eclectic, occasionally crass appetite for a luxuriant profusion of experience; this extravagance scored and counterpointed by his (no less provincial) sardonically terse skepticism. Indeed, on these terms, the two interviews may almost be seen as complementary panels of a diptych-screen depicting variations of the same personality: the 1910 interview, the crisply reticent occupant of a walk-up studio, who "seemed not at all disposed to enter into minute facts about his own career"; the 1946 interview, a jovially voluble, Pickwickian-sounding gentleman who enjoys hoaxing casual acquaintances with tall tales; surrounded by Italian, Flemish, and Oriental art work (with a good word or two for himself as a bargain-hunter).

The imaginative centerpiece of Cady's fifteen years with *Life* (during which period, and thereafter, he contributed to *Judge*, *Country Gentleman*, the *Saturday Evening Post*, *Ladies' Home Journal*, and the long-since-defunct *People's Home Journal* in which appeared his first illustration of a Burgess story), was itself a village: the community of Beetleburgh, which threatens at times, in its thronging multiplicity, to overrun the borders of Cady's, and *Life's*, respective domains. Although Cady, in *American Artist*, reports having joined the staff at 24, the first work with his signature I have found appears in the May 21, 1903 issue, at which time he was 25. As against its ebullient title, "Business Boom," it is a tiny drawing of something like a third of a column: and exhibits Mr. Beetlebug, seller of boots and shoes, happily confiding to a fellow bug that Mr. Centipede has just fitted out his entire family. We see the bonanza customer sashaying down the path at right and realize that this image, more than the gag itself, is the cartoon's "point": i.e., the centipede as tall-story embodied, hyperbole domesticated and brought to bay in the telling. Centipedes and Daddy Long-Legs will appear and reappear among the voluminous Beetleburgh chronicles (the patron of the insect hotel, unable to sleep because the centipede in the room overhead keeps taking his shoes off; Miss Long-Legs, with whom all the swains at the Beetleburgh Ball are eager to dance, because she can accommodate so many at once): embodying Cady's two-edged appreciation of extravagance, of sheer multiplicity; and, too, his less ambivalent respect for virtuosity, for the artisan's many-handedness.

The comic and preposterous and utterly natural radiations of these creatures' multiple legs seem, like medallion-symbols, to bid the expansion of the Beetleburgh universe to the full-page and two-page dimensions it will occupy by 1906 and 1907. It must be noted, at this point, that Beetleburgh, far from being an innovation of any degree, was founded amid a plethora of drawings featuring insects, frogs, hippopotamuses, all performing various satiric or burlesque assignments; all in keeping with that heterogeneously humorous flavor, laced with polemic of varying strengths and syruped with good liberal intentions, which distinguished the early 1900's *Life* as waist-coated forebear of the *New Yorker*. As cavorting competitors of Cady's June bugs and crickets — and, later along, rabbits and frogs, with the advance of his endlessly self-integrating commonwealth — we find Kemble's acrobatic frogs; Lutz's own Bugville; and contestants from the various menageries of Gus Dirks, Dart, and other staff regulars. Given the various talents and energies displayed by his zoological colleagues, it is senseless, obviously, to seek any specious uniqueness in Cady's work. Yet, it makes considerable sense to try to identify that distinction which is his; which, I think, is the hectic empirical inquisitiveness — and acquisitiveness — busybodyish as Peter Rabbit himself — and, with it, the sensuous joy in garnering things, data, samples, potential identities — which, given his centripetal skill and Daddy Long-Legged venturesomeness, virtually dictate that the only way for the Beelteburgh universe — for the Cady universe, its nucleus in Beetleburgh — is expansion.

Probably because Cady's delight in abundant specifics dominated, or overrode, his sense of composition (how can the naturalist, bug-collector, connoisseur of data truly consider the world as being composed?) the earlier smaller drawings look somewhat over-congested and plushy. Cady's sense of design and patterning, as against the hubbub business of his details, always tends toward the static: his two favorite compositional devices are the Brueghelian open field, and a sinuous, infinitely attenuable kind of track, by either of which means he can freely proliferate and fondle examples. Yet, even in these overcrowded miniatures, one may notice traits that the enlarged space of later years will justify and honor.

For Beetleburgh is not only a puppet theatre in which insects disport themselves in human frock-coats, tippets, stove-pipe hats, aprons, bonnets, and watch-chains, in terms of absurdly human occasions and patterns; it is also, and by that token, a New England hamlet; and, an observed-and-recorded landscape of actual potato bugs, grasshoppers, and whatever. What kept these notions in harmonious, if frenziedly, jiggling co-existence are the crossed control-bars of Cady's devout observation and his artifice. Cady's artifice — that arabesque wing and arc of his line; the feathery notations of bark or plumage — is Cady's device for observing and identifying and preserving. Thus, in his Beetleburgh or, later, Rocky Pond or Huckleberry Hollow drawings, the landscape, the terrain, is ubiquitous, as it never is in Kemble's dry, dashingly spare Frog drawings. Thus — the grocer's son amidst his Flemish and Chinese art works — we see nature at its most natural and most artificial, at once.

The sense of theatre, the relish of theatrical occasion, of scene, tableau, and all those ceremonial felicities which are packeted in terms like "showing off" and "dressing up"; this range of gratification is expressed in Cady's finest work through the most electrically febrile excitement. Amid that slightly somber physicality which characterizes most of *Life*'s pictorial art (and, for what my scant knowledge is worth, that of most of the early American 1900s), Cady's is easily the most, if not the only, forthrightly erotic art that I can recall. It becomes more evidently so during 1905 and 1906, as he acquires a fonder, more leisurely control over his black and whites: those insidiously satiny blacks, those whites that can either shimmer as with August afternoon heat, or scintillate as with moonlit New England frost. Consider that charming (with more charms than one on its chain) drawing, "Ready for Spring," in the March 22, 1906 issue, with its unpretentious appreciation of so many vernal sweetnesses: from the frog, lower right, being cosmeticized by a mouse-barber (whose sign offers to powder wings "While You Wait"); to the upper area of the page, where a décolleté Goddess of Spring (most startling because one feels no inconsistency at all with her gently voluptuous context) is twining a ribbon around the neck of an old rabbit gentleman who could be one of Uncle Wiggily's more footloose (not to say, less rheumatic) cousins. Consider further a still earlier full-page drawing (August 24, 1905), "The Rocky Pond Rowing Association Holds Its Annual Carnival." The carnival is held against a richly appointed tree-trunk pavilion, housing an insect orchestra. In the middle ground cavort frogs, lady rabbits, and beetles (all creatures in these Cady drawings are bound by the fairy-tale egalitarianism of at least approximately equal size). In the foreground are some smirking, lecherous-eyed hares, very unlike the Easter doll models Cady used for Burgess's Peter. Far back right, beyond the orchestra, a procession makes its methodically solemn way up those stairs where a sign directs them "To the Bar." And, to the far left, exquisite ivory-white boaters are suspended, in their crafts, on the mated blacknesses of night and water. What is both so insidiously ingratiating and so touching about Cady's art in these and other drawings is the matter-of-fact eclecticism of the appetite which, one feels, has directed them: the candor, the warm crassness, with which he welcomes such diverse objects of his pleasure, giving to them his most open-hearted delight in them as facts; and bringing all, the fairy-tale imagery and the erotic playfulness, under the authority and benediction of his style; without — God bless him, and Pan, too! — so much as considering, I'm sure, any such thing as "absolute experience."

The more I consider it, the more likely it seems to me that the bugs were not only Cady's original, but his favorite, repertory company. Their neutrality, their preposterous-seeming graces and aptitudes, their amorality: all of these traits are recollected wistfully, as it were by Cady himself in the first decade of *Peter Rabbit.* They are not characters, but *personages*: theatrical figures which enact their author's appetites for spectacle, for practical jokes (including the crueler ones: a bug family admiring a firecracker that a "nice boy" has lighted in front of their home); for dress-parades (a bug husband critically surveying his Hepsy, who is posing beneath a human-sized picture-hat in a haberdashery); his zest for events, ceremonials, and great occasions like the spring planting, or the summer arrival, at some flint-faced New England resort, of succulently plump, straw-hatted tourists. On such occasion, the potato bugs, mosquitoes, and the ants array themselves in those formations which seem especially dear to Cady's eye and, possibly, heart: ranks, phalanxes, in which identity becomes a glimpsed, virtually casual distinction.

For Cady, these parades and festivals and public ceremonials are not only available scoops for amassing identities and situations. They offer him invitations to consolidate, crystallize and, indeed, to diminish, what is mythically vast and vague. One of the earliest drawings in which human figures prevail, the "Original Moving Day" (May 3, 1906) presents us with Noah on the point of embarkation, as a bottle-nosed old Yankee skipper, shod with one hip-boot and one ankle-high galosh; much encumbered by his immediate family, diverse ape and hippo couples, and their sundry luggage. The ark displays one of those advertising signs to which Cady's imagination cleaves: "Choice Apartments to Let to Select Couples, No Children." A drawing of October 24, 1907, the "Day Jonah Moved Out" shows the departing tenant loaded with golf clubs, sea-chest, potted plant, and clock. "Apartment to Let" is placarded on the whale's upper jaw. The "Original Thanksgiving Day in Old Plymouth" features pilgrims trying to sell real estate to the Indians, and the Café Standish advertising its table d'hote dinner for fifty clams. And a wonderfully Hogarthian-toned drawing of July 4, 1907 — the "Original July Fourth" — singularly compact for Cady, shows the Fathers at Independence hall engaged in a thrashing, writhing, headlocking, wig-tearing donnybrook that Peter Rabbit and his woodland compatriots could scarcely hope to rival.

Those comic mercantilisms which speckle such commemorative scenes — the placards, the commercial booths and banners — are too ubiquitous to suggest any savagely deflationary skepticism (with a few exceptions which deserve and shall receive separate attention). They represent Cady's own comic testimony to the ubiquity of the here-and-now, and ever-reductive sense of the present, with its two-bit expediencies, which his native New Englander's soul can attest. They are inseparable, too, of course, from that imagery of the world-as-fairground — a bazaar of infinite scope, of endlessly abounding ware — which his drawings cherish. "Poverty was my legacy," the *American Artist* interview quotes him, "And I have ever been grateful for it. Poverty teaches great lessons that so many fail to learn. To an eager mind it reveals that many of the best things in life have no price tag on them." Yet, what so many of Cady's drawings reveal is a kind of continuous astonishment — scornful, yet, in general, sardonically tolerant — that the torrential abundance of this world should leave room for any price tags at all; and, at the same time, the Yankee acknowledgement of man's right to price, and to advertise, that which man has made or collected. Last but surely not least, these tiny enterprises and exhibits represent a recurrent miniature symbol of Cady's double feeling about the mingled grandiosity and opportunistic, self-vaunting flash which national myths and holidays represent.

At the same time, as I have said, one does not sense Cady's motive in such reverse-laureate drawings as being purposely deflationary; largely, I think, because one never feels any awareness on his part of any standard against which to deflate: of authentic grandeur, largeness of scale. Not that they seem dominated by coarseness or pettiness, any more than do similar works of the Brueghels (who, I suspect, may have influenced him prevalently). That very sensuous beauty, robust and somehow courtly at once, which informs some of his most droll or roguish devisings, is also what neutralizes, I think, the possibility of grandeur and of awe in Cady's work. Nor, when I refer to "awe," do I refer to something beyond his province as a cartoonist. One recallsThomas Nast's occasional drawings, notably the famous one of Boss Tweed as nesting vulture; or Winsor McCay's productions — not only the *Little Nemo* strips but the often banally conceived editorial cartoons he was drawing for Hearst in the '20s — which affect one with a solitary, intense, and starkly defined massiveness, and scope, the scene of mighty space which suggests a veiled consciousness — which, to me, is what the word "awe" connotes. It is ridiculous to speak of "missing" such a quality in Cady's work, as it would be to speak of missing it in the Ziegfeld Follies. But it is hardly ridiculous, in regarding work of Harrison Cady's shimmering volatility and richly exploratory range, to define the nature of that range; and — let the art be "popular" or "high" — to inquire whether or not, and how, the creative imagination, the artist's drive to articulate this imagination as identity — evolves itself. And in Harrison Cady's work — as wonderful as I find so much of it, and as distinctive as I judge his contribution to American popular art to be — nevertheless, certain lacks which I have mentioned, convey to me not only the consciously elected, or accepted, limitations of an artist's autonomous response to experience — not the limitations which he evolves for himself; but, rather, the limitations which he initially brings to bear upon experience, which are implicit in his nature; and which the accretion of skills does not so much overcome, or even neutralize, but merely holds in check, still to be divined in his work, along with his other traits of perspective and attitude. And to note there is the only way fully to honor that scope of energy and humorous resource that makes his total identity so impressive and warmly engaging.

The wind that twirls and tinkles the wind-bells of his talent is that of illustrator. The basic component of his work is the illustration, and what it suggests to me about his personality as artist. The illustration represents an attempt to see the typical, or archetypal, in terms of the particular; and it can represent, in the instance of work like Cady's, an important threshold; one at which the observer and collector, like Cady, chooses to stop, or beyond which he dares not proceed. I mean, that threshold beyond which the creative imagination formulates, or merely supposes, which is the first step anyway, its own context: that which proposes its own terms of inquiry, of definition — of illustration. Thus, the power to envision becomes, through its extrapolation, a power to reshape, to redirect and to rediscover the world.

I think that Cady displays the last of these powers — enough in itself to guarantee him rank among some of the outstanding artists and documenters the United States has produced — but that he lacked that primacy of imagination that would have enrolled him beside Winsor McCay, George Herriman, and Maurice Sendak. Visually gorgeous as is so much of his work, it lacks that *sovereignty* of the visual that distinguishes the artists I have mentioned. As an illustrator — by stressing which, I emphasize again, I have no intention of stressing any demeaning or devaluating kind of inferiority — Cady subscribes to certain *given* actualities, certain basic pragmatisms, which those other artists are at very least less quick to accept. Considering the fantasticality of his material, it is remarkable how little his work exhibits of sheer dream, of the polymorphous wildness, which those other men share, on frequent occasion, at least. His very best work is earthy, warmly matter-of-fact; conveying that sense of possession that is linked to discovery. When he introduces dreams, as in his drawing of 1914-1915, they will be of the most conventional Victorian muslin. When Peter Rabbit's kiddies dream, their fantasies are of the most briskly anecdotal kind (and as briskly detonated as *Little Nemo's*).

The beautiful paradox of Cady's matter-of-factness is that it gives him heart to welcome what is gratuitously eccentric, odd-shaped, tangy about experience; and excites his cricket-quick resource as a maker — which, for him, means, primarily, inventor. Invention in itself is a secondary or tertiary form of creative imagination; imagination as subordinated to the will. It represents a kind of accommodation of circumstances, by devising and improvising momentary adjustments; and so it does in Cady's work. And not only in the decorative resource of his Beetleburgh pavilions and staircases, its ballrooms and racetracks; but in Cady's unapologetic affection for, and animated proliferation of, gimmicks and gadgets; ranging from the giddily serpentining contrivances of Professor Quack's locomotive reducing salon, to the iridescent horrors of an industrial Dachau for children. And except, perhaps, to the most Rousseau-sodden intelligence, no deep contradiction presents itself in the way Cady's vivacious, rather chaffingly quizzical regard for machines nearly keeps abreast of his regard for insects and animals and birds. He cherishes in all that which is gracefully direct and, at the same time, ornamentally quaint; that which responds smartly to the purpose of a particular occasion, and that which answers only the occasion of an identity, of an idiosyncratic history. And these double-coursing loves of Cady's unite in his love of making: taking possession of a situation by seeing it as a form; then devising for it some resolution, even if that resolution consists solely of focusing and crystallizing the situation. Not the grandest, not the most richly transmuting of creative processes; nevertheless, the function of maker operates, through Harrison Cady's best work, with an infectious intensity of animation; recalling in us, perhaps from very many years ago, when the impulses to possess, know and name — the initial steps of creation, fused in a gem-like one.

In 1907, he begins drawings that would seem to claim the collective title: "The World as a Fairground of Folly." I use "satiric" both advisedly and apprehensively — as of electric shocks and jangling alarms; since the word seems at once to ask and to defy redefinition, especially at present; when our manifold perspective of society, our claustrophobic awareness of current history as *multitudinously* with us, have combined to alter so drastically, if not to abolish, the authority of the satirist: a figure, it seems to me, whose authority resided precisely with his power to convey the sense of re-discovering evil through the lens of individual sensibility, and humor. And in this latter capacity, it seems to me, Cady — although lacking either the imaginative vocabulary or the ferocious moral independence of Goya, or even Nast — has both re-discovered and predicted a comic mode as apposite to our century as were those artists to their own. Cady's mode was basically as antique as that of the *Nirrenshaft*, or Brueghel the Elder's rustic surveys, from which it derived; but it focused and enriched and enlarged the ancient device — the panorama of vanities and self-delusions — by re-affirming the sense of location, and the sense of personal perspective; which Harrison Cady, who had made of style his attire, was all-but-uniquely equipped to supply.

Equipped, in this partnership of sensuous versatility and stringent decorum, which have brought us heretofore, as framed by *Life*'s various cartoon conventions, Cady's own fecund responses to occasion and situation, and his joy in documenting, these responses.

Now, directed to the chronicling of follies, that same combination of appetites and disciplines brings us an assortment of drawings which, however traditional their premise and antecedents, seem of an almost novelistic density. Contemporary enough in the spirit they radiate — amused though wary-eyed perplexity at the sheer multitude of evils and fooleries — to turn our eyes back to a present-day Fools' Parade: the shag-haired, houseless, housebreaking but unhousebroken offspring of Robert Crumb.

The first of the procession is dated April 1, 1907; with the overall title, "Why not Make April First a Legal Holiday?" Its content, covering two full pages, is a spectacular march along what appears to be the Fifth Avenue of that era. Leading the parade is a jester on a sumptuously caparisoned donkey, a clown-dog in circus ruff and hat trotting beside him. He precedes rank upon rank of fools, bearing banners like those of the trade guilds: "There's No Fool Like an Old Fool" — the central body, comprising strutting dotards with their sweeties; to their left, Society Girls who Married for Titles, and are seen squired by diminutive tuxedoed gigolo types; behind them, Married for Money, and behind them, the Get Rich Quick Brigade. A phalanx of bandaged simpletons, bearing firecrackers and cannons, make up the "Didn't Know it was Loaded" unit. Farther back, the "Patent Medicine Fools" can be seen; and, maintaining the rear, "Plain and Simple Damn Fools"; while very, very far back, left — one of Cady's characteristic diminuendo touches: "Fools Who Don't Subscribe to *Life*."

What I notice myself, in summarizing this content, is, of course, that the summary seems so commonplace: a roll call of popular clichés and pedestrian suppositions; whereas to see the drawing before one is to make instant contact with its glisteningly ornate mixture of pomp and meticulous solidity; and with the number of glancingly peripheral effects which seem, almost, to usurp the importance of the larger content. Cady's style has never seemed so much a filter, or a grille, as in these drawings. Nor, by the same token, has it ever functioned so aptly as a means of identification; in fact, of naming; for it is through the style that he names that catch-phrases and categories take on their corporate force, and their sheer recognizability. I realize particularly from work like this (and this, too, is a factor of his vocation as illustrator), how much the word permeates Cady's work, how omnipresent is text throughout his work. How much sentences, statements, aphorisms, assume priority over the visual, yet — at his best — drop into natural collaboration with the visual; some of the more obvious by-products being those advertising signs and banners which I have discussed, and which play a more assertive role than ever in the satiric drawing.

The most notable impression, however, it seems to me, of even a single example like the April Fool drawing, is how Cady avoids according evil, as such, any power whatsoever; avoids personifying it, and envisioning it as a force. This has very much to do with the neutrality to which he has elected for so long; which is partly the neutrality of the village wiseacre or sage; and partly the neutrality of a more diversely driven sort of man; who would be compromising by any violent moral passion, his capacity for receiving, for apprehending, for suffering. You will miss grievously, if you so misunderstand Cady as to expect it, that genuine animus which propels every one of Art Young's swart, saturnine cartoons, appearing at the same time in *Life*, and slightly later on in *New Masses*. But you may find again — in these drawings, no less than in Cady's animal illustrations for Thornton W. Burgess — a kind of esthetic empathy become, through the medium of his style, both so acute and so not-quite-drunkenly comprehensive, that it remains a tissue-thinness this side of sentimentality; and, in some of his 1914-15 drawings, severely buckles that partition, at very least. On the other hand, when he portrays the "Road to Hell," in 1910, the rather Ziegfeldish staircase that represents it is not paved with good intentions, but layered with popular and mostly innocent transgressions: swearing, smoking, attending prize fights; its heaviest chord struck by an elevator sign, inviting those in a hurry to "Take This Elevator with Another Man's Wife." The demons are barely glimpsed, in a handsomely stalactited alcove, at the bottom of the page.

The tenderness of Cady's to which I've been alluding was knowingly characterized once, by James Agee, as the Siamese twin of cruelty (Agee was referring to D. W. Griffith; and I am reminded both of Griffith's imagery and the characterization, by the voluptuous, shadow-steeped gentleness of many later Cady drawings). In both emotions resides a kind of avidity for retaining the sensation of emotion, without the chain-reaction of empathy, of true identification with the other person, which genuine emotion must quicken. The cruelty which discloses itself increasingly in his work, from 1907 on — sometimes as an aridly crass New England roughness; sometimes as merely unexpectedly deeper coldness, or arbitrariness, than the village-skeptic patina suggests — reminds me of the neutrality, as well as the near-sentimentality for which that neutrality acts as shield and control. Fairs, themselves, in the raunchy medievality which they have kept over the centuries, enlist much of such cruelty; and in the work of Cady's maturity, it is honed by the quickness of curiosity — that other companion of much cruelty, especially in children — which he brings.

It plays like a narrowly glimpsed St. Elmo's fire around the edges of that superb drawing of September 14, 1914, which Jim Ivey has reprinted in Number One of his *cARToon magazine.* The central oval insert shows a boy of perhaps ten or eleven, in collapse; supported only by mechanical arms that grip his own arms, and his waist; and which extend from an apparatus, slightly taller than an average man; which is simultaneously spraying him with ammonia and the contents of a drum labeled "Reviving Fluid"; while a lower arm of the machine injects him in the calf, the joint of the hypodermic emerging from his shin. OUR MOTTO: DO IT NOW, declares a sign on the machine; which the caption announces as a "combination ginger machine, exhilirator, reviver, resuscitator, and ambition injector, absolutely prevents nervous collapse and ennui." The locale is a 1914 factory engaging in child labor; and the drawing, over the title "Some suggestions for still greater efficiency in child labor," comprises a page of vignettes — claustrophobically packed, and with the simmering vibrancy of July asphalt. In the upper left hand corner, a bespectacled and Dundrearyed old gentleman, a cold-eyed Mr. Pickwick, rubs his hands as he contemplates another young boy in an elaborate steam-bath, the stud-pimpled surface of which seems to be suffering from its own heat. The boy looks on the point of liquefaction. OUR MOTTO: SKINNY LITTLE LABORERS MAKE LIGHT FACTORIES. The cultural resources of this notable community are on view in the rectangled lower-center panel; in which the factory entrance (OUR MOTTO: "EXPERIENCE IS THE BEST TEACHER") is flanked, in what might be the landscape of contemporary Belfast, by the silhouetted ruins of a desiccated church, and a school, which one of Cady's more superfluous signs marks "CLOSED."

The drawing is almost unique in Cady's work, I think, for its exploration of a locale; and for the pulverizingly oppressive physical imminence that he gives that locale, and the attendant implications of the period. One can read as much about the impersonally diffuse brutality of the early 20th century here, I think, as in an account by Dreiser or Farrell. And, at the same time, viewing the drawing again and again, I have never lost my initial consciousness of Cady relishing his performance; not that I felt him to be savoring the children's oppression and pain and spiritual stupefaction; but rather, that — for all the patent candor of his indignation — he accommodated this indignation, and the horror which must have predicated it, to the vocabulary of his style. Some mechanism of response strains out what the writing of Farrell or Dreiser — or the frequent drawing of Art Young — convinces us again and again is monstrously unassimilable by art, about the actuality of social oppression; and to which, therefore, art must bring a humility beyond the humility of its own gifts candidly offered. Such a challenge, I feel, is somehow sidestepped by Cady's work; what I feel, even amid the stunning actuality of his factory — is that, for him, not, undoubtedly, as a man, but as an artist, the abuse of machinery takes close second place to the abuse of young boys and girls. And such abuse he is able to assimilate, in a sense, and compensate, through the exercise of his invention: that faculty, after all, which is framed and fashioned for compensation. So, too, one recalls his numerous shies at irresponsible and ruthless motorists; which, however generally — in the earlier years, at least; they later become more somber — produce drawing like the October 17, 1907 one of Mr. Boodlecinch's progress through a New England neighborhood — leaving a comically-entangled and picturesque debris of architecture, livestock, and natives; with a frieze depicting a hayseed posse in avid pursuit. What strikes and, not a little, disturbs the reader, is the way Cady assimilates his affection for the landscape, distress at its violation, and ire at the desecrators, into a comic montage of such aplomb; in which the velocity he deplores becomes the most comically-exciting factor.

In a beautiful essay on Robert Frost, Professor T. K. Whipple once noted the intensity of response, the priority given the most eccentric violences of wounded pride or sense of fitness, which inhabit the stereotype of the woodenly unemotional New Englander; and he cites the muted savagery, behind the angular folksiness of tone, in poems of Frost like "The Code," in which a hired hand overturns a haystack on a farmer, in resentment of the farmer's command. I find that I can super-impose much of what Whipple writes about such *reaction* — as a trait of behaviors, as a spiritual condition — on my own feelings about Harrison Cady's work; in so much of which what delights or disturbs or, on rarer occasion, appalls me, proceeds from the importance he gives to his personal hierarchy of reactions; and his wonderful presumption, even from within the Chinese armor of his technique, of those reactions' importance, and his willingness to project them upon terrain of such scope. Such presumption, so common in the era of Cady's career, is, I think, hard for us to imagine, much less acknowledge as a viable attitude for polemic; when the best of our editorial cartoonists, like Herblock and Conrad, are rigorously selective, gnomically whimsical, cheekily *ad hominem* in their common approach. With Cady's work, however, the chromatic scale of reaction on which he played is to be borne in mind no less, I suggest, when reading the generous-spirited best of his drawings, then when encountering their shocking, painful and at least equally brilliant opposites. I refer particularly to the virulently anti-Semitic drawings, which appear with especial concentration between 1910 and 1915. The apogee of these, I think, appears in the May 5, 1910 issue of *Life*. It is called "Surrender of New Yorktown" — surrender, that is, to invading hordes which are unmistakably identified, although Cady's for-once diffident labels designate them only as "Trusts." All — Diamond Trusts, Jewelry Trusts, Gold Trusts and Theatre Trusts — present the same badger-like profile, greedily squinted eyes and derby hats. Their solid ranks are shown marching on City Hall, where the sorrowing but resolute-shouldered incumbent is having his baggage transferred to the sidewalk (by a covertly smiling black porter). At far left, Our New Mayor sits enthroned. The wrought eagle on top of his throne's back has outspread wings crooked in a shrug of, one suspects, other than stoic resignation. Cady has never shown such acumen at drawing corporate ranks of figures which at once present a solid mass; and, in the sheer definiteness of each figure's tracing, a potential entity. His hardest, hottest black-white contrasts dominate the conquering armies. The Diamond and Jewelry Trusts stand before the heaped litter of their properties. As a grace note, the front ranks of the Theatre Trust — before which an aged actor knees ignominiously — wear ballet tutus.

"Surrender of New Yorktown" was, of course, no more unique in Harrison Cady's career than are its images and attitudes unique in *Life*'s or many other periodicals in that era. Cady had done relatively innocuous Semitic caricatures in 1907, when Jonah disembarks from the whale to an audience of Hebraic faces, embroidering adjoining cliffs. And, in his splendid New Year's cartoon for 1910 — evidently modeled on Bosch's *Garden of Earthly Delights* — the spectators at the New Year's birth include the Wandering Jew and — standing slightly below him — his smirking near-replica, in morning-coat and striped trousers, who carries the Guild sign of — to be sure — the Theatre Trust. No unfamiliar opponent — or emblematic image of that opponent to *Life*, over the preceding years; during which one finds numerous attacks on the Theatrical Trust, or Theatrical Syndicate, trademarked by the Mask of Comedy: *Life*'s own beaked, bearded, crafty-eyed transmutation. One notes, among the loose, casually ignorant, not-altogether-hostile contempt of innumerable "Jewish jokes," the Prodigal Son returning to Cohenhurst Manor; drawings like William H. Walker's of 1901 ("Oh, Mr. Carnegie, This is so Sudden!") in which Andrew Carnegie is seen espousing the Drama, to the horrified chagrin of the now-familiar countenances.

Yet, the standard argument/evasion that the prejudices propounded by Cady's drawings were those "of his time" seems particularly pointless — whatever one's urge to make the best possible case for him — in context of his total work; so much of which reflects or exemplifies the bidding of "his times," whether those times represent a specific assignment, or the cultural imprimatur of a period; and yet, so much of whose essential personality resides, to be wrested by us from its servile craft. Virtually every authentic artist's work, great or small, expresses a never-ending barter between the artist and his era; so much the fiercer as the artist is greater. His victory is measured by what resides of his identity, of the grace which it confers; for in that record we read the value of his expenditure, the enrichment by him of his period. So, when a champion bargainer — if not a great artist — like

Harrison Cady, who was less generous than the best, yet pursued his own life-long, hard-lined, margin-hugging barter. When such a man succumbs, and succumbs with such an ardor, to the most squalid meannesses of his times, one feels, beneath all feelings of sorrow and embarrassment, that one has been, this time, cheated; that Cady and the period have acted, as it were, in collusion. What make it worse is that the ardor to which I refer is not that of a compulsive hater; of, say, a Wyndham Lewis, whose laboriously documented anathema bestows, if not grandeur, a perverse richness upon his victims. Cady is no such hater; neither here, nor in those drawings of September 19, 1912, in which Father Knickerbocker is Gulliver, spread-eagled by Lilliputian Jews; nor the one still earlier (October 5, 1911), of the same Knickerbocker being dosed by a babushka-ed Mother Europe with Jewpills — spheroid replicas of the accustomed head, of which he protests: "The more I take, the worse I feel!"; nor in the later drawing of Jewry as a monstrous baby, threatening to overgrow its metropolitan cradle; nor the St. Patrick's Day drawing of the Last (i.e., Irish American) Survivors, straggling past a committee whose banner exclaims "Welcome to Rabbi Patrick." What we find bearing Cady onward through these unhappy performance is never the authoritative, the at times all-but-self-justifying rancor of a Goya, of a Swift; but rather, a medley of other feelings, notably fear and jealousy: the typical fear and jealousy of that often self-educated esthete, many of whose number voice a certain kind and degree of anti-Semitism. A part of his motivation is, I think, to embody in the Jew that erosion of cultural quality which, to be sure, is always taking place; but which he feels — usually, in proportion to his self-education — as an assault upon, or a theft or vandalism of, a bitterly earned property. I feel something of such jealous fear in Harrison Cady's anti-Semitic cartoons: the adoption by a man whose usual work is infused with a lover's drive and solicitude, of a device dictated and inscribed by ancient animosity; rendering in perverted form, his accustomed loves: of multiplicity, of animal vivacity.

Seen in terms of his 15 years' career with *Life*, he presents himself, I think, as an amateur who has in no wise ever abandoned that role in its original sense; so that, with each successive work, the style and artisanship of that particular work becomes more evidently important as a confirmation, a seal, a kind of lamination which insulates that vignette, or gag, or grass-roots formulation. The work of a devout amateur like Cady features that rediscovery of style and craft; for they have become, not merely means whereby he ascertains or simply tests some perspective of the wold's proceedings; but have become part of those proceedings; because they pertain to the lover's confirmation of his love. And it embodies, reinforces the will of the self-educated, self-cultivated man, to make that cultural lamination, that sense of style, a verifiable part of what his tirelessly estimating Massachusetts eye divines. Style in its authentic sense most often represents how an artist seeks to preserve a little while — or give the illusion of preservation to — those reflexes or tics or momentary prejudices or, sometimes, discoveries of his perception that he prefers preserving over others. In Harrison Cady's case, I more often get the impression that his style — styles — are framed to preserve everything, even as he professes to ridicule, fondly, everything.

The amateur's all-inclusive tenderness is what explains the irreconcilable-seeming shift of Cady's style, which startles us first, in the drawing of 1913: that shift, I mean, from the bristling outdoor busyness of the earlier drawings, to the darkness-enfolded passivity, the island stillness of his lamp-lit women, in the extraordinary lobby for women's suffrage which he conducts intermittently over the next three years. Of course, the work of any hack, which Cady, avocationally at least, was, provides its own standard explanation for all stylistic changes, if only because — counter to much contemporary opinion — only the hack regards style and content as truly inseparable; meaning that style, for him, represents a mechanism of adjustment to the object which content offers. Yet, it seems to me, that to acknowledge Harrison Cady's singular, though not first-rank, stature as an American artist and what it signifies, is to part company, from the first, with glibly docketing generalizations; or, at very least, with the supposition that terms like "hack" can express anything comprehensive or useful about his stature and achievement. Because a highly gifted second-rank artist like Cady embodies the primacy of sheer quantity in American life and art, and of writing one's particular history through various adjustments to that almost-pulverizing physical space, which Charles Olson and other critics have apostrophized;

by which, even the highest of American artists know a kinship with hack practice and hack rhythms which, it seems to me, are far less common (though, perhaps becoming more so within the last generation) anywhere else in the world. So, too, from one view, Cady's middle-decade drawings are, themselves, neither more nor less than emblems of that laureate-like status into which seniority and productivity have straight-armed him; away from the mock-laureate role of his early 1900s public-event cartoons. 1914 drawings like "How the Cap'n Lost His Leg" or "Dreams" offer that obligatory piety, that toast-masterish nod to Serious Values, which one comes to recognize in the work of cartoonists (think of Burris Jenkins, or McCay) who have attained a certain eminence, and density of habit: plus, perhaps, corresponding remoteness from their original humorous enterprise. Such does one feel from Cady's genre sketches as this time: until, that is, with the women's suffrage cartoons, one meets once more that catalytic intensity, that (surely, at least, in this series) all-but-obsessive protectiveness, not toward figures but toward his world; which, almost as with the genre-images of Griffith, makes it impossible to assign to Cady the coagulated soul-grease of the professional sentimentalist.

The signal of Cady's intensity is the sense of mythic isolation, of dream-like starkness — always, however, enfolded by his consciousness of the event as an identity in itself — which has emerged more emphatically in his work since 1912 — an October 31 drawing, showing Rodin's Thinker contemplating modern New York — and, presently following, in the November 21st issue, a macabre companion Death as a sign painter, lettering a patent-medicine ad on the wall of a building. As mutedly sardonic as the earlier drawings were clamorous, such drawings as these retain, however, that absorption in the scene as such which prevails in Cady's work, and which (with only one or two exceptions, like a 1916 lampoon of Navy Secretary Daniels) avoids the hectically ingenious, expostulatingly surreal allegories drawn by Young, or Walter or Dart. For Cady, it seems, is never engaged in the investigation of an event or situation — much less any analytic dialogue with it, or with his audience — but rather with ingesting it, and comprehending its effect upon him, and savoring its *thingness.* There is always that iconographic tone to his drawings, which makes them as remote from the present-day personifications of Herblock, or Mauldin, or Conrad, as from the savage theatrics of Art Young in their own time. And the intensity which they convey, is an esthetic intensity of possessiveness, through which Cady's apprehension of the scene becomes one with that scene, and impounded in it, as within a Chinese emperor's amber; not the dramatic, erotic-touched intensity of, say, Charles Dana Gibson, whose characters' physiques demonstrate such theatrical, and voluptuous, pliancy and expressiveness. Cady never registers Gibson's sheer anatomical curiosity — his faces and postures catalogue of seductiveness, scorn, or naïve openness. Yet, to realize this limitation of Cady is immediately to remember that with which he supplements it: the dream-like totality, the corporate personality, which these situations and archetypal stationings assume in his eyes, and hence in ours.

For all the three-centuries' distillation of Rembrandt which they conspicuously embody, the women's suffrage drawings beginning in October of 1913 imprint the derivations with a melancholy tenderness, a contemplation of loss, and undercurrent to these feelings, a horror of isolation, of removal, which, I suggest, utters the darkest anxieties that Cady's drawings — possibly excepting the anti-Semitic polemics — have ever voiced. I have every certainty, however regretful, that the drawings would, today, be received with small sympathy by many women, and most understandably; because, indeed, they assign to women a kind of sanctity which must, I should suppose, lay an ultimate insufferable restriction upon any human being. And yet, they are redeemed, I think, from the most demeaning of sentimentalism, from that which withers identity in an incubatored holiness, by the reality of the need with which Harrison Cady underscores his appeals.

The first of the suffragist cartoons (October 16, 1913) portrays, like a decoration of Genesis, the division of darkness from light: here, the darkness of a city street unvisited by female ballot: pustular with the fuzzy lights of bars, shady hotels, brothels, haunted by various prowling or crouching silhouettes; and, adjoining it, the pristinely white, rapturously lighted houses and shops of the street where Suffrage lives. Brushing aside the sentimental cobwebbing — or, rather, letting it hang in place, as necessary filter for the genuine sentiment, which, in, my opinion, still, after more than three generations, supports and almost redeems the simplistic pseudo-idealism, the twittery bathos. What Cady effects here — and, very largely, through the shrine-like stasis of his composition, the formal severity which is so startlingly poignant — is to present what was once the commonest of myths about American women, a myth of which today's latest, and possibly last, filterings are those plumbers and housekeepers of the detergent commercials — and, invest it with the distinctive intensity of a personal yearning, of a signal need; resulting in an image of woman as a stanchion of sanity, much less a dispenser of socio-moral detergents than a refuge, an assurance of reality; of, that is, the reality which remains when the reality Outside — Matthew Arnold's land of dreams — has gone to scrofulous darkness.

The darkness infiltrates those pro-women suffrage drawings; reminding us, by contradiction, of how enamored their author has been with that teeming world which he must here depict as nightmare; and the paradox, though expressed with a fervor which bears it something beyond the mere fatuous paradox of common propaganda — that Cady is seeking, in the woman-image, a reality more real than the pestilent reality which, however, in this context, becomes as insubstantial as delirium. For the images of saloons and red-light hellholes show none of Goya's jolting concreteness; rather, they contribute to a central and sovereign horror; that of woman's isolation from this world, and the deprivation which Cady reads in it. What is more forcefully saddening than the excrescences of poverty and vice in themselves, is their blurry remoteness; the way in which, for example — in the drawing of October 23, 1913, only a week after the one I have discussed — the darkness immediately surrounding the woman at her lamp — which the lamplight makes seem as warmly substantial as a sable lining — how this darkness, as it extends outward from her, seems to become a very darkening of the imagination itself, and a dissolution of precious reality.

Although he gradually relinquishes the suffragist theme, that displacement which those drawings show, of the world — what once was his world, proclaimed and reveled-in — so that the old swarming diversity is transferred to the swirlings of reverie, or hallucination — this sense of abdication persists, never altogether giving place, throughout all his subsequent serious work for *Life* ("serious" meaning, to me, all the work which makes up the remainder of his authentic, not chronological *Life* career: 1914-1918.) To me, the genuinely effective strain of his World War I propaganda drawing — for which he was given the Allied Artists' Award — is never the strain of flatulent glory-mongering which further poisons, with a poison as of gratuitous indignity, my own memories of World War II. Rather, the relatively few drawings by Cady which help authenticate his work of the period, all incorporate wistfulness, loneliness, psychic and emotional bereavement. Such a drawing is "Belgium: The Field of His Fathers" (1915), with Don Quixote, on horse-back, filing the desiccated landscape with remembered windmills; or, the 1915 "Joffre," with the general visited by Napoleon and his phantom troops (such spectral "guest spots" were much favored by Cady, who would later introduce Abraham Lincoln; with comment, to be sure, more wistful than helpful). Or, the surprisingly few savage drawings (which somewhat accelerate from 1917 on): the December 1917 "Twas the Night Before Christmas"; a photographically stark depiction of a butchered French family, lying in the snow; or, some ten months earlier (February 1, 1917) the superb study — reproduced in the *American Artist* portrait I have mentioned — "A Family in Germany that Hasn't Lost a Member": the family comprising the Hohenszöllern males; whom we see, in white uniforms, strutting, like hybrids of goose and weasel, down a corridor of ghastly pale light. The Crown Prince wears a tiny skull and cross-bones on his shako; and a cigarette cants from his lips, which wear the watchful smirk that Cady sometimes give his foxes and weasels, in the Burgess illustrations. And the fatuous, grotesque advance of this procession — perhaps the most ferociously derisive parade ever imagined by Cady — flings our eye over the massed, silhouetted hordes of arm-waving spectators, on either side: from which emerge, first the raging face of a whiskery patriarch, then a moribund and ragged shadow, standing on someone's shoulders; then, the ubiquitous eyes — emerging from the irregular blackness, like the eyes of night animals, only far more sinister — all of which are pupilless. The mob takes one's mind backward, first to the thronging Jewish invaders of "New Yorktown"; then, forward, to those innumerable, never tiring but ever-more-tiresome crowds of vengeful neighbors whose shouts and cudgels pursue Peter Rabbit to the doors of his home.

And the mob image itself is, I think, crystallization of that *removal* from the jubilant profusion of his youthful drawings — the sense, not of his having lost his appetite for it, but of his realizing perforce the incapacity of his appetite for what has become too overwhelmingly and stridently and sometimes alarmingly profuse — which I find in the largely dreary, ceremonially handsome propaganda cartoons of the middle and late decade. It is in this period that I find the ebulliently omnivorous folklorist of the early 1900's, curdling into a version of that podiumed prophet whose echo-chambered tones all-but-audibly recall to us the suffocating endeavors of Stephen Vincent Benet or Edna St. Vincent Millay, for World War II radio. To consider an Eisensteinian lollapalooza like "In the Spirit of the Great Crusades" — with those iridescently featureless — and, I'm sure, smell-less — marching phalanxes, reminds me only of the ranked potato-bugs, moles and pumpkin-bugs in the 1910 "Battle for Hunker's Hill"; and of the identity, the very tangibility, which numbers could acquire, then, for him. His fatal loss is the loss of solidity, because there is only one solidity for him, and it is absolute, and distinguishes his rapport with both the world he knows and the world he does not know. The major, if only partial, exceptions to the empty majesty of 1918-1919 are a few naval drawings, which, at least, breathe a freshness of space — actual, not allegorical — and water; reminding us, albeit glancingly, of seascapes like "Wounded Whale" or "Grappling the Lost Anchor," which he was to paint in his latter years; or, Peter Rabbit's joyous, if misadventure-pitted, Sunday excursions on his craft, the *Sally*.

Yet to say that the war inhibited or deflected the true course of his work, would be simplistic and patronizing to Cady himself; for the truth is, that the cataclysm of World War I proved an agency of encouragement and liberation and self-discovery for the art department of *Life*: partly, I think, because of the crucial discovery, by many a resigned or timid or self-despising artist, that style and technique could serve as the instant tools for serving an impassioning cause, inapropos of that cause's validity. Of more concretely immediate importance, perhaps, the provincial part of *Life* magazine had flung open waterways to the popular art of Europe, and especially that of the German caricaturists: a fiercely purposeful, stringently patterned, austerely decorative art: about as germane to the ambling documentation of *Life*'s early 1900's cartoons, as a dreadnought to a

Massachusetts fishing schooner. The effect of such intense and schematic art, which imposes the terrain of its own perspective, rather than acceding to the given terrain of neutralized experience, is to awaken and re-animate even some of *Life*'s oldest contributors, as though they had discovered themselves citizens of a new country. So we find, in those vertiginously exciting issues of 1917-1920, the work of Ellison Hoover (later, with Arthur Folwell, to succeed Clare Briggs as author of *Mr. and Mrs.*, in the *New York Herald-Tribune*): tiny, globular Germans, bewhiskered and Prussian helmeted, tumbling like pinballs over the aproning space of some capacious Wilhelmstrasse, or beerhall; and occasionally, among such innocuous-looking kobolds, so formidable a drawing as "Gott" (the white-beareded Prussian God, guzzling beer among the blasted remnants of a city). And thus, too, we encounter the sleek-lined japonaiseries of Red Irvin — the harsh-stroked, gallows-toned sketches of Netherlands import Louis Rawmaekers. But we also discover a new access of vitality and invention of old *Lifers* like Harry Grant Dart, and William H. Walker; and, most distinguished of all, Charles Dana Gibson; who contributed to *Life*'s World War I campaign, what amounts almost to a propagandistic mythology, featuring three incomparably vivid personifications: the Junoesque (undebatably virginal) and falcon-eyed Goddess of Civilization; the burly, malignly carnal Prussian, spike-helmeted and spike-moustached; and the Goddess' sinister counterpart, War herself as the Prussian's harlot-mistress; the hypnotically macabre contrast of whose voluptuous body and smirking death's-head (which Gibson was able to endow with a tonal scale of expressions) surely influenced the creation of C.D. Bachelor's Millie War, in the early '30s. Not only Gibson's impeccable sense of proportion and gravity; his ability to reconcile the physically natural and the physically graceful; but, his instinct for erotic actuality, and how it permeates a variety of social tableaux here empowered him to imagine situations at once melodramatic and concretely certifiable; and, in the scenes featuring the Prussian and the Whore, a succession of pictures which, even today, exude the fetid sexuality of Eric von Stroheim's films.

Even at its brilliant best, Cady's work of this period, it seems to me, evinces no such freedom of self-discovery, no exploration of a new imaginative continent's terrain. Even his technical advances, like the silk-screen imprint that he employs, don't appear to discover for him, any more than they do for us, those new continuities whereby technique is revitalized and justified as art. Each technical advance is, for Cady, as it seems always to have been, a self-confirmation, a successive lagoon, rather than another mouth for some hurtling imaginative river. The world, for him, lies elsewhere; and the very most grandiose of these patriotic hortations only confirm one's general impression of his withdrawal: not, to be sure, withdrawal from "the masses" — with whom, I should suppose, he entertained a closer rapport than ever — not yet that withdrawal for spiritual inventory and self-replenishment which almost any artist requires; but, a withdrawal, as it were, from his art itself, as an agency for verifying and certifying reality, for making it *more* real.

Nor, as far as I can tell, was the precious rhythm ever resumed during his last couple of years at *Life*, with their ever-slowing seepage of repetitions or cursory variations on earlier subjects. In the Watson interview, Cady is quoted as declaring that the death, in 1918, of the founder and editor-in-chief, John Ames Mitchell, marked the virtual end of his career there. Yet, with or without Mitchell, it is hard to read, in Cady's disappearance from *Life* and the particular stylistic refinements it was adopting, any factor more important than an unexplained, possibly quite justifiable recalcitrance. With the artistic quickenings of 1917-1919, the magazine had discovered a tempo and tone which, so far as I know, it was never to relinquish: urbanely cosmopolitan, crisply judicious, and very remote from the shaggy whimsicality and village prankishness of its earlier years. Gibson's Goddess of Civilization had, quite obviously, become a permanent staff-member. Gone, too are the clubby confidentiality of its old voice, the mellow assurance about its cultural holdings. Succeeding these slightly port-scented tones are the breezy directness and ironic familiarity of a magazine which has discovered itself as a *journal:* i.e., an observer and suitor of current history's tempo. Gluyas Williams is conducting his miniature chronicles of suburbanites in *Life*'s pages; H. T. Webster, of *The Timid Soul*, undertakes his small-town comedies of manners in May of 1920. Gibson, done with the Homeric adventures of the Goddess and the Whore, has resumed the elegant, low-keyed satiric journalism of his earlier work. In effect, *Life* in early 1920 was, unknowingly as yet, readying itself to enter the lists against its soon-upcoming, formidable and ultimately lethal rival: the *New Yorker*.

Surely, I am not alone in concluding that nothing about the stylistic conversion I have just described, should in any way have inhibited or discouraged Harrison Cady from some major enlargement and enrichment of those patterns that his career as a satiric cartoonist had already laid down; especially since so much of this conversion now seems a broadening and refining of that alert and graceful provincialism which had distinguished Cady's work from 1903 on.

Yet, indeed, the 1920s, that jubilee period for such humor, saw, as far as I am aware, the submergence, if not disappearance, of Harrison Cady's career as a cartoonist of the adult world. He would contribute to *Judge* and *Puck*; but I am not aware of Crowninshield's *Vanity Fair* ever using his drawings; or the *New Yorker*, which surely would have found him a post beside one-time *Lifers* like Irvin and Gluyas Williams. And never do these whizzing, multicolored, shining birds, which he started on their various voyages in the early 1900's, ever meet in some unique configuration, some brilliant congress. As far as Harrison Cady was concerned, such alternate possibilities had permanently given place along with the alternate styles and voices of his earlier career, to the role which dominated his published work for the rest of his life: that of children's illustrator.

The nadir of fatuity, for any critic, is to ream the characteristics of an artist's style in search of reasons for some "mysterious" change or hiatus in his career: overlooking, all the while, those plain contingencies — money, prestige, working conditions, or simple boredom with one's work — which generally reduce such mystery to it proper scale and place in the career's pattern; not as some cosmic riddle, or conundrum; but as merely another delineating factor of the man's character and work; as, so to speak, the zero which gives identity and location to a decimal series. Yet, in confronting the course of Harrison Cady's work, it is to style that we must return, as it is style which has sustained and defined so much of his work's progress up until this point.

And, I feel very sure, the question of his continued residency in the world of Peter Rabbit and Unc' Billy Possum, Danny Meadowmouse and Johnny Chuck, is to be — by no means solved, but defined, by scrutinizing Harrison Cady's work of over fifteen years for *Life*; and noting very particularly how each phase of his career represents a successive attempt both to keep intact not only the universe of various experience, which he knows and cherishes, but also his own veneration of the beautiful and the pleasurable. The insect-carnival; the spectacle of folly by which he attempts to admit and to assimilate the threats to beauty and to order; the microcosm of women, at once insular and excluded, which turns the ugliness of actuality into nightmare; and, finally, the specious microcosm of propaganda. In each of these phases, I think, one finds Harrison Cady attempting to mold and keep inviolate a sense of the universe that may be continued by form. Whereas in other artists, in Gibson, for example, form represents a plastic attempt to identify and to articulate the changes in one's sense of the universe, in Cady's drawing it represents rather the attempt to comprehend and to protect; an attempt which would result in the brilliant artificiality of Beardsley, the stylistic rigor of Doré, but for Cady's sweetness of humanity, his candor, his appreciation, even unto relish, of his own vulnerability, and all others'; so that even at his worst, he never withdraws into mere defensive coldness, or compulsive stylistics.

It is by such a route, I think, though, that he eventually puts down stakes in fairyland-which-is-not fairyland: the fantastical yet impeccably observed child's world of nature. This was not in the nature of any ignominious withdrawal; rather, I should think a setting in what was, itself, a populous and challenging actuality to any honest and intrepid settler; that of children's literature. And it represented, I think, that moment in Harrison Cady's life when like many another artist and especially at a certain age, a point of ascendancy in his career and consciousness — as regards his own hand, and the shape made in that hand by the little orb he has become used to holding, his stored apprehensions of reality — and sees where, and how, the hand has taken the shape of the orb, and then decides whether to elect for a larger orb, or a smaller — or whether to leave off altogether, and re-train his hand's muscles. Even in his last years at *Life*, after 1918, with one exception (and the last adult-directed drawing I have found in April 10, 1919: "Transatlantic Voyages, 1620-1920," a vision of airpower), he does nothing but successive variations on the Beetleburgh and animal drawings of earlier years; all reflecting, I suppose, no basic indifference to, or abandonment of, his role; but disappointing and a little unsettling, after the 1903-

1918 rocket-course of his drawing career. Meanwhile, he has begun *Peter Rabbit* for the *New York Tribune*: August 15, 1920.

PART TWO

The very earliest encounter I can remember with the collaboration of Thornton W. Burgess and Harrison Cady is receiving, when I was about seven years old, a copy of the *Adventures of Unc' Billy Possum*. About four- by six-inches — larger, though no thicker, than the average breviary; smaller than the average soft-cover reprint — the book presented Unc' Billy Possum himself on its jacket, engagingly disreputable-looking in a set of single gallus breeches, a handkerchief training from his back pocket; contemplating a hen's egg which split its luscious yellow yolk with the softness almost of fabric; with a smile at once plaintive, sly, and winsomely greedy: one chord from that tonal scale of smiles which Cady — who was to rival *Little Jimmy's* James Swinnerton as virtuoso of smiles — would deliver to us all, in volume after volume of his animal pleasantries. As I remember now, the prevailing impression on which my delight focused was the solidity of this wondrous gift: as a possession, for it was one of the first books of my very own, not a hand-me-down (though they were cherished, of course) from my older brother; and, as such, was as wonderfully glossy and fresh as my brother's books were wonderfully worn and elderly, or rather, ageless-looking. Its solidity as a book, too, enthralled me, I recall: that marvelous combined allure of book-and-object, at an age when anything of corners and pleasant, strokable surfaces that can be carried about, which can be "owned" with none of ownership's distress is momentarily magical — how many of us can recall, how few of us can recreate, this early character of love for our books?

But the dominant solidity lay, even before I had investigated the text, in its illustrations; from the jacket decoration described above, in its innocent sensuosity of color and line, to the last scintillating black and white print, Cady's drawing exercised upon me the compelling sense of these animals — possums, raccoons, toads, foxes — being real, certifiable, beneath and beyond the innocuous token anthropomorphisms of clothing, and chimneys on their cave or tree-trunk houses. They were identifiable animals of an identifiable landscape; and I could feel, as I feel now, even amid Cady's plethora of whimsical grace notes, that he had kept his hands off what was authentic, what could be correlated with experience in the animals' identities. This was of enormous importance to me because, at that age, I had just been acquiring that curiosity about unfamiliar animals — i.e., all those not local to my observation, as were squirrels and dogs, for example — which is so often presumptuously ascribed, in children, to a "love of nature," but actually expresses, I think, something very different, though hardly less important: a curiosity about alien identities, about the variants of identity, to be found in the animate-which-is-not-human. It is often the first, far too often the last, glimmer of reverence that a child knows, and when badly served by parents and educators, it can curdle into mere peevish avidity for novelty; and, at worst, into that sadistically abusive disdain for animal life, with which no zoo or wild life preserve can be unfamiliar. The burgeoning child's hungry curiosity for identities — strange, alternate identities — was matched by the same crystalline observation and humorous empathy which Cady had brought to the Beetleburgh drawings for *Life*; and these virtues entered into partnership with the generous but canny vivacity, the vigor and the tenderness, of Thornton W. Burgess — in his unassuming way, one of the best children's writers, and teachers, America has ever produced.

A native of Massachusetts (Cape Cod 1874), as was Cady, Burgess had produced, before engaging on his full-time *oeuvre*, a series of popular adventure books about the Boy Scouts, and a handbook for young brides, besides acting as advisory editor for several publishing enterprises, among them *Good Housekeeping*. A body of necessary, even, in context, respectable hack-work; which, moreover, judging by the tone of his autobiography, *Now I Remember*, never soured his later writing personality with the meanness, the resentment of guttered creativity, or the rancid smugness developed as protective disguise, which mark so many vocational hacks. Burgess seems to have enjoyed that capacity, typical of the best New Englanders, for absorbing workaday pragmatism with an unpretentious tolerance and a tough humility.

Rereading him today, even without my father's voice, with which I so long identified the stories, I can understand better than ever how Burgess' voice came naturally to permeate my imagination and, in fact, my reception of much experience. For Burgess, it now seems to me, developed, at his strolling, hands-in-pockets gait — the gait neither of laziness nor of languor, but of essential patience, of sensible ease — a storytelling style equal, in its way, to Kipling's in the *Just So Stories*. That voice coheres and justifies the innocently free-handed borrowing with which the books are filled: from Beatrix Potter (whose legacy of Peter Rabbit, even the lipperty-lipperty of his gait, Burgess freely acknowledges in his autobiography); from Joel Chandler Harris' Uncle Remus [The Dear Old Briar Patch, Peter's home; also, the various skirmishes with, and escapes from, Reddy Fox]; and Burgess' own naturalist writings in the *Burgess Bird, Animal,* and *Seashore Books for Children*. Such borrowings, almost child-like themselves in their pragmatical forthrightness, are given a new and worthy home, as it were, in the New England theatre which Burgess' watchful sympathy created, throughout the 55 years of his career as nature writer.

Whereas Beatrix Potter — herself an accomplished and loving naturalist — was mainly concerned with knitting exquisite fairy tales from the twinklings and scurryings of her English gardens, Burgess was concerned with *exemplifying* the actuality available from his Massachusetts scrubs and thickets and meadows. Toward this end, he staged a whole succession of miniature comedies, melodramas, vignettes; all employed, through his intimate raconteur's voice, to focus for his audience the darting particulars of hoptoad, crow, or raccoon behavior; as well as the formidable generalities of survival.

The earliest stories, making up the volumes *Old Mother West Wind* (published in 1910 by Little, Brown of Boston); *Old Mother West Wind's Children*; and *Mother West Wind's Animal Friends*; are more shaped to the conventions of traditional fairy tales, fables and exemplars than are the later adventures of the Green Meadow or the Smiling Pool. I find these early tales (which Burgess had told to his children as bedtime stories) rather skimpy and pedestrian, for the most part — with none of the jaunty inventiveness, or atmospheric richness with which Kipling endowed his *Just So Stories*. Too, I find Burgess' didacticism slightly souring — especially in those occasional glints of Calvinism, when he ascribes animal traits (like Jimmy Skunk's white stripes) to some ancestral crime, or sin. But in the later books, Burgess' prosy lack of fantasy and invention, and even his didacticism (more mellow, as well as more matter-of-fact, later on) became the verities of his tone. The little homilies he addresses to his child audience, about obedience and responsibility, are sweetened both by his loving concern and by the veracity of his eye; he has the New Englander's predilection for reconciling the natural and the virtuous. They are saved from meanness, or the prissy banality and casual dishonesty which beset the exemplary story-teller, by the generosity of his spirit, which yearned to *see* a community of human kind and Nature's creatures, in no way inconsistent with the savage exigencies of Nature itself. I marvel even now at how long I have retained the immediacy of hunger, hostile weather, and predation as related to me by that earnest careful and mellow voice, when I was between seven and ten years old. And I marvel still more today, at how positively Burgess' love could act, as guided by his decency and liberality, not to distort or euphemize these realities; but to deliver them, as portions of our world, as plainly as the children would hear.

Harrison Cady visualized Burgess' theatre of wildlife and provided it with a warmly droll, raffish, and intense expressive vocabulary, which is also the dream-image equivalent of Burgess' text. It is so tempting to think of them as virtually one — the more so because Burgess' colloquial ease seems to bid the illusion of universality — the reader is slightly shocked to learn that — as noted above — they did not meet until after Cady had illustrated Burgess' stories in the *People's Home Journal* (Burgess, in his 1960-published autobiography, places their fist exchange of letters "over forty-seven years ago," which would seem to place the encounter, at earliest, between 1910 and 1912). However, when the Bedtime Stories, in which they presently undertook their most widely known collaboration, were first printed through the Associated Newspaper Syndicate, Wednesday, February 7, 1912 as "Little Stories for Bedtime" in the *New York Globe* and *Commercial Advertiser*, the unCadyan decorations were apparently signed by "Ray" (Cady's first drawing appears Monday, August 11, 1913). The first three Mother West Wind books — Burgess' first hard-cover publications of nature fables — were illustrated by George Kerr; and, even when the mythic association was several years underway, Burgess continued to work with numerous other illustrators: Lemuel Palmer (*While the Story Log Burns*); Southwick and Sutton (the *Burgess Seashore Book for Children*); and — no doubt, his most renowned collaborator, apart from Cady himself — Louis Agassiz Fuertes (the *Burgess Bird Book for Children*).

Yet it is uniquely in Harrison Cady's illustrations, I suspect, that one finds what the illustrative art — as an art so far receded, now, even from the pages of pulp magazines, as to seem virtually unthinkable, even to those who grew up with it — what this art at zenith glitteringly offers: the extension of the text's personality; not the mere closeting literal representation of the author's work; but, the gift of a concreteness which offers an alternate universe, the possibilities of art regenerating itself in many aspects. It is not merely specificity, but another *kind* of specificity, which illustration perpetuates.

The unique, electric vitality that the best illustration encompasses — the capacity both for concretizing and for glorifying the writer's invention — these were the qualifications Cady brought to Burgess' work, and which enabled the two men, in partnership and friendship, to affirm and enlarge each other. A sampling of George Kerr's work in *Mother West Wind's Animal Friends* makes Cady's sovereignty clear, even as it demonstrates why Kerr should have worked successfully with Burgess. For Kerr's work is both meticulous and charming, of a sedate and rather dreamy prettiness which more suggests English than American tradition. The gentle decorous reverie of his tone would seem perfectly suited to the conventionality of Burgess' earlier, fairy-tale-fashioned work, which — though his observation is repeatedly on call — seems generally to take place in a nurseryland limbo. Kerr's rather ornamental-looking forests and meadows could as easily be those of Sussex, or China for that matter, as Massachusetts. And while the animals in general sport the single-gallus pants and stove-pipe hats that Cady later standardized (although Kerr has had the highly questionable inspiration of putting Johnny Chuck in rompers), there is a finishing-school correctness about them; they would surely be as disoriented in the free-and-easy woodland of the later Burgess books, as would the Five Little Peppers in the Katzenjammer household, say.

It was Cady who not only visualized, but enlarged upon, the tone and the tempo and (this odious phrase really seems peculiarly suitable) the life-style of the Burgess forest community: a generally rowdy, voracious, touch-and-go world, which yet — on more careful examination — shows us a grounding of sweet, unthinking dignity. Cady's mastery of actions, expressions and costumes solidified, and provided a sort of visual primer for, the mythology which Burgess had introduced by making archetypal figures of his Buster Bear, Sammy Jay and Happy Jack, the grey squirrel. Burgess' unpretentiously mythic approach enabled him not merely to spin adventurous or poetic fantasy but to demonstrate the broad cyclical patterns of animal existence, while keeping paternal watch for the little day-by-day eccentricities and comedies of local animal behavior.

The singular charm of Beatrix Potter's work was its fluid elegance, combined with warm English matter-of-factness, and its ubiquitous domesticity — the hearth, the garden, at which all gather. The magnetism of Cady's work for Burgess is the houseless wildness, the furious ebullience, which his style conveys and humorously translates, but does not impound. Potter's little garden and meadow creatures — rabbits, hedgehogs, frogs, and mice — seem to have been born to their clothes, little subjects of Her Majesty that they are! — and their spick-and-span jackets or aprons testify to their impeccable domestic world, where all disorders are resolved by dinner and a good nap. The clothes that Cady's repertory wear are used and makeshift and tatterdemalion: you can all but smell the fumes of coffee and tobacco from those vests, stove-pipes and mufflers, which seem to have tumbled from a caravan of raggle-taggle gypsies, oh. The medallion-figure, for me, from Cady's illustrations — the one I shall have put on the button I shall someday forge, reading: "Remember B and C!" — is Buster Bear: the backstraps of his vest dancing gaily, his polka-dot handkerchief keeping time from his hip pocket as he pounds down the trail after a prospective snack of rabbit or woodchuck. Even the apron and mob-cap worn by Old Granny Fox does not encourage us to reflect on her homemaking virtues, especially when she is shown tiptoeing into a midnight chicken-coop to re-enforce her larder. When the Golden Anniversary edition of *Old Mother West Wind* was issued, Cady — who had never illustrated any previous edition — observed the occasion in style by putting flowers on his character's multifarious headgear. Even Hooty the Owl — winging over a darkened meadow, a dead mouse in his charge — was not forgotten; and Old Mother West Wind herself, envisioned by Cady as a somewhat balmy Massachusetts matron, with red nose and near-sightedly peering eyes, adds a slightly askew daisy to the wayward adornments of her Boston bonnet.

What still causes one to marvel in his work, is that, from their initial cartoonish aspect, the drawings — the more familiar with them we become — divulge the fullness, the emotional timbre, of "serious" illustrations: the representations of a universe in solitary moments. The thronging excitement of his earlier drawings for *Life* has crystallized here in a style no less trimly meticulous and compact — or conventional — than it ever was, and more economical than ever before. And the simplifications, jettisoning some of the old avidity for detail, seem to have released a buoyancy in his drawing, toward which he seems to have been working in the last decade — the naval cartoons, especially — of his work for *Life.* The rotund shapes of his raccoons, woodchucks and possums, seem infiltrated with air, so that running, their feet do not touch the ground. Yet, he never affronts nor even, past a certain point, tests, that authenticity of shape, that animal integrity which all of Burgess' prose reveres; never resorts to any structural distortions, or flagrant anthropomorphisms like hands instead of paws. Here, even as in the earliest Beetleburgh cartoons, the sense remains with us of Cady sparring with the actual world; his style, even as is the style of much great comedy, a device for keeping faith with the world, even as he keeps it at bay.

Because the animation of his drawing is, though quite genuine, so very *conscious*, Cady's work tends to be weakest when his characters are immobile; for he lacks the capacity for a rhythmic stillness, for an alert serenity that admits the sense of their background to the figure's presence, which helps to endear to readers the work of British artists like Potter, or Shepard, of *Winnie the Pooh* and *The Wind in the Willows.* Cady's glens and woodlands and pastures, so cleanly and downrightly executed, never express that kind of animation, so warm and so subtle, which makes even the tree-homes of Piglet and Eeyore, the ponds and copses of Toad, Mole, and Badger, as much participants in the scene as are the creatures themselves. When Cady's Peter Rabbit quietly contemplates Old Mr. Toad, or when Bowser the Hound stands in repose, the deliberation and orthodoxy, the *learnedness* of the drawing, dominate much more than in views of action, or even, simply, active emotion. His work has neither mystery, nor poetic resonance; although whatever compensation for these magics may be provided by the exactness, authenticity, and *constancy* of emotional shading, as minted in his characters' wonderful faces, is surely furnished by Cady to overflowing.

The kind of animation which his work radiates comes much nearer to that of American cartoons and comic strips in its almost-peremptory directness, its dashing shorthand, than to the water-color and oil-painting traditions of Shepard or Potter, as does the unexquisite B-B-shot-like compactness of his effects. Indeed, much of the best work in the *Peter Rabbit* comic strips is found, distilled and, often, lent more inventive variation, in the nature books. Yet, this more recent heritage, added to his own immersion, as amateur, in the study of artistic tradition, contributed to the distinctive vocabulary, both visual and narrative, he was evolving for his young readers. And when the action-fuse jumps and sputters, whether in chase or in whirling, nipping, mauling combat, the singular personality of Cady's style take full command. His tight yet weightless line quivers with that energy which we can feel, somewhat as we feel the impounded tremor of a cat's purr, through his most staid-looking drawing. The very punctilio of detail and composition, the incongruity of the animal bodies, in their token clothing, engaged in the most elemental animal combat or chase, lends a comic intensity to these drawings which seems, at deepest, fostered by the actualities of rage and hunger and sorrow and pain — just as in the best of the *Peter Rabbit* episodes years later. The space becomes magnetized: rather than an inert compositional component, it becomes the space across which Reddy Fox pursues Peter Rabbit or through which Hooty the Owl glides, with his look of eerie pomposity, against an immense New England moon. Looking at Cady's best drawings long enough, we can feel a little of that awe, against which smiling is our only defense, which we feel at a baby's rage.

The faces of his animals, the personalities or rather corporate personality which they keep within our view, are his way of balancing the eccentric or savage extemporizations of wildlife with his protective stylistic orderings. The faces, and especially his lexicon of smiles: the most human expression available to animal faces; which Cady's humorous discretion and dry emphasis turn into a little seal of *entente* between animal and human. The smiles may be humble (with eyes upturned; a suggestion of eyebrow in supplicant S-curve);

or quizzical (mouth a tentative arc, eyes childishly peering); greedy (with tongue, usually Reddy Fox's, signaling furiously from half-opened mouth); or, my favorite: complacent, with eyes tight-closed, showing little fanning laugh-wrinkles; mouth beamingly tight, with a hint of underlip; with the tongue showing at one corner, like a tiny latch on the owner's self-satisfaction. Peter Rabbit would, in later years, become the grand master of this last expression.

I don't recall being peculiarly impressed — although, by the age of eight, I had begun to identify the names of comic-strip artists, and authors of my favorite books — by the fact that the name "Harrison Cady," from the Bedtime Story Books which I adored, also appeared on the *Sunday Herald-Tribune* comic-strip, *Peter Rabbit*, which I more or less tolerated. I was becoming used to the bewildering duplication of certain names in my world. Had I not been thunderstruck, at the age of six, by the untoward echoes of "Uncle Frank," which was *my* uncle's name, and "Dorothy," which was my cousin's name, both on the radio serial, *Chandu the Magician*. No, that state of wondering at mysterious correspondences, which every child, I suppose, passes through, and many a romantic novelist appears never to have left behind at all, had already begun to recede for me. What with the obviously unreasonable number of Uncle Franks in the word, not to mention the all-too-typical multiplicity of Peter Rabbits, any glut on the Harrison Cady market was of no overshadowing concern.

Yet it surprises me slightly, in retrospect, that the difference in quality, between the Cady-Burgess work and Cady's solo endeavor, did not give me pause, even at a somewhat pre-critical age. For the annoyance and perplexity which *Peter Rabbit* occasioned me virtually every Sunday achieved themselves a kind of fascination almost paralleling the enchantment fanned by the Burgess books. And, though pre-critical I may have been, I felt no uncertainty about *Peter Rabbit's* humor being feeble and inane, featuring pointless and (for me and conceivably anyone two years or more out of infancy) infantile gags, which often consisted of some slapstick farrago: sled-rides or skiing expeditions which climaxed in the demolition of sleds, skis, sportsmen and the adjoining landscape. I wonder, even today, that neither that particular acreage, nor those kamikaze-inspired athletes, were ever declared public perils by some local humanitarian authority. It was slapstick without the joy of fantastic improvisation, of wayward choreography — the foolish catastrophe exhibiting its own foolish, self-justifying life — which graces the triumphs of slapstick, whether in *The Katzenjammer Kids*, or the manic pursuits of Chic Young's *Blondie.* The word which it urged upon me then — and which, even in so different a context, and with such different inflections holds its own now — was "mean"; not only for the arbitrary and direly unfunny disasters themselves, visited as they were upon innocent excursions and revels — but, I think now, because of a small-spirited kind of hopelessness which I sensed, without being able to give it words, from that pattern. I could not help comparing and contrasting these doom-dogged episodes with adventures of my childhood's other most illustrious rabbit, Uncle Wiggily: that Sherman Billingsley of the forest world; who, though appreciably older than Peter Rabbit, and crippled by rheumatism besides, could be counted on to pit his every resource of whimsical guile, smiling fortitude and invention that could be prudent and daredevil by turns, and as the occasion suggested; all in defense of his right to conduct ice cream parties, beach parties, sleigh-rides, quilting bees and to protect them not against piddling interventions of mischance, but against the headlong barbarities of alligators, baboons, bears, pipsissewahs and skeezixes.

The less explosive of Cady's jocundities seemed to depend very heavily on hopelessly weary puns, from which he would try to induce life, rather like a near-sighted snake-charmer coaxing undulations from a length of shower-hose, by dint of repeating the key-word in every other panel of the Sunday page, prior to the intended comic epiphany. This last was often attended by one of two of the principals shouting "Hurrah!" — which, on concluding twelve-panel travails every Sunday, seemed the most intelligible reaction of any.

All in all, my major sensation, as it was clarified for me through my later teens, on reading *Peter Rabbit* was the kind of pained embarrassment, half-resentful but half-pitying, too, which most children experience at the behavior of a grown-up who is trying, as frenziedly as uninspiredly, to "be fun" for them. And, mingled with such amusement, I now suspect, reconsidering *Peter Rabbit* throughout its history, is the half-acknowledged fear, on the child's part, that he is really learning more about the adult than he can handle.

Because, resent it and chafe it as I did, I followed *Peter Rabbit* through far later years than did many of its genuinely enthralled junior readers; a later age than I can recall without — no, not embarrassment, but a certain vestigial bemusement. My fascination consisted, I'm sure, partly of sheer bewilderment: that half-annoyed, half-empathetic mystification that has kept newspaper readers in footsore step with the most appalling comic strips, like *Smilin' Jack*, year after year. Partly, it was surely the residuum of that comic intensity which I've noted in the Burgess illustrations. Over a very long period, this represented one of my closest bonds with the familiar extremities of childhood. But partly, and still more important, it was the awareness that what I was reading now *was* a residuum: the sense, I mean, of some hollow, some wanting space, some crater of past enthusiasm, appetite, inventive joy. The drawing itself — a crisp simplification of the Burgess drawing style — dispensed with much of the illustration's lovingly assessed detail, although retaining instrumental touches — the flashing diagonals of the chase compositions; the facial expressions, to which Cady added some further shadings of anger, astonishment, or chagrin; key symbols, like the little tears, representing a considerable range of distress, which dart from outer eye-corners. *Peter Rabbit* of the 1930s retained these by-now-stripped mechanisms of a former vitality; and, too, enough intimations of zest, authentic joviality, sportive energy, to haunt, amiably and rather touchingly, those weary remnants that continued their reflex cavortings before the 1930's reader's eyes. I think that these clues, plus the reading of *Peter Rabbit* from its 1920 inception — with sequential reactions of delight, beguilement, and ultimate regret — would be enough to confirm my original feeling of a lack, and to discover, thus, restore, that which was lacking in the later strips: namely, the sense of a world that could still be comprehended and savored, if only in miniature, through Cady's instruments of style and taste; and the corollary sense of a style that had, for its author, so long been a preservative for the cherished flavors and fragrances of life.

Peter Rabbit's August 15, 1920 debut received no preliminary advertising in the *New York Tribune* that I have been able to find, nor was Cady so much as mentioned in the advertisement of Monday, February 16, for the serialized Thornton W. Burgess "Bedtime Stories" that would commence the following day — Burgess having quit Associated Newspapers over a contract dispute — and would continue thereafter for 36 years. The attitude to be inferred from both circumstances is, I think, no contempt for Cady as an artist, but rather that sanguine acceptance, by many editors and laymen, of the most gifted illustrator as a sort of appendage, or *ka*, of the author; who received his nutrition, correctly and in due course, from whatever fame the author ingested. The comic-strip's first two episodes — a rarity in Cady's career — do not show his signature; although that condition is remedied by the third Sunday: a possible suggestion that the publishers were considering the usability of another artist, should Cady for any reason fail the assignment; and further evidence, in any case, of how far the strip was regarded as a spin-off of the Burgess tales.

Peter Rabbit's neighbors and predecessors on the *New York Tribune* were divided about equally between genteelly whimsical strips, expressly for children, and adult-directed comics, which — certainly, in comparison with the opulent rowdyisms of Hearst comic strips — were generally, also, genteel: oriented to a mild (though jiggered with discreet slapstick) and plausible comedy of milieu, with the drawing geared generally to human probability rather than to the jovial dilations of, say, the Katzenjammers, or Gus Mager's "Monks." Its emphases were at least as much on comic dialogue — i.e., a little more extensive and accommodating than simple gag exchanges — and, possible humorous variations on social relationships, as they were on burlesque cudgelings, or spills from motor boats. More important, in terms of the *parvenu* Rabbit: the two prevalent strains found in the *Tribune's* comic pages, over a period of years, are: the humors of the upper-middle-class, sympathetically portrayed, as in "Polly" by Cliff Sterrett (one of "Polly and Her Pals'" innumerable metamorphoses), or "That Son-in-Law of Pa's!" (Wellington's long-enduring update of *Our American Cousin*: *nouveau riche* America vs. British decadence): and, the affectionate depiction of village life (Fox's *Toonerville Folks*; Gene Byrnes' early preparations for his "Reg'lar Fellers" schoolboy strip; "*Jus' Boy*" by Fero: the original version, more carefully and more lovingly observed, of Doc Winner's *Elmer*). The strains I mention had not yet coalesced into that WASP urbanity that came to prevail over the comic-section of the *Herald Tribune*, throughout the latter '20s, and the '30s. *Peter Rabbit*, however, had arrived in good season to take advantage of the *Tribune* comics' solvent, molten condition. Peter's neighbors, on his first appearance, included *Mr. and Mrs.*, Clare Briggs' marathon bickerers; *Lazy Larry*, doggerel whimsy by Tony Sarg and George Mitchell; and *Betty*, C. A. Voight's portrait of a glamorous and frolicsome blonde, who, a little later, took on a Woody Allen-ish swain named Lester DePester. Peter himself replaced *Dinny Doodle*, Collinge's engagingly capricious fantasy.

The earliest *Peter Rabbit* comic strips are, in effect, efforts to convey the Bedtime Story illustrations into comic strip form; using Burgess' familiar intecessor and guide between the world of nursery fantasy, and that rustling, scurrying, pouncing world of actual nature. Evidently as a direct result of his popularity, Peter had begun appearing in *Life* cartoons — always unnamed, usually as onlooker — as early as 1916. He had always been the most emblematic, least literally accurate of Cady's figures, with his doll-like, rounded body, and staring baby eyes; the image of an Easter Bunny doll, rather than, indeed, the agonizedly maturing hero of the Burgess stories who takes a mate after savage contest with a bellicose jack-rabbit competitor. At once, an exceptionally inviting and inordinately challenging comic-strip protagonist.

Peter and Danny Meadowmouse (the Burgess names will be abandoned before the end of 1921), whom we discover sharing bachelor digs, are discussing an invitation to Betty Squirrel's party, with Danny bemoaning the obligatory gift. "Nothing doing!" announces the penurious meadow mouse. "My presence will be my present." Peter — a roly-poly, notably long-eared Peter, much more like his Burgess prototype than the confident home-owner of later years — decides to buy a camera; a gift of which Danny takes brisk advantage at the party, by professing to be an ace photographer. The predictable climactic explosion — Danny was using too much powder — produces a gallery of blackened faces and darkened spirits; to say nothing, one supposes, of Danny's future social prospects at that address.

The opening episode offers a pocket encyclopedia of Cady's humorous themes for the next 28 years: the vagaries, fatuities, and pleasures of fashionable society; the fascination of contrivances and machines; the disastrous consequences of overreaching, in any direction, for any goal; slyness and shrewdness, even deviltry, sometimes triumphant and sometimes discountenanced. The drawing, however, continues to nestle, even timidly so, in Thornton Burgess' forest world, with a bright-eyed glance toward Cady's Beetleburgh drawing. Peter, Danny, and their friends are all rather inert-looking, and seem themselves to have posed for a chromo, by a photographer whose camera was overcharged, not with powder, but with essence of violets: the art-work would not look ill-selected inside one of those Fabergé Easter eggs which used to be so popular. One also notes that Peter and Danny are approximately the same size: the egalitarian scale that has been noted in the earlier single-panel cartoons.

It occurs to me to wonder once more, in recalling the earliest *Peter Rabbit* comic strips, about the possible importance of Cady having specialized, before, in single cartoons and illustrations; his having come new, not only to the comic-strip, but the *full-page* comic strip, a *form*, that is and not a mere magnification of the familiar daily, four-panel tract; and a form psychologically as well as artistically relevant to any consideration of the comic-strip; because the now-virtually-lost twelve-panel page reflected, among other factors, the artist's sense of his work's *potential* size.

It must provide (I refer here, or course, to the humorous comic-strip; not the adventure strip, whose problems and resources were radically different) not only a funny and visually diverting story, to be told in the deceptively-copious-looking space of twelve panels. "Deceptively," because those dimensions, which seem to invite an agreeable expansiveness of narrative, actually demand the explicit and the essential in both dialogue and pantomime, draining both as rapaciously as the queen bee. They demand a story that will not simply develop, but exhibit and explain those characters and those basic situations, which the weekday strip may already have explained and re-explained as though for a future generation of Homers (nor, indeed, can it "develop" a situation as can even a two-reel film comedy, because the temporal progression is lacking: each panel must be a manifest situation in itself). Beyond, and as implicit in all this, the Sunday comic page had to present and support the *impression* of largeness, of meaty abundance; and toward this purpose the artist had to be able to recognize, and to embrace, the prospect of experience and naturally enlarging, exfoliating in comic design from the page.

Recalling, from all of his work which I have tried to appraise here, Harrison Cady's particular mating of propriety and finesse; his love of the particular circumstance and the typical figure; his delight in and obvious rapturous amusement over the weight and the absurdity of numbers as they represent laughable paradoxes of identity, I wonder how that jovial yet dry and down-scaling temperament which emerges, could have reconciled itself to, even rejoiced in, or continued for 28 years to resist and to circumvent, the conditions and requirements of the full-page comic strip. I think that had he become a novelist, his would not have been the richly plotted, event-marbled novels of the nineteenth century; but rather the implicitly skeptical (its gradient bearing towards cynicism, and even pessimism) form of the picaresque novel.

He had a proclivity for terse, astringent comment, for hard, dry shapes impeccably adopted to their occasions; and, at the same time, a sense of obligatory form *as* an occasion, like a social occasion, to be met and answered; both of which inclinations, I suspect, produced, especially in the later *Peter Rabbit* strips, that logey monotony of routine and ritual motions to which I have referred. And yet — as I hope to illustrate here — Cady's humorous and resilient veneration of experience, his self-directed and self-educated discovery of experience, give the earlier *Peter Rabbits*, in particular those from 1920 through 1929, a cachet and a tempo — and invite an identification with the artist — which is, in any age, as fugitively sweet as the scentless-scent of dandelions.

In short order, Peter's personality shrugs free of its vague affable courtliness of the first episode. The imp-embryo of the New England practical joker shows itself as he teases his oafish friend, Buster Bear (an appealing and, potentially, thunderously comic figure, in his helpless, expostulating largeness; and a possible model for Walt Kelly's Barnstable Bear, of the Sunday *Pogo*); whom, regrettably, Cady altered (in whatever sense comes to mind) to the burlesque heavy, "Old Mr. Bear," after a few episodes. With the coalescing of his personality, Peter shucks Danny Meadowmouse as gentleman's home companion, and — without the menacing intervention of jackrabbit rivals — acquires a family: one of the most expeditions coastings into domesticity I can remember seeing in comic-strips, not forgetting Walt Wallet's Valentine's Day discovery of Skeezix.

His domesticity, for the first three months or so, seems unstable enough, surely, to justify the increased giddiness of his character. The fluctuations among his children are, in themselves, sufficient to unstring a Dr. Spock, or the Old Woman Who Lived in the Shoe. On September 5, of the same year (1920), a boy and a girl bunny are in evidence, unnamed and indistinguishable from each other, except by their clothing. On October 10, a single boy rabbit is on view as a budding Boy Scout; but on October 24, like some species of undulant fever, the domestic census has mounted to seven babies, all of whom Peter assumes the charge of minding. On November 7, three infants are seated at dinner, but as of November 14, the much-beset peterfamilias finds himself with only two little girl rabbits (either Farmer MacGregor was near the premises, or the rest of the offspring were deported to Dr. Doolittle's, for rehabilitation therapy). On March 27, 1921, a new arrival is on hand, upon whom (possibly in the uneasy realization that he had better establish some identity check on this remarkable clan) Peter plans to bestow the name of Algernon Reginald Cuthbert Rabbit; only to be dissuaded by another new and longer-abiding arrival; Mr. Possum the know-it-all,[1] who will court disaster at such depressing and unvarying length, throughout the later '20s and '30s. Thereafter, however, this delirious menage comes to focus in the twin brothers of the strip's longevity — who are seldom addressed by any names at all, although one or the other is recognized, at rare moments, as "Petey," and whom Vincent Fago, Cady's replacement in 1948, christened rather more firmly as Petey and Buddy. They provide a secure enough scionage, though distinctly un-rabbit-like in number; unless, of course, one prefers to regard them, from episode to episode, as random representatives of a far more populous household, whose other members are depleting carrot-fields elsewhere. As against the manic fluctuations of her progeny, Mrs. Rabbit is, and becomes increasingly, the image of domestic stability and sensible strength, which we have seen in more reflective mood in the suffrage cartoons. October 31 confers on her, permanently, the name "Hepsy"; which for years before has circulated rather promiscuously among insects, fish, and other casual forest citizens; only lately coming to light on Mrs. Buster

1 This marks his first appearance as arch-meddler. His first appearance as disaster buff occurs on February 11, 1923, when he directs himself into the millrace on Peter's icemobile. Without the occasionally amusing sententiousness of Uncle Phil, in Lank Leonard's Mickey Finn; the eloquent aplomb of Major Hoople; or the self-absorbed serenity of J. Wellington Wimpy, Mr. Possum (intermittently known as "Professor Possum") is that dreariest of comic braggarts: the kind who co-exists with his disasters, providing no vital give-and-take. As a character, he was the equivalent of an unfilled cavity, and approximately as amusing.

Bear. Although she has her own New England homemaker's vanities and fanaticisms (joining the Self-Denial League; sending the children to dancing class), Hepsy, whether as foil or consoler of her erratic mate, lends the warmth of Cady's long-time empathy for women to the helter-skelter vagaries of setting and household; and seems, indeed, to embody the strip's deepest investment of Cady's longtime observation and remembrance.

Although it can, and presently does, spill into silliness and distractedness, the molecular looseness of those early *Peter Rabbit* strips — especially those of the first year — deserves major credit for the recurrent pleasure — whether explosive or wheedlingly sweet — which it affords. I think one might justly say that, to a very considerable degree, *Peter Rabbit* never coalesced, never came to focus at all, as have any number of comic strips, from Gray's *Little Orphan Annie* to DeBeck's *Barney Google*, which managed to train the author's reserves of experience, prejudice, fantasy, and appetite to follow the processional pattern of a mythic, more or less continuous story. Cady, however, never displays any sense of his material, or the shape which his reception imparts to it as commanding, bidding, a *certain* fable. He was already spooning from the rich roe of fable itself; and the sense, which those years of cartoon-work for *Life* must have confirmed in him, of anecdote and example as the bounty, the trophies of experience. So, the first year of *Peter Rabbit* is a cornucopia of humors: of satire, slapstick, Aesopian fancy, exemplary tale, cracker-barrel anecdote; all a-gleam, as it were, with Cady's personal identification with the storytelling act.

The overwhelming sense of language as the extension and warrant of the image's reality, recalls to one the labels and placards which flourished, hardy perennials, throughout Cady's allegorical cartoons for *Life*; and provides a kind of reflective leaven for whatever — and however justified — boredom and annoyance one feels with the flabbily desultory punning of *Peter Rabbit's* later years. And, when fused with Cady's birchy toughness, mischief, and generous skepticism, it can present us with Peter Rabbit as orator for the Young Possums' Political Club rally, one momentous afternoon of September 12, 1920; when, to the cresting euphoria of his audience, he managed to insult every animal resident of the adjacent countryside, merely by stocking his address with every metaphorical cliché in the politician's manual. A reference to "those birds in office" who "spend their time feathering their nests," elicits a point-blank egg from a neighboring bough (somebody in the crowd, yielding to the feast of metaphor, murmurs, "Things are coming to a head"). A jibe at being "stung by grafters" with "honeyed words" draws the incensed attention of some nearby bees, who lose no time in calling Peter's attention to them; and so on, each successive onslaught earning the political martyr fresh ovations from his audience; until, to a general paroxysm of delight, he tumbles into the pond before an inflamed coalition of forest folk. My wonder, in reading for a fourth time this fifth episode of Harrison Cady's new series, is at the terse dispatch with which Cady has duplicated some of the funniest two-reelers that I can remember; with an interacting slyness and bluntness about political actualities, which they have rarely bettered: all of it — despite a few examples of technical lag, such as misplaced dialogue balloons — charged and sharpened by Cady's debonair acceptance of his own experience, and its capital of images.

His contrivance lacks the richly billowing ebullience of Knerr in Hearst's version of *The Katzenjammer Kids*; or the wise-cracking riffs and licks of Sidney Smith's *The Gumps*. But, so long as he can give full play to his flair for multiplicity of detail, with a situation which accommodates such development naturally — Cady achieves a free, bubbling jubilation warmed and buoyed by one's sense of his authentic enthusiasm, his delight in both rhythms and particulars. One of the most joyously headlong of the slapstick episodes (January 2, 1921) involves no more elaborate premise than Peter accepting a dare from a May beetle (for, yes, Beetleburgh had received an extended lease in these earlier years; the bugs, either half or one-third Peter's size, acting as punchinellos, minor imps, side-line hecklers and commentators) regarding the strength of his golf-drive; with the following panels showing the ball on meteoric route through every perishable surface within a radius of country miles. The concluding panel — to become a virtual insignia in later years — shows a storming mob of Peter-bound complainants. (The episode, like others of Cady's best, was to be repeated with a variety of missiles — including model airplanes and snowballs — within the following years). Another such adventure, January 8, 1927, shows Peter, in the opening panel, indignantly rejecting a petition to make the streets of Carrotville (the name his community acquired in the late '20s) safe (!); then in each of the succeeding panels, undergoing one abrasive skirmish after the other with street-excavators, coal-trucks, sanitation hoses. The abounding delight which I feel from these slapstick fugues is produced, I think, by Cady playing, against the obviousness of the slapstick pattern, his own delighted discernment of each detail as solidly distinct; and the way in which attention — surely, as much earnest as mock-earnest — seems to release from these details a life which was already in them, which does not ensue from any forcing, any rigging, any formal manipulation. I think that he thus imbued even this most modest-seeming of his undertaking with as much sheerly *painterly* feeling as has any major American cartoonist.

Yet, not less than his greatest contemporaries and predecessors — Bud Fisher, Billy DeBeck, George Herriman — he reveled in and lovingly deployed and multiplied words; which he saw, like those other, with a wisdom which today would have been second-guessed almost out of existence, as indispensable to the visual art he was practicing: words and images in comic strips being as inseparable as they are in thoughts, with each punctuating, insuring, and giving form to the other. In the May 1952 issue of *American Artist*, there appears a short historical sketch by Cady of "Cape Ann: American's Oldest Art Colony." The style of this article — agreeably old-fashioned, with its courtly periods, its leisurely apostrophes of landscape; yet, with no bluster, imprecision, or extraneous furbelows — is like a concert presentation of that rhetorical music which sometimes grunts as mellowly as a parlor Hammond organ, but rather more often skitters and wheezes like a square-dance fiddle, to the reverberations, which we can all but feel, of foot-stomping accompaniment, throughout *Peter Rabbit*.

I have mentioned my supposition that Brueghel offered Cady a cohering influence, and reassurance; and one of two most probable influences (I shall discuss the other presently) is manifest in Cady's eerie-earthy feeling for the solidity language realized among us: to be seen, for example, in the Elder's fair-ground displays of Fables and Proverbs. Cady relished words — perhaps with the residue of New England husbandry; certainly, with the painter's esteem of words as virtually mystical, in their intangible palpability; and in the Jupiter-like authority of their comic and terrible frivolity.

Talk is what supports and guides the chipper little vignettes of the early *Peter Rabbit* strips: talk as explanation, expostulation —

or, scanting neither of these functions, sheer ornament: although always directed by Cady's downright explicitness. The rhythms of his Sunday strips unite, at their best, the trajectories of casual story-telling with the tiny digressions and contributory incidents of oral narrative. Cady loved to stage-manage, with arrows pointing to crucial details, or poke us amiably by identifying readily-identifiable actions or emotions ("Very mad," for the little rabbit's glowering rage); it is his private indulgence, his way of admitting his voice direct, and the *presence* of his tale-telling, which he wants us to acknowledge. He loves talk as sustenance, the humble humbug of candy store owners and haberdashers; the profferers of free advice (Peter Rabbit to a possum sweating over a stalled car: "The pesky builders put all the work into the trimming, and never think of the engine…") And — here again, the duality of the close-mouthed, diffident man interviewed by *Life* in 1910, and the voluble, gregarious one interviewed by *American Artist* in 1945 — he loves to foil and counterpoint the foaming words with one or two brief, but steadfastly repeated words (which generally turn out to be the last word), from the auditor.

The lore and the coloring of Massachusetts furnish the double setting — the village, or little town, and the deep woods — which, even in such naïve-looking context, strike one with the vividness of their familiarity. As I have mentioned, the village permeated many and many a comic strip, in the *Tribune* and elsewhere; yet even in the midst of so much pastoral preference, what strikes one is the selective exactness of Cady's perception, or recollection; and the matter-of-fact expedition with which he seeds his art with his observations. In memory, the episodes of ten or fifteen years merge into a kind of comic tapestry of Massachusetts views and ways: the candy store at which maple-sugar candy and molasses are sold; abandoned barns, in which unicycles may be discovered and the busy barns in which crops are stocked against the frost; birds skating on the frozen pump water; tippets, well-sweeps, dories. In those years, the setting and its impounded lore enhanced its animal cast all the more by putting in relief the breezy anecdotes mimed against it. And — what one identifies only with some of the best comic-strip art, as with some of our best writing — the setting prevails as a far-flung corporate image. For, even later on, when the adobe-like mounds in which Peter and his friends dwell become recognizable houses, and

Carrotville a decided village — the village and the nearby forest complement each other in a curious, haunting way; haunting, because they reflect Cady's devotion to the *idea* of his setting, as a continually present scene. The forest is the home of all amoral, free-booting, outlaw animals — birds, who, along with the bugs, form the imp contingent of Cady's world; scheming or irascible bears, and frogs; who are capable of absconding with Peter's clothes (as does a robber band of birds whom Crusader Rabbit has set out to apprehend); or diddling him out of free ferry-service, as does a rascally frog-skipper. Unlike the bears or chipmunks which Mickey Mouse or Donald Duck regularly engage in sportive pursuit, the "wild" animals in *Peter Rabbit* speak even as do their urbanized brethren. Nor are those latter, themselves, ever very remote from their original nature; for Cady never practices — even in comic strip, where he adopts some additional latitudes in depicting attitudes and expressions — the wildly elastic characterizations of Floyd Gottfredson, or Chuck Jones; nor, except for Peter and his family, do the characterizations ever range beyond the breadth and flatness of old-fashioned "humors." The southern accented possums, unctuous or crafty; the pompous woodchucks; the bellicose bears; the figures in each category are mainly interchangeable with each other.[2] All Carrotville citizens, except for occasional fishing, are herbivores. (There occur infrequent buffo villainies of bears and foxes, with *hasenpfeffer* as object, but these never-too-convincing episodes are not adopted as continuous themes; indeed, the nearest to serious criminality, apart from the rogueries of birds and frogs, which the strip ever offers is the 1923 appearance of a raccoon hold-up artist). Neither do the animals own pets, as do Mickey and his circle; nor, apart from a few episodes at the zoo, and some sleigh-ride sequences, enlisting what looks like an alarmingly outsized rat, called "Dobbin," have I found any animals in the usual domestic subservience, say, of livestock and the like. Nor do human beings appear — except during the '30s, in the little rabbit's dreams about such personages as Barnum and Izaak Walton, and, in the '40s, an appearance by Cady himself. All in all, one's impression is of a tiny world doubly suspended within

2 This excepts various single appearances; old Aunt Mandy Possum; Peter's braggart cousin, Jack from "Faroff Australia;" the resourceful Colonel Popweasel, who builds an igloo one heatless night from Peter's library books; a lariat-tossing June bug sleuth, called Daredevil Dan — some of whom seem to have been contemplated for repeated engagements.

its own natural environment, and Cady's mellow, orthodox consideration: a miniature world in which the natural co-exists with the artificial, in a way which answers admirably to William Carlos Williams' wonderful characterization, from *In the American Grain*, of the Puritans and their little gardens.

Partly as direct consequence of Cady's limitations — his lack of formal initiative, or of a very adventurous imagination — Peter Rabbit within the first decade of his life assumes shape as one of the few folklore heroes whom comic strips have neither totally diluted, nor appropriated in name only. For he is far less a character such as we recognize and hail in Popeye or Barney Google, than he is a smiling conductor of energies, fancies, vanities, and wisdom. Apropos of Barney Google, in fact, Peter of the first two years very much and deplorably resembles the early Barney: a dreamer, an incorrigible loafer, a follower of false leads to success and fame, a connoisseur of hopeless enterprises who winds up what seems like every other episode with a jaunt to the "tea-kettle" or "quad," under collar by some squirrel or woodchuck constable (often unjustly, to be sure, yet with keen appreciation of an alarmingly venturesome character). The pattern of an irreclamate rogue and idler is modified through the first year, however; largely, I should suggest, because Cady himself wanted a more pliable and fluid character, who would register more of the tiny variations he loved to note in the progressive scene before him. Even as community and home both assume more sturdy contours, Peter expands from comic ne'er-do-well into humorous dilettante: an inveterate sampler of experience (much of it, to be sure, ultimately explosive); a tinkerer and dreamer and offhand philosopher; who does not, like the rogue and loafer, so much dictate a given sequence of events, as awaken them catalytically. And, gradually, accordingly, his figure becomes portly-sleek, his ears shorten and stiffen, his mouth widens to the ready-smiling burgher's mouth, in other words, a foaming beaker of Harrison Cady himself, with a few squeezings of Don Quixote, and a twist of Henry Adams. I now look rather differently than I did some years ago, upon the monotonous catastrophes of the later *Peter Rabbit* adventures, because they now seem to me much less Cady's *preference* than they seemed on first reading them. Not that Cady was averse to deviltry, as witness the bug and bird chicaneries, or even cruelty: within the first year of *Peter Rabbit*, a scoundrel possum steals his clothes by convincing him that his children (in reality, two balloons) are drowning; another possum, at the seashore, sets Peter up in a Dodgem game, in which he is woefully battered; and a well-intended bear is permitted by Peter and sons to poke his head into a hornet-occupied log, in search of the little rabbit's lost hat. But even here, the meanness is partly, at least, a flinty enjoyment of the whimsical shapes assumed by the which is inevitable to our lives — i.e., mischance — and our occasional manipulations of it. Yet, I find neither specious paradox nor evasion in saying that there emerges more of candor and compassion from Cady's work, than that cruelty which is partly his insularity, and partly his artist's erotic contemplation of all experiences. But he never represents pain or injury as merely unreal, or as a joke in themselves. Rather, with a kindly vigor that is not unlike the tone of his partner, Burgess, he counsels us on how these miniature crises and cataclysms demand, by their very reality, that we absorb them and laugh, not even, perhaps at them so much as at the endless pattern of inconsequence in which they figure. A term like "sadistic," while it may apply eminently on occasion to such an artist, may neither cancel out his complex of strong and benign virtues, nor act as a leveling common denominator to his art.

Peter is an indefatigable gallivanter in all sorts of vehicles, but especially his long-suffering, long-enduring craft, the *Sally* (which periodically rises phoenix-like from being detonated by inquisitive fireflies in her gas-tank or graffiti-plastered by mischievous turtles), and putterer (in the first three years, especially, an obsessive short-wave radio buff, and at times an insufferably self-absorbed one; on one occasion, literally chasing Hepsy and an old school friend out of the house because their conversation interfered with the precious messages from Frog Hollow and Possum Four Corners). He is an amateur mechanic and inventor cut to Harrison Cady's own pattern, and once puts in a charming eight panels showing some June bugs how to build a modern radio set (with pine-board base, wire, from vines, and a scroll of birch-bark for a horn). The mechanical zeal of these episodes, while never venturesomely inventive, as are the Katzenjammer boys' destructive toccatas, expresses, in its preoccupation with small adjustments to, and of, reality, the mixture in Harrison Cady's personality of the hearty and the exquisite; and his genial submission of human intelligence to the gorgeous market of eventualities which nature offers us. Peter is also both an avid consumer and doughty doubter of popular pieties, a proclaimer of sampler-virtues; as in one resounding episode of November 7, 1920; in which he presses his Sunday dinner and the family's upon an indigent young woodchuck who has just announced that he was "at the front." Peter, at soaring patriotic Fahrenheit, also insists that the wayfaring hero accept several packets of leftovers; and, as the satiated veteran's paw is on the doorknob, implores him briefly to summarize his experience at the front. Of course, the happy warrior obliges, hurriedly crossing the hospitable threshold: "I was at the front, and I rang three times, but no one answered, so I came around to the back." And disappears, leaving Peter to face the red glares and rocketing dishware of his dinnerless wife and children.

Peter's forays into charity, however, (on other occasions, he is solicited by one of Cady's beloved Daddy Long Legs for alms to buy a pair of long pants; and for collar-money by a heron who is already collared, and cravated, up to his non-existent chin) do not offend with any sense of chinchiness or smugness, so much as they merely propose, as fit for our amusement, the oddity of persons' differing views of charity; and, the importance of not letting that awareness be submerged by fanatic blanket decrees (although what one misses from Cady, and not from Walt Kelly, for example, is the recognition that those conditions which most exhort our charity, are those which themselves obliterate individuality). Peter and his author thus become bearers of what is surely as important a message as many children's or adult's comic strips have taken in charge to deliver: the universality of the eccentric, the uncategoried, the odd-numbered detail. I have mentioned what I infer to be the Brueghels' two apparent major influences on Cady, and this is the second: the wayward particular, which can make the majority of data, the throng of accreted wisdoms or observations, kick the beam. One remembers from the numberless examples of his *Life* cartoons, the potent detail or utterance concealed in a host of details; as in the child labor cartoon, where, far back among the ranks of pious injunctions and mottoes, a barely-glimpsed sign carries the stark instruction: GET BUSY. Arcing through such examples, one can discern Brueghel's *Descent of Icarus*: a key image, I think in the advance of Cady's work: the tiny legs vanishing into the remote lake, right of canvas; all but devoured by the prolific serenity of the countryside. But there follows in train the realization that Brueghel's and Cady's purposes are, in effect, opposite: that whereas Brueghel is illustrating the single mythic event submerged, in actuality, by factual numbers, Cady is demonstrating the resistance of the particular to orthodox enumerations and statistics: and the sometimes perverse energy of the isolated particular. One of his very favorite episodes, repeated numerous times with numerous tinkering over the years, is one in which Peter and the Carrotville "home team" (baseball, boating fishing) are bested by a zanily improbable "scrub team," comprising, perhaps, a kangaroo-mouse, a toad, a spider, and Cady's ancient darlings: centipede and Daddy Long Legs. The unvarying consequence is, of course, that nature, personified by Peter Rabbit and his squirrel or raccoon colleagues, rediscovers Nature, as demonstrated in the scrub team's wild adaptability and devising vitality.

But the citizens of Carrotville, themselves, are little vessels of ferociously independent and touchy pride, which reminds us of Whipple's remarks about the hypersensitivity of Massachusetts natures. Whether Peter is ousted from his seat at the circus after a set-to with the possum behind him, who chortlingly likens his ears to "a pair of pesky umbrellas"; or is belabored by the furious Unc' Billy Possum, whom Peter has pedantically addressed by his Latin name, he and his fellow Carrotvillers enact again and again the preposterously short-fused, comically vulnerable aspect of the individuality cited above — an individuality that more involves the distances between persons, and the respect for distance as something forged with methodical exertion, than anything more broadly or more richly assertive. Just as humorously suggestive and atmospherically savory are the episodes in which Peter, aspiring to be glass of fashion, is talked into shucking his new straw hat, or shaving his London tweeds, by jeering ill-wishers who, themselves, eventually appear in the renounced styles. (The young rabbits as a rule show more audacity and verve than their father does in this respect: buying a straw hat from a farmer for spring headgear, or preferring the hurdy-gurdy man to the concert conductor). These tiny comedies of manners radiate both Cady's addiction to elegance, and his thick-barked New England self-sufficiency; and in this regard, I think, offer something potentially much more exciting and enlarging that sermonettes on individuality: for he fuses intuitions of his own temperament with those of the animals' and, accordingly, finds a comic correspondence with childhood temperament, its qualms and pressures. And by such a route, he projects his own instinct of felicity — his understandings of that solidity which, even as at certain points in one's childhood, can mystically flesh those intimations of art which we later recognize as intangibles. I think that he introduced this special, evanescent sense of art into the microcosmos of *Peter Rabbit* a little more fluently, a little more poignantly, than he had into even the best of his *Life* drawings. I do not believe he and the former actress Malina Eldredge, his wife from 1915, had children, and this may be a fraction of a reason — no more than that, surely — why I feel even from the earliest *Peter Rabbit* strips[3], a certain lack of the ready rapport with the actions of childhood imagination, that almost reflexive fluidity, as of a shared vocabulary, which Howard R. Garris' and Lang Campbell's Uncle Wiggliy stories or Palmer Cox's Brownies, invoke. Yet, considerably more than compensation for any such lack is the contract which Cady formulates with childhood — that most tactful and self-extending effort to realize their common ground — which locates him in many instances, I think, with the best Edwardian and Victorian children's artists.

Why does the work of this man, so enrapt of nature, skid and falter within the last two decades, toward the vacuum which nature proverbially abhors? For just as in the World War I propaganda drawings of his later years at *Life*, the loss which so shocks us and shudders our previous enthusiasm is a loss of solidity, of his significant core; which results in a sense of remove more shocking than the sometimes sweetly pathetic latterday dithering of many aging cartoonists, groping along the spoors of lost inspiration and zest. His age alone cannot be accountable; he was still quite vigorous enough artistically at the age of 73.

In part, perhaps, the attrition may be laid to the erosion — and replacement of his setting which had been occurring around him at accelerated rate since the merger of the *Tribune* and the *Herald*, in 1924. For a number of those moods and attitudes which had commemorated the American village and which had, in major degree, been enshrined by the *Tribune's* comic section — the provincial suspicions and animosities; the jostling and sometimes abusive

3 I have not thus far seen those books — *The Adventures of Caleb Cottontail*; *The Bug Book*; *The Animal ABC* — written by Cady which Houghton, Mifflin published in the '20s.

humor; the casual skepticism or no-less-casual harshness towards the alien, along with the always somewhat unstable tolerance for local eccentricity — all such roughnesses were being planed and made tractable to the tone of suburbia, which, reconciling the former village to the companion strain of upper middle-class comedy, would come to dominate the *Herald Tribune* — giving it a demeanor and ambience as locally distinctive as the morose, dangling-armed gauntness or lumpiness of the *Chicago Tribune's The Gumps*, and *Moon Mullins*. The style of a slightly sweeter, more leisurely-gaited *New Yorker* — a future, or alternate station, for several of the *Herald Tribune's* cartoonists, like Crawford Young and Ellison Hoover, who had also been Cady's contemporaries at *Life*. The White Plains-Central Park WASPishness of the *Herald Tribune* became so permeating after a time that when Harry Hershfield, author of *Abe Kabibble*, was tarrying there in temporary alienation from King Features Syndicate, he brought in tow a new protagonist named Hoyle, starring in *According to Hoyle*: pink-cheeked, string-monocled, Lord Plushbottom-mustached; who steadfastly passed along, in sedulously deYiddishized English, the very same lines, in the very same situation, which Kabibble had been delivering for years.

The style coalesced over the decades into the most distinctive corporated image of a certain corner of New York life then appearing in a newspaper comic supplement; and acquiring on the way what was at the time a unique gentleness and liberality of humorous tone, a consistency not merely of comedic situation, but of taste and intelligence, unrivalled by its more vigorous fellows, which is seen crystallizing by the '20s' close. Upon the death of Clare Briggs, in 1929, *Mrs. And Mrs.* was taken over by Ellison Hoover — whose minuscule Prussians had print-patterned the pages of World War I *Life* — and *Herald Tribune* editor Arthur Folwell: producing what, in my opinion, is one of the rare continuations of a comic strip that exceeds the performance of its original author; for, the monotonously wrangling earlier strip — with anger or sour peevishness its pivotal emotions — evolved under Hoover and Folwell into the still-bilious, but more humorously observant, stoically mellow comedy of the '30s and early '40s: one of the most altogether authentic satires of middle-aged domesticity American comic strips have ever produced. In similar vein, *Clarence* — who, in the nervous vigor of Crawford Young's drawing, had been a grousing, blustering domestic pasha, foil and opponent to his flapper niece, Mabel — softened, under the hands of Weare Holbrook and Frank Fogarty, into the Robert Benchleyan soft touch — affable and quizzically amused — whom, I believe, most readers who can recall *Clarence* at all identify with his name. For a rarity, I should say, the loss of hostility — of the '20s' hectic jumpiness and galvanic excitements — did not mark a simple slackening of vitality, a striking of colors, in the *Herald Tribune's* comic section; because these were supplemented by other tones, no less genuine and much more scarce (and, today, surely unduplicable): a benign sort of critical patience, a whimsical flexibility, an even-tempered realism: virtues which, if a little thin-blooded, gave those comic pages a sense of shared good-nature and easy conviviality that seemed refreshing enough then, and are delectable in retrospect.

Yet one can see with little exertion how this settling down of the *Herald Tribune's* comics — a pedestrian patience, touched with genteel wistfulness, surely dictated, however indirectly, by the Depression mood and tempo — may have marked, for an artist like Harrison Cady, an end to the venturesomeness which the loose volatility of the earlier years had beckoned from him. I don't think that editorial pressure would have, or could have, directed the quiet shrinking of *Peter Rabbit* into a comic strip designed solely and very, very simply for nursery-age children; besides which, among the section's other "kid strips" of the period, Mal Eaton's *Peter Piltdown* lost none of its antic deadpan insouciance; nor Johnny Gruelle's *Brutus* its runaway, jocosely elaborate fancy, in deference to any prevailing mode. But in the instance of Cady's work, that decorous prudence we have noted again and again, in its very evolution, which so directed him even as he advanced in skill and rage of response, to redefine and rearticulate his limitations, and those of his imaginative sphere — this prudence worked against an expansiveness, an overflow, an appreciation of his art's power to invade and shape the very world — which, given his intelligence and cultural attainments, might have led him from the identity of outstanding American artist and folklorist, to that which he might have shared, in rank, only with George Herriman: originator and language forger.

In summary, I think that Harrison Cady, in the last decades of his work, retreated and retreated honorably, before the sheer size, the spatial enormity, with which his country confronted him; and, ensuing from that, the sheer divergency and weight of concerns and occasions, all demanding equal consideration, all demanding, somehow, imaginative absorption, imaginative reconciliation, with which the American artist, citizen of the most consciousness-hounded nation on earth, must deal. The artists who have been out-and-out destroyed by such impasse — driven to insanity, to dissolution, or to their deaths — we know, and know, perhaps, too well. We know far less well, or consent to acknowledge much less freely, those artists like Cady: villagers of the most wonderful drive and capacity, who seek throughout their work a universe which will also be a village; who, when they decline, do so not in violence or debauchery, nor, often even in despair or melancholia; but, by a gentle diminution and withdrawal of not only their imaginative energies, but their wills.

When he retired, on July 25, 1948, he was leaving, in the comic supplement of that period, not a sinking ship, but a becalmed one: unable even to sink with dignity, because its holes were stuffed with the shredded wastes of distributors' greed and publisher's cowardice. Rechecking the *Herald Tribune* comic section recently, I found that I could not recall, even by name, a single comic strip of that time, other than the survivors from earlier: *Peter Rabbit*, *Mr. and Mrs.*, *Clarence*, Haenigsen's *Penny*. Even now, the participants in that vacuously handsome comic supplements, glazed with self-congratulatory comeliness, seem to smirk and to shuffle their way out of my memory. Everything to be welcomed in the style of the 1930s — everything easy, unselfconsciously decent, urbanely familiar — had gone to vinegar: thin-lipped WASP-liberal righteousness, slick fatuity, and implicit behind these, the worst sort of schoolmasterish censoriousness. I now recall it to be almost evenly divided between muscle-flexers like *Bodyguard* — flatulent with empty adventures, its casts multiplying more erratically than Peter's children — and lovable-adorables like *Honey 'n' Hank* — a late but zealous comer to the pillaging of Chic Young's *Blondie* undertaken, in the '40s, by the *Berries* and *Dotty Dripple* and their inestimable like. Amid this glutted, clamorous atmosphere, *Mr. and Mrs.* and *Clarence* appear to smile, sadly and half-apologetically, from their war-imposed half-pages, like old homeowners watching the bulldozers and steam shovels at large in their neighborhood.

Consummate epigraph to *Peter Rabbit's* disappearance, and the environment from which it disappeared, is the little prospectus of his intentions delivered by Cady's replacement, Vincent Fago: and recorded in *Newsweek*, September 20, 1948. I am told, by reliable persons well-acquainted with Fago, that he is a man of plain language and good-will; so I am encouraged to account his speech merely a statement of unpretentious, if singularly unimaginative, candor, and not the bleakly smug and petty declaration it seems in print. Yet, it haunts me as a response — possibly the only one with which its author would go on record — not only to another man's work of nearly 30 years, but to the promise and challenge that man's retirement left to his successor. It is the acceptance speech of an assistant barber who has just been promoted to first chair: and reflects exactly what the *Herald Tribune's* editors wanted, and what they bequeathed to their readers. Fago's diligent and not unenterprising, but supremely insipid continuation, the drawing hardly reaching the level of Saturday morning cartoons, seems the prime, denatured summary of everything they were capable of thinking or feeling about the childhood world Cady, almost inadvertently and with no prior experience, had entered and, for some 30 years, commanded.

He died on December 10, 1970. The last published children's work I am aware of his having signed are his illustrations for Little, Brown of Boston's Golden Anniversary edition of *Old Mother West Wind.* To them, one fancies appending — possibly, as a kind of end-paper — the full-page, full-dress farewell which he never gave his reader, and which the cluttered ignominy of his surroundings would surely have rejected: a farewell at the Rocky Pond pavilion, with Japanese lanterns and buffet tables; Peter Rabbit in his "old regimentals," augmented by a cummerbund, toasting Thoreau and Emerson, to a small party of frogs, June bugs and wild birds; Hepsy, wearing her first orchid, about to do the bunny hug with Colonel Popweasel; while Mr. Possum, at a side table, is explaining to Cousin Jack how to balance a beer-stein on top of two sherry glasses, supported by two shot-glasses, supported by two shell-glasses, all balanced on two upright pinochle cards. The little rabbits are tugging at their father's pants legs for a nickel to give the hurdy gurdy man, outside — as the bug orchestra glides into its last dance of the evening:

Somehow, they'd rather be kissed
To the strains of Chopin or Liszt…

HOWDY-GENTS
MORNING-PETER RABBIT-WE'VE JUST CALLED TO ASK YOU TO SERVE ON THE SCHOOL BOARD

IT WILL GIVE ME GREAT PLEASURE TO SERVE-MODERN TEACHING IS ALL WRONG AND ESPECIALLY IN SPELLING - PUPILS OF TO-DAY CAN'T SPELL ANY MORE THAN A MOSQUITO

SPEAK IN MY EAR TRUMPET PLEASE-I DIDN'T CATCH THAT LAST WORD

WRITE IT DOWN-HE DOESN'T HEAR WELL
YES HE'S AS DEAF AS A BAT
SURE
-MARCH 12-22-

THERE IT IS
!
!
!
Mosquitoe

BAH! YOU'RE FIRED
THERE'S NO ROOM ON THE SCHOOL BOARD FOR A GINK WHO CAN'T SPELL
THE IDEA AN E ON MOSQUITO
SCHUCKS-WE PICKED A LEMON THAT TIME BOYS
HARRISON CADY

CLOCK DEPT
YOU'RE RIGHT AND IT'S A SPECIAL BARGAIN TO-DAY
BY JINKS!-IT'S A FINE LOOKING TICK TICK

BING

YES IT'S A BEAUTIFUL STILL LIFE-MISTER-OF A PIECE OF CHEESE-VERY STRONG AND REALISTIC
THAT'S THE GEM OF THEM ALL-WIFE

!
MAR-26-22

OOF!
HOT CHOCOLATE

SCOUNDREL
KILL HIM
WRETCH
WHEW! I GUESS I'D BETTER SCO
THERE'S NO ORDERS HERE FO
ME TO-DAY
HARRISON CADY

WE WILL COMMENCE OUR STUDIES BY FIRST TAKING UP A CURIOUS BUT INTERESTING SPECIMEN - NAMELY THE PUFF-BALL

THIS AS YOU READILY WILL SEE IS A FUNNY SPHERICAL SHAPED FUNGI AND—

—IF YOU WILL KINDLY DRAW CLOSER YOU WILL NOTICE THAT IT'S COLOR IS A BROWNISH WHITE AND—

—LOOKING YOUR VERY CLOSEST YOU WILL OBSERVE THAT IT'S SURFACE APPEARS TO BE HARMELESS ENOUGH BUT—
-MAY 14-22-

!
- UPON APPLYING THE SLIGHTEST PRESSURE IT CRACKS OPEN AND A HEAVY BLACK CHOKING DUST IS GIVEN OUT

WOW! JUST LET ME GET MY HANDS ON YOU
THANKING YOU FOR YOUR KIND ATTENTION I WILL WISH YOU GOOD-DAY-YOU BIG FAT RABBIT
HARRISON-CADY

IT'S A FINE RIDE FOLKS AND YOU'LL ENJOY IT- WHILE I STAND AND LOOK ON
AH! GREAT! HIS SELF-DENIAL BUTTON IS WORKING
NICE, POPSY
SALLY

!
SALLY
THE WHIRLPO

WOW!

WHOA!
JULY 23-22

BUMP
BUMP
CAVE OF THE WINDS

WRETCH! YOU DIDN'T RIDE YOURSELF
NO, MADAM, I WAS PRACTICING SELF-DENIA
SALLY
EXIT
HARRISON CA

YOU MUST PERMIT OSWALD TO PLAY YOUR DRUM FIRST-BABY-YOU KNOW HE'S OUR GUEST
WHOOP-HE'S A BUSTING MY BOOM-BOOM
HURRAH AIN'T WE GOT FUN-BANG BANGETTY BANG BANG

THAT'S THE IDEA-BABY-OSWALD GETS THE FIRST SPIN IN YOUR LIL' BUZZ WAGON
WAH-H HE'S RUINING THE MACHINERY
OUT OF THE WAY—

NOW-BABY-I WISH YOU TO TAKE YOUR NEW CHRISTMAS SHOVEL AND GO OUTSIDE AND CLEAR THE WALKS AND LIL OSWALD WILL GO WITH YOU
AH! THAT'S JUST WHAT I'VE BEEN WAITING FOR-POPSY

LISTEN-OSWALD YOU'RE MY GUEST SO I'M GOING TO BE VERY VERY GENEROUS WITH YOU AND LET YOU USE MY NEW SNOW-SHOVEL AND—
JAN-21-23

—END ALL THIS NONSENSE ABOUT TREATING YOU LIKE A PRINCE-SO YOU JUST GET BUSY AND SHOVEL FOR YOUR LIFE OR SOMETHING DREADFUL WILL HAPPEN TO YOU-NOW THEN-
DIG FASTER- -AND FASTER
Copyright, 1923, N. Y. Tribune Inc.

WHEW! WHAT'S ALL THE TROUBLE HERE?
OH-POPSY-HE'S A BAWLING BECAUSE I TREATED HIM LIKE A PRINCE AND LET HIM PLAY WITH MY NEW SHOVEL FIRST
BOO-HOO-OO OO-OO-O
HARRISON CADY

HO-HO! MISTER TURTLE-
MAY I ASK WHAT YOU'VE
GOT THERE?
SURE! IT'S MY NEW
LAND AN' WATER MOTOR
I INVENTED IT MYSELF—

— IT RUNS ON TH' LAND AN' SWIMS IN TH' SEA AN' IT CAN DIVE LIKE A FISH AN' IT DOES IT ALL ON A PINT O' GAS SO JE'S HOP IN AN' I'LL GIVE YOU A FREE DEMONSTRATION
YEA?

NOW IN YOU COME AN' I CAUTION YOU TO HOLD ON TIGHT AN' KEEP YO' FEET INSIDE TH' CAR

HURRAH! THIS IS GRAND
YOU BETCHA-NOW HOLD ON TIGHT AN' I'LL HEAD HER FOR TH' WATER

AWAY SHE GOES-RIGHT OFF TH' END OF TH' DOCK JE'S LIKE A PESKY YOUNG DUCK

SHIVER MY TIMBERS-BOSS-WE'RE MAKIN' SIXTY KNOTS AN HOUR AN IF YOU'LL GET DOWN INSIDE AN' CLOSE TH' HATCH I'LL SHOW YOU HOW SHE'LL DIVE
MY TH' LIL' JIGGER CAN GO

J. BUG'S GREENHOUSE
!
FLORIST
WHAT IN-

BY CRINKUS! RIGHT THROMGH MY MASTERPIECE

WATER TANK
UN FOR YOUR VES-ITS A FLOOD

CHARGE EM BOYS- SOMEBODY IS GETTING GAY WITH US BEES
OUCH!
MAY 8-31

LEAVE HIM TO US BEES
THERE'S THE OWNER'S NAME PETER RABBIT
PETER RABBIT

IT'S NO PLACE FOR US
!!!- I'M RUINED
SCOUNDREL
WE'LL FIX HIM
BILL
BILL OF DAMAGES
HARRISON CADY

HM-M THEN YOU SURELY ARE VERY PROFICIENT ON FACIAL MASSAGE
NOPE-I KNOW NOTHING ABOUT IT

PERHAPS THEN YOU ARE A TRAINED MOUSTACHE CURLER
NIX-I'M NO MOUSTACHE TWIST

HUH-THEN YOU MUST BE A WHIRLDWIND AT SHAMPOOING
NO-I'VE NEVER SHAMPOOED A THING

WELL-THEN FOR THE LOVE OF CARROTS WHAT MAKES YOU THINK YOU CAN HOLD DOWN A JOB IN A BARBER SHOP?
·MAY 21-22-

!
WHY-PLEASE SIR-MY ANCESTORS WERE ALL HARES
HURRAH THAT'S A PUN

HARRISON CA

“One day Mr. Rabbit surprised Mr. Weasel making a meal of young mice.”

GEORGE 'N' JOSIE

HARRY J. TUTHILL AND THE BUNGLES

Little Orphan Annie's true parents are, of course, alive and known to the general public, among whom they could be seen for some three decades, leading what often seemed a semi-fugitive existence, watching and being watched by their neighbors; following various Grimm's Fairy Tale trials in pursuit of wealth, status, and honor. Between times, they prowled through the chambers of their apartment at Sunken Heights — a dwelling which might be pardonably confused with a nautilus shell's interior, or Kafka's Burrow; beseeching, or thunderously demanding, that the universe witness their afflictions, of which Exhibit A was their being married to each other. In all these respects — especially as spies, eccentrics, and fevered diarists of the world at large — George and Josie Bungle, of Harry J. Tuthill's *The Bungle Family*, proclaimed their bloodline to Orphan Annie, that bleak little newscaster, as well as considerable ties to George Herriman's beleaguered modern day Crusoes, *The Dingbat Family* (whose inception, in 1910, preceded that of the Bungles by three years). They had as much to do as the protagonists of either contemporary strip, with an American middle-class sense of style,

which Tuthill, like Herriman, perceived as an always somewhat frantic clutching at whatever G-strings, towels, and patchwork remainders could be furnished from one's fantasy capacity, and memories of better days. And they made their day-to-day last-ditch stand, their ongoing Alamo against neighbors, bill collectors, cops, and highly combustible perfect strangers, with a mixture of plentiful venom, rather addled gallantry, and withering melancholy that would have done their Ungentle Annie proud.

Increasingly, over the years, *The Bungle Family* expressed a flexible-steel perception of American romanticism from inside out, not even equaled by *The Gumps*, with its lavish reviews of Victorian plot-lines involving besieged maidens, vulturish bankers, and philandering counts. Sidney Smith's imagination loved to fondle, even while smiling, the warm sable lining of romance which he supposed underlay the plain serge of daily Americana. As for the Bungles, however, what we see every day *is* the lining: the funny and appalling ways in which George and Josie's imaginations can shape their lives is never in any doubt, nor its remoteness from the imagination of Victorian novelists, save in the Bungles' — and their neighbors' and relatives' — untiring postures of indignation, injured dignity, and aristocratic scorn. Visually, they are cut to the pattern set by the Gumps, with a probable eye cocked to Bud Fisher's Augustus Mutt and his Sweet Woman. But their black hair — George's curls and Josie's puffs — combined with their operatic marching and arm-flailing, give them a European look augmented somehow by the deadness of their backgrounds. Tuthill's vinegary lines, his flat colors and scanty use of shadows, plus the cold, lofty spaces in which the Bungles usually found themselves engulfed (you could fairly hear the echoes in that apartment) produced a gauntness of architecture and faintly dream-like solemnity, compared with which Di Chirico might seem to be staging a series of Mardi Gras galas.

I am always struck by the animosity accorded Tuthill's drawing style, even by alert and sympathetic critics like Coulton Waugh (who compared it, in terms of the strip's pleasures, to eating ice cream with a sore throat) and Bill Blackbeard, who, in Maurice Horn's *World Encyclopedia of Comics*, enlisted the adjective "grubby." I have always found myself refreshed by Tuthill's freedom from the conventional dexterities of comic-strip shorthand, and grateful for his translation of what must have begun as awkwardness and maladroitness into a vocabulary of space and line that contained what he had to say about his characters' relationships to each other and to their real and imagined worlds. Barren of any sensuous delights, the spidery line gets across a fascination, as hypnotic as the more sophisticated bareness of *Little Orphan Annie*, of potential animation in the dead-looking surfaces, from which may spring the impromptu, dippy choreographies of George's occasional sidewalk battles with bill-posters and strolling contortionists. The stiffness produces some marvelous images of vacuous pride: spike or beak-like noses atilt — as though the adjacent world was a sulfur swamp — eyes closed, shoulders high. The space becomes a virtual character in *The Bungle Family*, the Bungles' major antagonist, which they seem to be combating even during afternoons at home, when they register their degree of marital harmony by walking counter-motion to each other: Josie striding, cougar-like, with folded arms, George executing a unique walk, somewhere between a stalk and a strut, as though secretly practicing a Ubi mating dance: one raised fist or pointed finger menacing the heavens. They are surrounded by open doors, which, unlike the glowering alcoves of *Little Orphan Annie*, open, not into darkness, but merely into the hermetic grimness of other, similar rooms; while the windows open on adjoining wings of the apartment house, any prospect of which makes San Quentin appear a Louisa May Alcott reverie. George and Josie are continually peering through these windows at the cryptic or titillating performances of their neighbors, whom we can glimpse, fleetingly, through the Bungles' window-frame and the vistas of their shoulders.

But what Tuthill's vacuous-looking, delicately sinister, droll draftsmanship accomplishes above all, is to portray middle-class Americans as autonomous entertainers; and their imagination as an agent at once of ballooning hope and of squashing frustration. American comic strips have always provided a gallery of artists taking shies at delusions of wealth, athletic skill, erotic prowess; but I doubt that very many of them have presented imagination as the self-goading, often enough self-defeating, yet unquenchable energy which Tuthill portrays; or managed to embody it, as he does, in his character's personalities, and especially in the recurrently frenzied, chronically disorder-prone George. Here, as in other instances, the nearest parallel I can call to mind is that of George Herriman's *The Dingbat Family*, which began, on June 21st of 1910, as a tentative

run-through of Bud Fisher's and T.E. Powers's domestic cacophonies, but presently settled — unsettled — into a Pepys's diary of domestic paranoia, with Mr. Dingbat — who shrunk from his original, average height, even as the lowering world around him expanded — clamoring for his rights — ill-considered and worse-rewarded — from every quarter of his daily experience. The first fatal manifestation of the *Family Upstairs*, on July 26, 1910, completed the hemstitching of the Dingbats' patchwork gentility, vs. the uproarious chaos of the ungenteel, unhousebreakable world outside their apartment domain. Meanwhile, the cellar — the lower margin of the strip — was being taken over by a cat and mouse, eventually to be identified as Krazy and Ignatz.

I have no doubt at all that Harry Tuthill's temperament and imagination took ready impress from *The Dingbat Family*: certain "childhood friends" of the Bungles, the E. Pluribus Dowdys, bear the name, slightly transmuted, of the original Dingbat couple, who retreated within the year to plain Minnie and Denny. But Herriman's influences, such as they were, are placed in relief by Tuthill's originality, which proceeded from his acerb, X-ray-like reduction of the Bungles and their terrain. You don't get the humorous and erotic juice which ripples like a benign lava through Herriman's ragtag-elegant drawing style: a perfect counterpart as he described the Dingbats' own desperate improvisations against the family upstairs, their increasingly giddy excursions at running the family to earth, of the exquisite seeming-makeshift improvisations which he adored in Chaplin. It is style evolving and justifying itself, out of an apparent nothing.

The Bungles reflect the Dingbats' capacity for breeding situations out of air; save that the Bungles' air is the chill middle air of obsession and bug-bear; all seen in the refrigerator light of Tuthill's composition and tone: the calamities and confusions that George and Josie were capable of spinning like silkworms out of their guts. With most stereotypical married couples in comic strips from the 1910s through the 1930s, the awfulness is implicit, and safely interred, in a given situation; but, with the Bungles, it is a vital component of their joint energy, and informs the feckless, deranged quests which they pursued together. Tuthill had a falcon's eye for their compulsive imprecision, landing their arrows a fair half-inch alongside the center-mark; geared as they are to encountering, and anticipating, theoretical events of all kinds, so that the actual is slightly out of focus. They are capable of exhausting a Sunday afternoon determining the correct spelling of "catatonia," or trying to determine the contents of a box, long consigned to the rear of a kitchen shelf, which is finally identified as sawdust ("Put some milk and sugar on it," is one of Josie's earlier suggestions). But, where Herriman makes the reader aware of the (minimally sentimental) love and creative élan in the Dingbats' actual and fabricated dilemmas, Tuthill makes us aware, above all, of the vacuity, of the way their fantasizing highlights the nullity at the center of George and Josie's shared life (many of the Sunday pages resemble syncopated charades of Henry James's *The Beast in the Jungle*).

Harry Tuthill was one of the most deeply sardonic journalists of his day or many another; and never so much as when he showed the self-germinating futility of much that passes for taste and cultural heritage in contemporary life. A tenement child in Chicago during the mid-nineteenth century, a former newsboy, he displays little of the piety toward traditional culture (in the sense of: "Hands off, boys, this is bigger than us") which distinguishes so many of his contemporaries: meaning, not disrespect, or careless, anarchic disregard, but respect cut with irony. Both Bungles exhibit enormous pride in their articulateness and can expostulate at length (as, indeed, at only token invitation, can most of their associates) as though unfurling scrolls of testimony for some cosmic Clerk of the Court to review. Their volubility, like that of Minnie and Denny Dingbat, is part and parcel with their fantasy life. But unlike Herriman's company, it is laced with resin. "Oh, I understand now why my friends smile and shake their heads sadly, and say 'Poor Mrs. Bungle!'" exclaims Josie, whose aptitudes are those of a novelist, circa Jane Austen. She can build little vignettes around data like the waddle of the landlord's son, and Balzacian passages around a Bungle acquaintance, named Irene, having cosmeticized her name from Eileen. "I see poor Irene, née Eileen, trying to get out the car," she remarks, as inexhaustible a newscaster as little Orphan Annie, and, if anything, possessed of greater verve. Like the traditional wife-images of comic strips and radio and television, she excels at bringing her husband to earth; Josie's distinction being that she feels no qualms about the suddenness of George's descent, or how far he is from the ground.

Josie supplies the ice, George the fire, in the relationship. Whereas Josie's commentaries and apologies are richly expositional, George's rhythms are vigilantly terse, as of a Continental Op perennially composing reports for The Old Man, or a warfront journalist typing dispatches. As with Harold Gray's little vagrant, every experience, no matter in what state of consciousness, must be recorded. "Whoo! Couple of good lefts that donkey got together. Now, let's see. Where am I?" This reflection follows upon George's conference with a neighbor, after erroneously introducing a doctor, with a bill, into the latter's apartment. George's style is his armor, and through it he both fabricates and perpetually exonerates himself from adventurous crises. His speech amounts, in fact, to a picaresque novel, which he may have commenced writing about himself the day he was born. "What!" represents, for George, both an exclamation and a punctuation. Something more, perhaps; or the "what" is the object of continual search, the elusive occasion of renown and esteem, the wandering fortune, which lead himself and Josie on expeditions more hypnotic, and darker, than anything in Andy Gump's campaign for the presidency, or Uncle Bim's contests with Count Zander, because they proceed from deeper within the characters. The "What!" of the Bungles' quests, the missing justification, is like unto the spot on the horizon, the Real Right Thing, after which the characters of Henry James, or the exclaimers and self-protesters of J.R. Williams's cartoons, are forever striving.

Yet, the energy which George invests in his delusions sets him off from most of his white-collar fellows in comics strips; certainly from genially self-indulgent, and ever indulged, Major Hoople. For, unlike the yarning Major, and in a way different from that of the loud-talking, but often shrewd and watchful Andy Gump, George repeatedly attempts to shape life to his fantasies, and with a steamrolling energy which, however it may rebound on him, is a touch more formidable than that shared by his numerous middle-class neighbors. I cannot recall a comic strip artist who has portrayed, as has Tuthill, the Walter Mittyish imagination as something potentially, if ever-so-faintly, menacing: a loaded gun likely to "Bang!" at any moment at all.

For George Bungle is an agent of disorder, the walking embodiment of disorder, the magnet of poltergeists and boggerts. Non-stop, centerless quarrels mushroom wherever he appears, walk-

ing his stiff-jointed walk (Tuthill, in his scant commentary for the daily strips, would usually refer to George as "the Colonel," a title never otherwise dwelt upon, that I know of; but, I have conjectured his walk as the product of a war wound). His Sunday page adventures are little glories of inanity, the megalomaniac zip of a Preston Sturges hero turned back upon itself, a syllogism of absurdity. George strolls down to the lake one fine evening to hear an elderly gentleman, swimming, cry out for someone to rescue his Ambrose. Gallant George is halfway peeled out of his coat, even as the distraught old man announces a fifty-dollar reward for Ambrose's recovery. After a series of futile plunges and splutterings, Ambrose reappears in his delighted guardian's grasp, and turns out to be a fish ("Ambrose! Naughty, naughty. Look, he knows we're talking about him") and finally the man awards himself the fifty bucks. George's response, in the last panel, is to hurl him back into the lake. That is George.

He is an incorrigible sidewalk superintendent, and extempore officiator: a forty-carat buttinsky, in other words. He interrupts a petshop owner — a man with a thick Slavic accent — as he is quarreling with his painter over a matter of what George understands as the "poppies" which are to adorn the store window. George, his creative electricity in full flash, preempts the painting job, and supplies a border of red, white, and blue poppies, only to be enlightened that the design required was of *puppies*: "Docks! Bow-wow!" George, with that philosophic calm which is always on call after the storms he has projected and engendered, strolls away.

George represents creativity. He is romance gone totally off the axle, skidding into this irrational gutter and that. And yet, as ruthlessly explicit as Harry Tuthill may be about George's eccentricities, he concedes him his eccentric will; which is what sets him apart from the ranks of so many other ineffectual, pathetically dreaming work-a-dayers of the comic strips. George's demonic strain, his not-to-be-dismissed crazy force, represents an autonomy as considerable as that of Molière's or Meredith's comic protagonists. He displays a Quixotic combativeness: an afternoon walk may launch him into the weirdest skirmishes, little cyclones of tussle in which fists seem to be impaled on spike noses, like jelly apples, and war-cries ("All right, you phony!") fly hot and heavy. They may involve an uncivil bill-poster, who accosts George with brushes and placards, or a con-

tortionist who rebounds, an animate punching-bag, from his every blow; or, eerie as a vignette from Gogol, the embattled inhabitants of a sewer, whom we never see, but who seem to have resolved on their working-place as their fortress. All these fracases take place in whirligig confusion such as would send Quixote himself, in despair, back to his windmills. And the most eerie effect is that George generates and thrives on turmoil. Yet for all his quota of losses, Tuthill makes one believe that George can be a formidable opponent: his neighbors and relatives are leery of him. A rebellious clique of Bungle relatives, formed to challenge Goerge and Josie's title to an inheritance promised by a genealogist, scatters when George stalks into their storefront headquarters. He brings us up short: how extraordinary to realize the untilled acreage that exists in popular art between the abject victims of "off-days," hard luck, defective equipment, or their own amiable incompetence, and the Flash Gordons! In George, I suspect — it is the most plausible explanation I can put forth for the continued, rather wide popularity, over three decades, of this aloof, irony-juiced strip — American readers felt an independent mind and imagination, however loony their occasional excursions, tendering confidences, genial enough, but never wheedling.

Originally lurching and skittering like the roughest tablecloth jottings, when Tuthill's style found solidity, it became a startlingly supple instrument of suggestion: a vehicle of the fantasy's elusiveness. Even when melodrama takes the keyboard, the soft-pedal is played. A daughter, Peggy, drifts through during the 1930s; in her rather languid wake, a suitor, one of the most dubious of "good guys," named Hartford Oakdale. Oakdale was a mustachioed smoothie of wrinkle-free manners, instantly championed by George (who may have viewed him as a self-projection). He sprayed the Bungles' lives with the heavy cologne of intrigue: stolen jewels and kidnappings. Yet, Tuthill, with his zest for deflecting clichés, swipes aside every opportunity for the *schmaltz* in which Sidney Smith, from an overflowing tureen, bathed his characters. A kidnap attempt by gangsters is, as one can imagine, close to the probable real-life equivalent — a series of "close-ups": George, Josie, and Peggy, unfevered but bemused, exchanging speculations about why they are not headed for their host's yacht, as promised. When Lord Addlewit regales George with some Trader Hornpipe about a face-down with jungle natives, all that the "flashback" panels reveal are some static clusters of Addlewit's party and some staid-looking, mostly naked black men. All of which reflects, not Tuthill's disinterest in, or self-consciousness about, melodrama; but his determination to play it out his own way, using his wry-minded sense of scale; for which, one gratefully realizes, his drawing, once a maneuvering action through his limitations, has become an agent, a positive instrument of selection, such as how many comic strips offer us? It is romance permanently off-center; even Peggy's ambiguous courtship by Mr. Oakdale fails to turn up the James Stewart/Cagney Mr. Right whom, even in full knowledge of Harry Tuthill's works, we may fleetingly expect. The only rival to appear, however, is one Barko Sowers, a snakier version of Oakdale, against whom Hartford glows, however dully: not Mr. Right, but Mr. Best-We-Can-Hope-For.

The Bungles' advance into the '30s — that era which saw, in films, the rebirth and life-eternal fantasies of *Topper* and *On Borrowed Time*, and *The Scoundrel*, the power-through-grace fable of H.G. Wells's the *Man Who Could Work Miracles* — found George's restive fantasy life beginning to colonize the "real world." Not only do his daily confrontations grow increasingly eccentric, but his dream life more and more infiltrates the Sunday pages: he counts sheep which, typically enough, begin wrangling among themselves as to who will precede whom; a Busby Berkeley-type extravaganza on the idea of "bringing home the bacon" finds him a pork tycoon, making a luncheon appointment with President Roosevelt, until awakened by Josie, who needs two dollars for the landlord.

During the waking life of the daily strips, George's dreams begin to spawn curious visitors to Sunken Heights. He is whisked into an undercover assignment guarding a top-secret rocket — which, to be sure, promptly goes AWOL, with George as its sole passenger, and deposits him in the woman-dominated future civilization of Queen Chloe XXIV, who instantly appropriates George as her prospective king. (This episode actually represents one of George's, and Tuthill's, least successful fantasies, since, for once — perhaps because of the unaccustomed scope — Tuthill's tilting cliché is, itself, a cliché of sci-fi burlesque.) The most eerie, funny, and mordant of George's excursions, however, are those which confront him with dinky, scruffy-looking, but redoubtable men, who, like George McWhirter Farthingay, the Man Who Could Work

Miracles, possess reality-shuffling powers, which one and all they place at George's disposal. These *schlepper* elves would seem natural ancestors to another disadvantaged Oberon, Jackeen J. O'Malley, Barnaby's fairy godfather, in *PM* of the '40s; but they are much more efficient, generally much meaner, and treat George with a condescending but whole-hearted cordiality. There is a genii-like personage who inflicts "squitches," mini-curses, on George's enemies, causing a nasty-talking neighbor, for example, to swallow his teeth; or the spirit of Dumb Luck, who amiably introduces himself as George's natural guardian. The visualization of these seedy gnomes is informed with Tuthill's usual sarcastic economy: they are not here to convert the Bungles' skeletal, shabby-genteel, claustrophobic world, but come as its natural children: and they have the spooky plausibility — to which the popular reading of our current, psychic energy-obsessed age will attest — of poltergeists.

Then in the mid-'30s, as though the Caliban energumen of George's willfulness had embarked, finally, on a life of its own — or, as though Harry Tuthill, jaded at last with the Bungles' spider-webbed life, were trying to thrash on to something else — George acquires a protégé called Doodle: neither a poltergeist nor an elf, but an earthy, cheerful recasting of their short-spoken, demonic efficiency. Doodle is built along their inverted-kettle lines, only human-size, with a mustache recast from discarded turnip-greens, and talks that pan-Slavic which is Tuthill's only venture, within my knowledge, into ethnic characterization. He endears himself to George originally on joining a decrepit baseball club, which George has acquired, and straightaway recharging the club's and George's morale with his dippy, Z-curved pitch. The unlikely partnership progresses through Doodle's short career as a wrestler, and the pair's more erratic enterprises as private detectives, in 1937.

Doodle was the first full-scale portrait of innocence that I am aware of Tuthill having attempted: a brother-in-arms of those formidably endowed but sentimentally vulnerable men, or monsters — *Popeye's* Toar, Lennie in *Of Mice and Men*, Karloff's Thing in *The Bride of Frankenstein*, which, in the Depression '30s, emblematized innocence and affection, linked — shackled — to a strength, a potency, which was abused and evilly manipulated. I think that Tuthill's oblique, sardonic talent, with its proclivity for skating the thinnest of ice, was at once fascinated and a little embarrassed, after the first farcical élan of the ball-club episodes, by Doodle's presence and meaning to George, and his possible permutations. He had one more try at the character, however. The Sunday *New York American* pages of 1937 are rather abruptly taken over by George's hulking cousin, Homer: a man, unlike George or even Doodle, of minimal speech, and quite unlike George, of rather consistent, if short-range, success at expressing his will. The profuse dialogue balloons of the Sunday pages are banished by the rousing pantomime of Homer; who, in one episode, watches his beloved, Miss Dilly Doe, being squired by an Oakdale-Sowers type. He sulkily consents when, with raindrops, she sweetly requests his umbrella; then, as he is getting it from his bedroom, yields up an explosive "No!" in agonized close-up. He shows himself both a descendant, albeit non-verbal, of King Solomon, and a cousin germane of good ole George, by scissoring the umbrella in half; forcing the courtly slicker to prove his mettle by leaving Miss Doe the protective half, while he is forced to walk in the rain.

Homer represents the most decisive splitting of the Bungles' imaginative walls in the course of their existence. He did not last long; proving, so I am informed by Bill Blackbeard, too violent a disruption of what had become, for Tuthill's readers of the past generation, accustomed if offbeat rhythms. I understand, but regret, Homer's departure. He might have augured that reshaping and re-liberation of one's vocabulary, which only the most earnestly committed and vigorous artist can consider, much less put into execution. As it was — until his final withdrawal, at the beginning of the '40s — Tuthill seems less soured, less lulled — as by protective self-inoculation — into the fatal mechanics of routine, than most other such artists, among them those I care for, who come to mind. And the Bungles' destiny has, in at least one instance, proven happier than their spiritual daughter's — for, in the wake of their cranky, off-sides existence there have been no attempts to "revive" them through other hands.

THE BUNGLES—Hired - - - - - - - - - - - - - - - - - By H. J. Tuthil

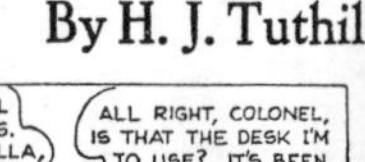

THE BUNGLES—Call Mrs. Bungle - - - - - - - - - - - By H. J. Tuthil

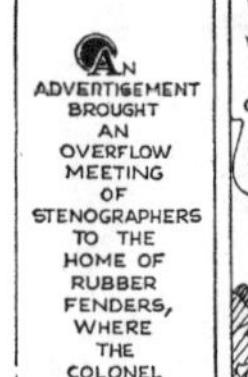

THE BUNGLES — Old Granite Heart - - - - - - - - - By H. J. Tuthil

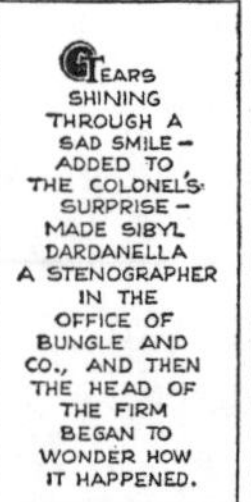

THE BUNGLES—Sibyl Looks Forward - - - - - - - - - - By H. J. Tuthil

THE BUNGLES—Home Is Not So Sweet Now - - - - - - - - By H. J. Tuttle

THE BUNGLES—Mrs. Weener Should Know About This - - - By H. J. Tuthill

THE BUNGLES—Sibyl Is Being Herself - - - - - - - - - - By H. J. Tuthill

THE BUNGLES—Poor Drury, It's All Settled - - - - - - - By H. J. Tuthill

THE BUNGLES—A Blue Homecoming - - - - - - - - - - - - - By H. J. Tuthi

THE BUNGLES—No Place Like Home When George Keeps House - By H. J. Tuthill

THE BUNGLES—The Bad News Is Leaking Out - - - - - - - By H. J. Tuthill

THE BUNGLES—Big Hearted Drury - - - - - - - - - - By H. J. Tuthill

THE BUNGLES—Expert Versus Expert - - - - - - - - - - By H. J. Tuthill

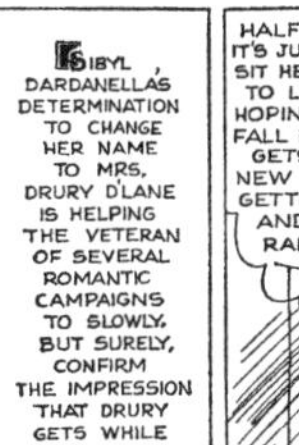

THE BUNGLES—Confess, Colonel! - - - - - - - - - - - - - H. J. Tuthill

THE BUNGLES — A Visit from the Green-Eyed Monster - - - By H. J. Tuthill

THE BUNGLES—High Time for Some Fast Work - - - - - - - By H. J. Tuthill

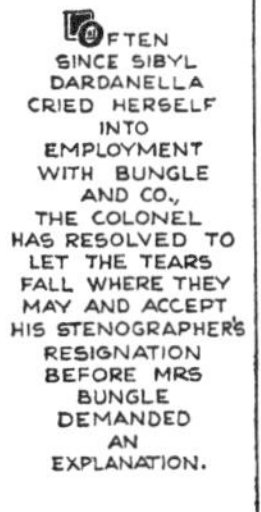

THE BUNGLES—Start Explaining, Colonel - - - - - - - - - - By H. J. Tuthil

THE BUNGLES—Ha, Ha! A Triangle - - - - - - - - - - - By H. J. Tuthil

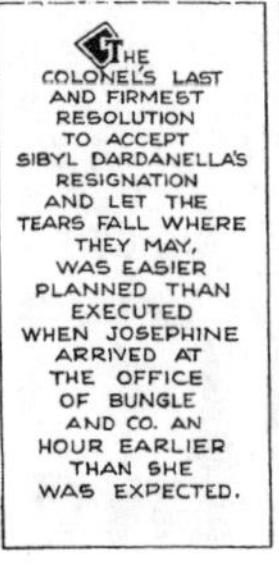

THE BUNGLES—All Over but the Shouting - - - - - - - - By H. J. Tuthil

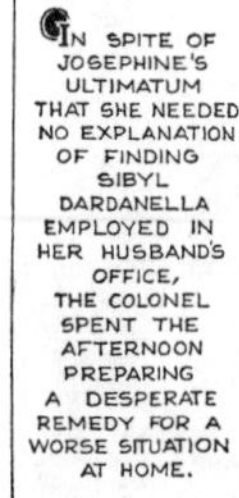

THE BUNGLES—The Colonel Just Will Interrupt His Wife - - - By H. J. Tuthil

THE BUNGLES — Ah, Those Were the Days! - - - - - - - By H. J. Tuthill

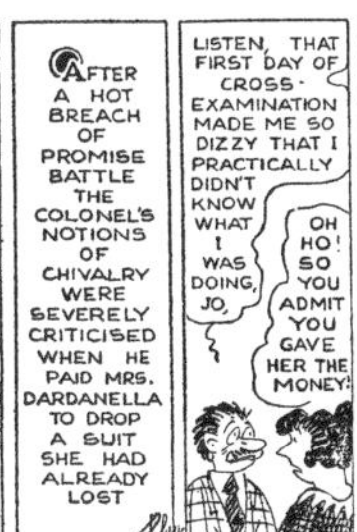

AND SO MRS. BUNGLE HAD REASON TO BE DISTURBED WHEN THE COLONEL WAS SO CARELESSLY SYMPATHETIC THAT HE RECENTLY EMPLOYED SIBYL IN THE HOME OF RUBBER FENDERS.

THE BUNGLES—Good-by, Sibyl—or Josephine - - - - - - - By H. J. Tuthill

THE BUNGLES—Cupid Calling Mr. D'Lane - - - - - - - - By H. J. Tuthill

THE BUNGLES—Louie to the Rescue - - - - - - - - - By H. J. Tuthill

THE BUNGLES—The Colonel's Story Sounds Just Too Good - - By H. J. Tuthil

THE BUNGLES—Sibyl Is a Dangerous Lady - - - - - - - - - By H. J. Tuthil

THE BUNGLES—Louie Talks as if He Isn't Fooling - - - - - - By H. J. Tuthi

THE BUNGLES—Shocking News - - - - - - - - - - - - By H. J. Tuthil

THE BUNGLES—Yes, Sir, I Told You So! - - - - - - - - - By H. J. Tuthill

THE BUNGLES—A Clue to Drury's Absence - - - - - - - By H. J. Tuthill

THE BUNGLES—Dissatisfied Investors - - - - - - - - - - By H. J. Tuthill

THE BUNGLES—Bad News - - - - - - - - - - - - By H. J. Tuthill

THE BUNGLES — Home and Office Trouble - - - - - - - - - By H. J. Tuthill

THE BUNGLES—Rubber Fenders Are Cracking - - - - - - - - By H. J. Tuthill

EACH DAY SINCE THE FINANCIAL ADVISER OF BUNGLE AND CO. HURRIEDLY LEFT TOWN, AN INCREASING NUMBER OF GET-RICH-QUICK INVESTORS CALL AT THE HOME OF RUBBER FENDERS AND ASK THE COLONEL TO REDEEM THE EXTRAVAGANT PROMISES OF DRURY D'LANE.

EITHER I GET MY $40 OR I'LL TEAR DOWN THIS JOINT.

I KNEW IT WAS A FAKE BUT HE KEPT TALKING FAST SO I WOULDN'T HAVE A CHANCE TO THINK WHILE SIGNING ON THE DOTTED LINE.

THERE'S BUNGLE HIMSELF!

WHERE? LET ME GET OVER TO THAT PHONY!

I WANT JUSTICE!

RUBBER FENDERS

GANGWAY PLEASE!

BUNGLE & CO.

THE BUNGLES—Paying on Demand - - - - - - - - - - - By H. J. Tuthill

THE BUNGLES—The End of Another Rainbow - - - - - - - By H. J. Tuthill

THE BUNGLES—News

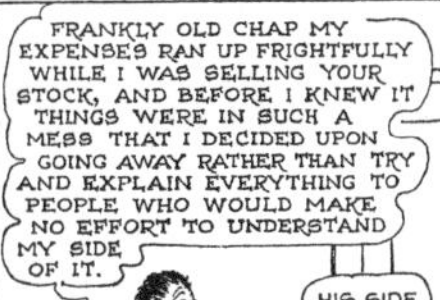

THE BUNGLES—The Colonel's Optimism Always Dies: Hard

By H. J. Tuthill

THE BUNGLES — Business Versus the Home

By H. J. Tuthill

NOBODY WATCHES THE BIRDIE

J.R. WILLIAMS AND OUT OUR WAY

They are always peering,
The kids: skinny, bespectacled,
        plump, earnest, aloof,
Standing on their raft;
Or, the cowboys,
Squatting, reclining,
Around the campfire, the flames of which
Increase their look of age.
Each separate in the orbit
        of his own posture
        from the others,
(Not even sure they want to be drawn,
        that they *are* a picture).
Peering with their popeyes,
The mouths either talking, or
        about to,
Showing edges of rabbit-teeth.
Their eyes, their mouths, peering,

Trying to get a hold on something
        (even if not the Truth),
Beyond the campfire's edge, the horizon-line
        of the raft.
With clumsy, dogged patience, extraordinary
        authority
(He never cheated them of that)
And better his hand go dead,
His brain with it,
The half-second before he'd permit
        the first flicker of
        condescension
Toward them,
And their energetic, old, hard-working clothes,
The wrinkles at the arm-pits,
The bats at knees and crotch,
All very concerned, all going about
        their business,
Of being alive.
(They're not even sure they want to be drawn).

I recall, while reading the single-panel studies by J.R. Williams in the *New York World-Telegram* as a child, my curious feeling of intimidation at not being able to get the point. Not "what the drawing was about," which was almost too easy, but the swarming, or eccentrically composed content, its can't-be-bothered-right-now preoccupation, contributed to my bother. More accurately, I found myself having to wonder *where* the point was, where I was, or was supposed to be, in relation to these drawings. These questions were answered so affably, so urbanely by H.T. Webster, or by Clare Briggs or by Gluyas Williams — other distinguished single-panelers, over whose work, in the *Herald Tribune* or the *Evening Sun*, I can still remember my father chuckling and spluttering with laughter. Williams, however, had no armchair to offer the reader; no one lined up, smiling. I felt that these panels represented a door or a window left open, with not so much as a word of direct invitation or acknowledgment of any reader's presence. *Out Our Way* (emphasis mine) as the collective title, as well as the title of the Sunday comic-strip, more crisply drawn and more familiarly amusing (I later discovered, through the

good offices of Bill Blackbeard, that this strip was, for years, drawn by Williams's assistant Neg Cochran, supervised by Williams). There was no balcony seat. You found yourself in the thick of things, along with Williams: a clamoring, gesticulating family group, a bunch of factory hands griping and expostulating to, or about, a foreman called "The Bull of the Woods," who seemed in a perennial state of near-collapse (in close competition with his defeatist overalls) at the wanton disorderliness of events. Or, an assortment of cowboys, who must have been, even as teenagers, more tired, older, more roughly branded by their experience, than any tenderfoot replicas from Republic Pictures could seem after decades, as they floundered across a raw cliff, racing after a maverick seen dancing along the panel's upper border.

Disconcertingly, vignettes like these seemed to stream beyond the edges of Williams's daily panels, which offered, themselves, only the most provisional enclosures: no stage spotlight, no arenas for varieties of bull- and bear-baiting; but momentary viewfinders for an existence which, like that renegade calf, seemed repeatedly beyond lassoing distance of the bone-aching, exasperated pursuers. Was there, ever, a stage center? All the jostling and scrambling seemed directed toward hanging onto one's own space; the key dialogue in a scene often came from left or right of a panel: two factory wiseacres, tendering their philosophic glosses on some kibitzer accidentally scorching his nose with an acetylene torch; or, a manager, in serene autohypnosis, oblivious to his ringing phone. More often than not, once the eye picked its way to the "pay off line," through an array of postures which were virtual acts of incivility toward harmony itself, there was no payoff in any accustomed sense; not in the acceptable meaning of a punch-line, or a sententious zinger, the main implication of which is: "Oh, it's been put into words at last!" William's panels bristled with words, however, as they swarmed with wrinkles. Nothing brought his compositions and figures to bay, reminding them of their place; instead, even the wit, or joke, or flat-voiced summation by a younger brother or old factory hand, came from within, and remained within the situation; not reducing it, not controlling it, offering no you-and-I *we*-know-better winks or nudges, but rather directing the eye back to those ungainly gestures, the lurching, unguided purposefulness of the action. In a very simple looking panel, entitled "The Shadow," a mother quick-

marches her son, trusty-style, to the back door (he is carrying a small tower of crackers). The mother, in her few but well-edged words, has just finished cleaning the whole house. You feel an emotional authenticity that defies the seams of a quaint-homey-gag-situation package. There is too much bedrock exhaustion and exasperation in her little speech, and her overly stiff carriage, underscored by the weary, practical, not-quite-resigned lines of her ankle length print dress. And there's too much guilty awkwardness in the son's face, his gingerly protection of his cracker tower — even in the way his shirt spills over his belt — for the impeccably blueprinted genre humor with which Webster would have regaled us, wrapped in the gloss paper of universality. "Americana" has been relinquished in favor of ornery particularity.

I am not interested in denigrating unjustly an artist of Webster's exceeding craft and dispatch and wit; or, for that matter, men like Clare Briggs, or the often excellent Gluyas Williams, when I say the the word "packaging" sums up much of the difference between their work and J.R. Williams's ever-accosting, unceremonious art. For what the best single-panel work of these men delivered the reader was a cunning distillation of certain "typical" attitudes, situations, daily confrontations, with the style as a high-gloss, highly-enameled maraschino cherry, and a discreet lemon-squeeze, for this middle-class self-consolation highball, of patronization (scorn would have equaled lemon-pits). Norman Rockwell's name is often clipped to such sentiments; but Rockwell was absorbed imaginatively in his subject matter, which he accorded a sort of rhapsodic expansion, such as I do not feel in Webster or his like. Most of the others were contributors to the old *Life Magazine*, after World War I, and not long before the razing of its humorous-Americana edifice by the incense-scented torch of Eustace Twilley, of the *New Yorker*. Some of them, like Gluyas Williams and Gardner Rea, preceded others like Crawford Young (the original *Clarence*), sashaying on to the *New Yorker's* nearest counterpart among daily papers, the *Tribune*, later the *Herald Tribune*: all headed for the depot where Suburban Humor was waiting with the car, bags packed. The chief casualty of work like Webster's, with all its dash and fencer's perceptiveness, is what Williams often disconcertingly supplies: *context*. Not the mere assumption that this is shared experience, which is after all, the cartoonists' hole-card; but the precious membrane of continuity which unites the artist's personality, his background, the circumstances of the work, and the corresponding experience of the reader. I am not talking about one-on-one correspondence, of course; the art work as a thrift shop, where the auditor seeks out this camel's hair coat, that set of earrings; but, rather, something like the home-builder's scouting for water sources, neighbors, means of communication. Context is a trading post of psychic energies.

The type of American cartoonist whom Webster may fairly be cited as representing evolved a sort of comedy of manners, much of it bilious indeed under the chipper and expeditious drawing style; favoring titles like "Life's Darkest Moment," "And Nothing Can Be Done About It," "How to Torture Your Husband/Wife," and geared implicitly to the assumption that a majority of Americans are obtuse and inconsiderate to the point of near-inanimacy, so that to extend one's self over-much in the direction of politeness, of deference, is to play the fool and/or suicidal masochist: i.e., Casper Milquetoast. The occasional "happy" panels of Webster took place in a Midwestern Never-Never Land, which offered a series of Fabergé egg views usually entitled "The Thrill that Comes Once in a Lifetime" (properly inserted in which, I see, a caret, and above it, the title's completion: "And Only Once!") Webster's somewhat eccentric premise — that Americans are subjected to excruciating inconvenience and deprivation by being overly polite and order-oriented — might have provided a workable basis for satire; save that Webster himself, the dexterous and affable artisan, always seems to overrule the potentially troubling, comically rich aspects of the situation he is putting forth. The same formula-making zeal which caused him to patent his subject-matter and theme, dissuaded him, I think, from continuing the patiently observed, amiable, unmanipulative appraisal of what may have been his best work: *The Man in the Brown Derby*, featuring Egbert Smear, which ran in the *New York World* during the 1920s. Egbert, despite his uninviting name, emerges as a more plausible prototype of Milquetoast — one in some reasonable transaction with an actual-seeming context. I must hasten to add, however, that as a good bet Casper furnished more and heartier laughs, because the reader was constantly, in some corner of the attention, aware of lion-tamer Webster intervening between one's self and the most befretting, and daringly funny, aspects of Casper and of the Milquetoast syndrome. Webster continues to deflect all true humorous identification by making Casper so outrageous a marionette, his pathological obsequiousness operating on a closed circuit, that even the most obvious springboard of natural comedy — Milquetoast as a projection of Webster, or some important aspect of him — was deftly closeted. He would never locate himself, and, therefore, no more can we; even as to how much that he likes or detests his own characters. When I think of him, it is always of the office card in his drawings: arched eyebrows, tight-lipped smile, out-thrust chin.

In work such as Webster's and others of his contemporaries, the imaginative space involved, the sense of a vignette's or observed pattern's reception by the artist himself, is subtly undermined by the packaging involved; so that what is offered us amounts to a palliative for such irritations as we can bear to remember, in the most tolerable (i.e. "universal") of perspectives. In contrast, what Williams aims for, in every instance, is the specific thingness of every episode he records. I do not call him a poet in this regard, yet he reacts as a poet would be expected to: seeking the peculiar, even crazy structure of each situation, however ordinary. He is not a satirist, such as Webster made regular feints at being, nor does he pretend to be. He does not, or very seldom does, bite on through to the core of a situation. Rather, he shows the incident, be it a father and son waiting for mother to come home from a bridge game to cook supper; or, mother, father, and older sister, shielding their eyes from the darting filing of son's metal-craft; all as crustaceans, briny and rough-shaped, and the folds involved trying, like ungainly, patient starfish, to surround events somehow, and get a purchase on them. I can imagine Henry James taking a second look at Williams, and wondering from the rhythm, whether he — James — had any Arkansas cousins.

I would emphasize how much he has scuttled popular premises of design, style, and, sure enough, humor; and the wise, tough-grudging way (which represents a major renunciation for any American cartoonist) he commits his drawing, rarely, to sentiment; such, in its general use, tends to diminish the human figures in the work since it is usually deployed to exhibit the artist's superior awareness of their feelings' significance or resonance. Williams will entertain no such consideration, which also has to do with the physical eloquence of his drawings. The gnarly, gawkish, mulish force of a

country doctor — one hand in the back pocket of trousers, which seem to be wheezing, handkerchief straggling from somewhere under his frock coat, bent over in lazy-L-shape as he applies his stethoscope — every bulge and wrinkle of his clothes, every untoward crook and list of his stance, reflecting adaptations, vicissitudes, which no tailor on earth probably ever envisioned. This may recall my reference to Rockwell, yet consider: that marvelous iconography of Rockwell, which enshrines the slop of galluses, the textures of broadcloth shirts and seamed faces also robs the images of something in the way of that untoward, jagged energy which Williams concentrates. In his work, this energy is always distractingly, galvanically present, making every little scene a mall of current history, manifest as a cat's purr, felt through the skin, and showing itself in those marks of usage which, in real life, resist every moment that enshrinement, that sentimental bell-jar isolation, that artists like Rockwell, gifted as they may be, confer. Rockwell's space is wonderfully staid and commemorative; but in Williams, it is commandeered and all-but-preempted by the figures, the clothing, the furniture, the machinery, or the wallpaper. A perfect Williams protagonist is the all-but-boneless Airedale, which the family is constantly attempting to disengage from, or rearrange more decorously within, rockers, umbrella-stands, table legs: a dog which has sensibly accommodated itself, within its age and realization of its privileges, back to the reptile stage of dogdom.

Williams's most radical departure from his contemporaries lies with his admission of *text*, in force, the ubiquity and the potency of language, to his drawings, thus admitting a full head of narrative density into the simplest depictions, which, in another artist, would be muffed by the insistence on crystallizing and encapsulating within the immediate image. His alertness to energy guides his Chekhov-like instinct for plot in the most pebble-like-appearing vignettes: the constant, bizarre knots which the "ordinary" entails. During the '20s, this was registered in his work as a penchant for Louis L'Amour-like short-type Western narrative; in the course of which, in 1924, occurred a pile-driver image: the corpses of four would-be bank robbers, sprawled on the floor of the cow-town bank. (It is shocking and moving — shocking in being moving — today; because of the way the dead men's postures catch the *residual* energy of their recent life; recalling, in this respect, Kipling's "Danny

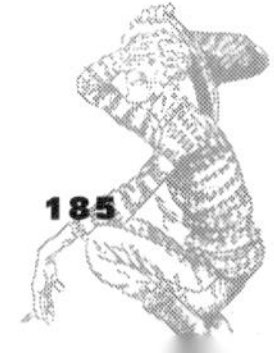

Deever.") In the later panels, however, the prevalent force is of the stories which people manufacture daily.

Time after time, he seems to recognize the key to his own art as lodged very deep in ordinary people's scrambles and grapples to unravel, or to slice, those preposterous knots; to make sense of things' and persons' perpetual displacement. Such displacement is apostrophized in title after title which appeared under the collective title, *Out Our Way*: "Heroes are Made — Not born"; "Why Mothers Get Gray;" "Born Thirty Years Too Soon"; usually, what they are entangled in — always — is their own history; a lockstep parade of gaucherie and importunity and defeat, which Williams, (for all the laborious whittling solicitude of his drawing) deftly, and gently, turns aside; for it is their willingness to contend, and the ways of contending which they improvise, which fascinate him and which command his art.

All are upheld by the authority of language, always a-sweat with its attempts to cope, so that no room is ever permissible for catch-phrase or aphorism: I don't know of one tag-line to which his work ever gave birth. Targets are not the issue. When his factory hands align themselves to discuss some momentary peculiarity or habitual perverseness in one of their number, the tone is totally without the curdled-puritan baiting, the wise-guy sadism, which TAD (a fine artist in his own right, and, at his best, a preceptor of Williams; the only such within Williams's life-span I can think of) fostered, and set the basic patterns for, in his series, *Indoor Sports*. Williams's men may complain and they may note with scornful wonder at times, but never merely to shrivel some elected scapegoat. What engages them, what fires them, is the arresting oddity of such people being as they are, of the situation in which they can flourish. They, all of Williams's characters, are expert talkers-to-the-occasion: not to mull and to ruminate, like the philosophic derelicts of William Saroyan or Carné and Prévert's films; not to lament and rhapsodize, like the barflies of O'Casey; but, demi-poets that they are (which is not to call them "unsuccessful" or "half-assed" poets; but only to suggest that the ultimate making of poetry is not their purpose, and does not inform their drive), they aim at finding some significant shape where there may be none, of simply assuring themselves that what happens every day is, bit by bit, manageable. "Ye gods, the power of language!" a tenderfoot exclaims, as the seasoned

puncher yells: "Tether-'er!" to somebody off-panel, with splendid inanity, but equally splendid hope — since that calf is still some four yards out of their reach, up that mountain face.

All of them are self-elected artists of the everyday, which is why none of them has any time to lapse into the quick-frozen type TAD served to popularize in this country, of the wiseacre chorus standing to one side, providing a mirthful *a capella* about some bore, fraud, or discomfited loser. Williams entertained no such piety toward cliques, those-in-the-know, or, it would seem, solidarity wisdom in general; solidarity was, perhaps, literally unimaginable to him. Canned truths are not what the *Out Our Way* gang is tanglefooting and scrambling after; but simply getting a touch more clarity, a stronger suggestion of some plausible shape into the knotted clothings, the trampled package wrappings. In the drawing of a graduating class posing for its photograph (which Williams and Blackbeard have reproduced in their *Smithsonian Collection of Newspaper Comics)*, heads are turning this way and that, a finger gophers beneath a collar, a nose twitches. Why should they watch the birdie... that birdie? The bird they have their eyes on will not come to roost during their mortal lives. Should they ask it to?

OUT OUR WAY **By Willian**

I SAY, I CAN'T GET AIR. I'LL SMOTHER! WE'VE GOT TO HAVE A BIGGER HOLE, AN' YOU'RE STANNIN' RIGHT WHERE I GOT TO GO.

GREAT SCOTT! DO WE HAVE TO RIP UP TH' WHOLE THING, JUST TO GET A BOX OF CARPET TACKS? SAY! CAN'T WE WORK TH' BOX OF TACKS OVER TO TH' EDGE?

HERE'S SOMETHING ELSE YOU LEFT UNDER— IT LOOKS LIKE IT'S ONE OF YOUR SLIPPERS.

RIP RIP

BORN THIRTY YEARS TOO SOON.

© 1934 BY NEA SERVICE, INC. J.R.WILLIAM T. M. REG. U. S. PAT. OFF. 5-

UT OUR WAY

By Williams

I SAY, I CAN'T GET AIR. I'LL SMOTHER! WE'VE GOT TO HAVE A BIGGER HOLE, AN' YOU'RE STANNIN' RIGHT WHERE I GOT TO GO.

GREAT SCOTT! DO WE HAVE TO RIP UP TH' WHOLE THING, JUST TO GET A BOX OF CARPET TACKS? SAY! CAN'T WE WORK TH' BOX OF TACKS OVER TO TH' EDGE?

HERE'S SOMETHING ELSE YOU LEFT UNDER— IT LOOKS LIKE IT'S ONE OF YOUR SLIPPERS.

RIP RIP

BORN THIRTY YEARS TOO SOON.

J.R. WILLIAMS

T. M. REG. U. S. PAT. OFF. 5-1

OUT OUR WAY—

By J. R. WILLIAMS

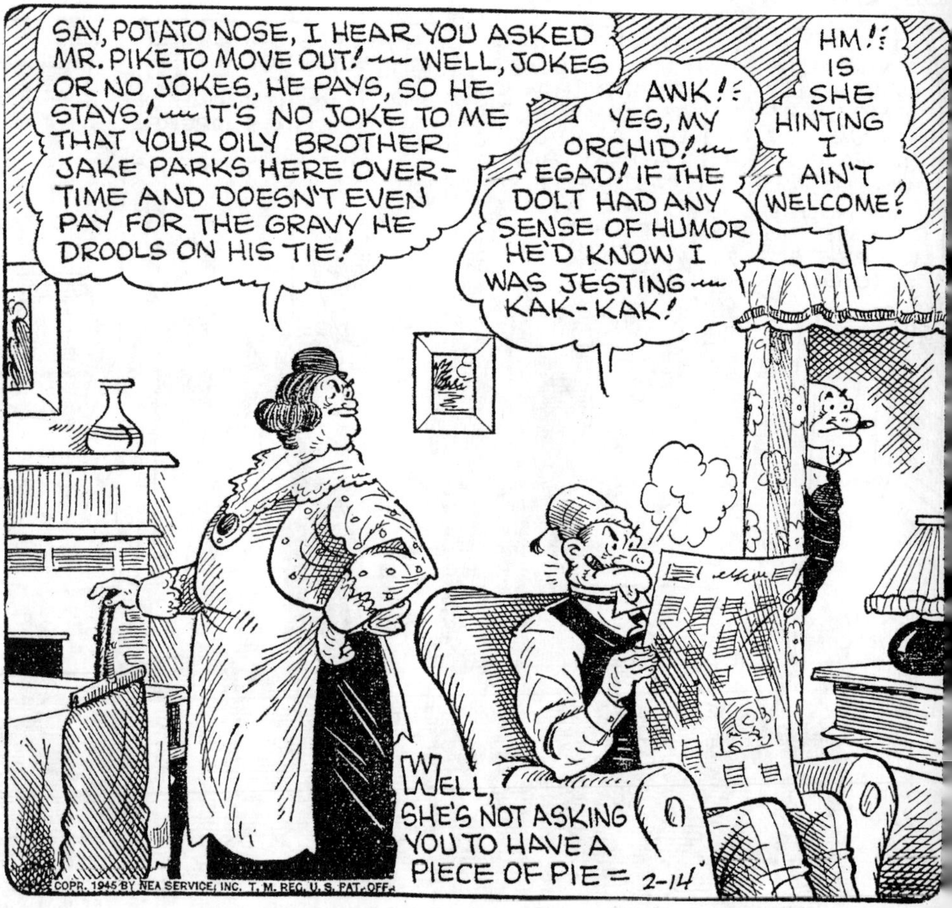

SAY, POTATO NOSE, I HEAR YOU ASKED MR. PIKE TO MOVE OUT! — WELL, JOKES OR NO JOKES, HE PAYS, SO HE STAYS! — IT'S NO JOKE TO ME THAT YOUR OILY BROTHER JAKE PARKS HERE OVERTIME AND DOESN'T EVEN PAY FOR THE GRAVY HE DROOLS ON HIS TIE!

AWK! YES, MY ORCHID! — EGAD! IF THE DOLT HAD ANY SENSE OF HUMOR HE'D KNOW I WAS JESTING — KAK-KAK!

HM! IS SHE HINTING I AIN'T WELCOME?

WELL, SHE'S NOT ASKING YOU TO HAVE A PIECE OF PIE = 2-14

OUT OUR WAY By Williams

OUT OUR WAY By Williams

FUELING ON THE FLY.

OUT OUR WAY
By Williams
YOU FELLERS SURE KEEP YOUR HANDS CLEAN FOR SUCH A SMOKY NEIGHBORHOOD. SAY—IS THAT A BIRD OR AN AIR PLANE UP THERE?
RAISINS
J.R.WILLIAMS
7-3
REG. U. S. PAT. OFF.
THE GOOD SAMARITAN
© 1929, BY NEA SERVICE, INC.

OUT OUR WAY **By William**

THAT CUTTER SPINDLE HAS A VERTICAL ADJUSTMENT FOR CENTERING THE CUTTERS, AND IS DRIVEN BY A WORM GEAR, AND THE THE CARRIAGE HAS A MICROMETER ADJUSTMENT FOR REGULATING THE DEPTH OF TOOTH TO BE CUT—THE FRICTION DISK WHICH—

THAT LADY MECHANICAL ENGINEER IS GIVIN' THEM OL' BOYS AN AWFUL JOLT JUST THINK OF A WOMAN KNOWIN' MORE ABOUT MACHINERY THAN THEY DO. THEY LOOK LIKE TH' WORLD WAS COMIN' TO A END.

IT IS COMIN' TO AN END, FER MEN! TH' KING IS ON HIS LAST LEGS—LONG LIVE TH' QUEEN!

 HUMPTY DUMPTIES T. M. REG. U. S. PAT. OFF. J.R.WILLIAMS 5-19

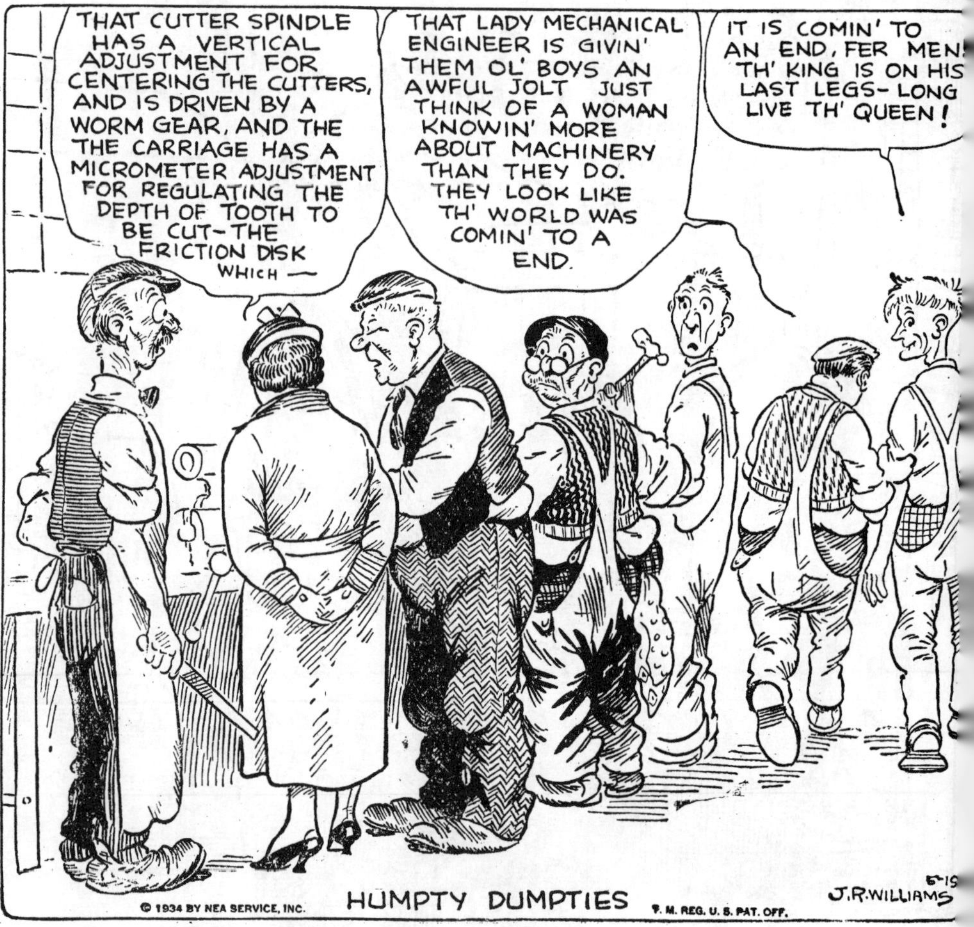

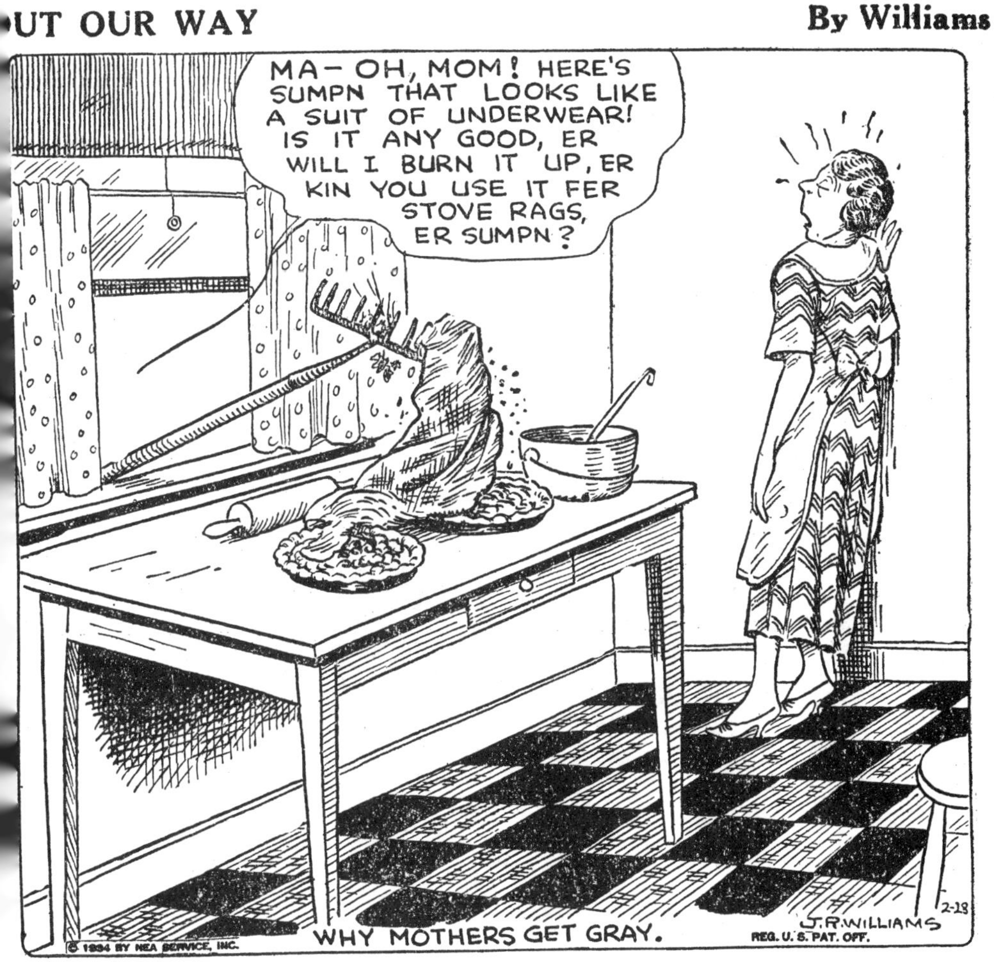

UT OUR WAY

By Williams

MA— OH, MOM! HERE'S SUMPN THAT LOOKS LIKE A SUIT OF UNDERWEAR! IS IT ANY GOOD, ER WILL I BURN IT UP, ER KIN YOU USE IT FER STOVE RAGS, ER SUMPN?

WHY MOTHERS GET GRAY.

J.R.WILLIAMS 2-28

THE BOYS OF WINTER

FRANK KING AND GASOLINE ALLEY

The key to the tone and rhythm of Frank King's *Gasoline Alley* — the ongoing tapestry of a garage-oriented small town over decades of family-raising, small-scale enterprises, national holidays — lies with the way King left his characters beautifully to themselves. The beings and engagements of Uncle Walt, Skeezix, and their supporting personages moved from one daily episode to the next as in a busy, but fluently tranquil frieze, like perch viewed in a mountain stream. Instead of every action, accident, and grimace being pointed up, outlined in clown black and yellow for our appreciation, here were people whose own earnestness about their lives and the beadwork of small actions making up those lives was obviously intended to serve in itself; to transmit, not broadcast, the fascinating energies of their common existence. The actions of Walt changing a tire or his cook and Skeezix's nursemaid, Rachel, paring carrots, or Skeezix himself about some two-year-old's experiments in mischief, assumed the luminous grave precision of simple rituals performed on a stage.

From *Gasoline Alley's* 1920s beginning, Frank King's prevailing style embodied a warm detachment to his subject, a rapt watchfulness, which he fully — and obviously, in large measure, successfully — expected his audience to share. This stance was opposite that of his Minnesota neighbor, Sinclair Lewis, whose own detachment was withering of subject and of self. Rereading the *Gasoline Alley* episodes of the '20s, '30s, and '40s prior to King's death, I feel the constant sheer presence of a world and the awareness of form, which gave the daily episodes their chunky, anecdotal shape and the Sunday pages their tapestry-like bustle and frequent, breath-catching beauty. And I can feel, in the slightest of the daily episodes, King's perception, backed by a humble, fierce perseverance of love, and an arresting (to all eyes not permanently arrested by habit) visual imagination, of how resistant to penetration and exploitation was that sandy Midwestern façade. His drawing style, as brisk and translucent as Wisconsin air, offered a vernal contrast to the wintry and crabbed linear narratives of Harold Gray, and Sidney (*Gumps*) Smith. Beyond that, it is a remarkable *conductor* of King's subject, in a way such as his earlier contemporaries among the *Chicago-Tribune/New York Daily News* strips, in their morose or satiric varieties of detachment, never tried for. I know of few such comic-strip styles, in any era, which call forth such overtones of grace and — the old-fashioned word answers best, here — *comeliness* from the no-nonsense, hands-in-pockets (or rolled in aprons) efficiency and dignity of the figures, and the treasured habitual rhythms, which their bearing expressed, of coping with their environment day after day. The strip had its inception in the permeation of these American lives by craft (the strip initially focused on the men's solicitude for, and contretemps with, their automobiles). Their typical posture provides King's daily translation of the theme, in its alert repose: torsos canted slightly forward, hands loose, but ready, at sides (or, perhaps, raised to chins); feet, in shoes that often seemed humped and spread to their own satisfaction like old, restful dogs, planted squarely on asphalt or backyard dirt. Unmistakable in every line is Frank King's conviction of his own community, the community of his own craft. The function of his art seemed not to impose the folksy haberdashery and cosmetics of a Norman Rockwell, nor yet to yoke with his interpretation of their lives, but to convey, by pooling his craft with theirs, and by rendering their corporate style as a way of life in itself. His reticence, his attentiveness to the particular gravity of this or that small job or ritual, identifies his style, in its tough decorum, as a more peaceful cousin of that made emblematic of the

'20s and '30s by Ernest Hemingway and Dashiell Hammett. There are echoes of the shrugging, low-keyed, "Well, shucks" dialogues in the oddly prim gallantry of *Dragnet*'s still-remembered police team. And King's easy spaciousness of composition, the reverence for distances, the tone of wry, sometimes cranky poise, recall the chill surface serenity of that most beautiful of American plays, *Our Town*; without, to be sure, the darkness of comprehension which made *Our Town* a great work.

The kind of American epic, in muted tones, which King was to propose can be traced very early on, in affectionate fiddling with perspective; which emerges in King's work as a way, not of questioning the gravity or stance or aspect of the material, but, rather, of refreshing the reader's appreciation of it. Not of penetrating the "ordinary," but of manipulating it, with a long-time tinkerer's patient adroitness. Ordinariness is a given of *Gasoline Alley's* world; something not to be converted, but to be endured as gracefully, stoically, playfully, as circumstances, and one's moods and talents, allow. The earliest of the daily episodes, those of 1920-1921, shift from a single-panel format — the present-day idiosyncrasies and follies and tastes — to a hybrid. From Monday to Friday, a conventional across-the-page strip would gently dog some character's (usually, Walt's) current infatuation, or dilemma. Then, on Saturday, in the single-panel format, a little garage conclave of The Boys — Walt, Avery, Doc, Bill — would take turns stirring the broth of that week's doings. The shift of narrative gait may have issued from publisher Joseph Patterson's infatuation with stage techniques (the choral review of local news reminds one of *Little Orphan Annie's* Monday morning mop-up teams of gossips and wiseacres) and restless inventiveness with narrative structure (the earliest *Winnie Winkle* strips, for example, would alternate from traditional dialogue balloons to typed narrative captions beneath the drawings). Whatever influence prompted it, however, the early *Gasoline Alley* style presents, itself, a cross-section of the tone whose counterpoint — unassuming independence, decorum touched with elegance — would prevail throughout Frank King's life as *Gasoline Alley's* author. Prevail, and flower, through those charming Sunday page fugues in which Uncle Walt and the six- or seven-year-old Skeezix ramble through a world projected through this or that artistic technique, or manner: a countryside seen as a woodcut series; a world of silhouettes; a landscape viewed in the splintery, listing shapes of Beckmann's Expressionism. These embody a patient, playful noodling with art-as-amusement, and art-as-decoration, such as could only proceed from a combined devotion and resignation to the static nature of normalcy, of ordinariness; and the use of art, not to penetrate, nor to covert, but to adorn and bless that life. King's approach to painting in these little *rigolades* suggests the draping of garlanded flowers around the neck of a beloved horse.

From the earliest drawings on, *Gasoline Alley* as King drew it is ruled by an enormous majestic self-containment, a *wholeness* of mood and characterization and atmosphere and humor, which maintained through Skeezix's adolescence, young adulthood (entering the Engineers Corps in World War II), and marriage. Even in daily gag episodes, involving back-fence feuds, or Walt's entanglements with the 1926 Puddlejumper, or Skeezix's infant pranks, the laughter seems to germinate from within the situations and characters, and to be retained there, within their monolithic earnestness. The dailies tended to be miniature anecdotes, chunks of history, even when occurring within some continuing story: Walt's black housekeeper, Rachel, discussing men and marriage with Phyllis Blossom's maid, Mandy, a pert, black asparagus stalk; or Avery, Walt's nickel-nursing neighbor, chortling and humming to himself — and unbending to present Skeezix with a dime — in the wake of a supposed bonanza. King's crisp line seems to permit a generous flow of air and light around the figures who are usually seen in full, at a camera's middle-distance, or slight upper angle. The faces are compact, sharp notations, with the mingled delicacy and glancing humor of Chinese silk-screen figures. The frieze of gestures, stances, and attitudes, seems to evolve organically: Rachel standing with her hand on the doorjamb, the other resting on her hip; Walt coping with Skeezix's two-year-old acrobatics while chewing over current events with Avery or Bill over the back fence; Phyllis Blossom holding a picture hat in place with one hand, while the other hand cocks a starter's pistol that will launch a Model T Olympic race. King's drawing seems to admit such movements rather than to project them. We feel his presence mainly as a loving watchfulness, which we may share. He manifestly could not care less about payoffs or blowups, nor, indeed, are there likely to be any. The fourth or fifth panel of each daily strip would generally feature some offhand little coda —

"Well, can you beat that!" — or resolution by one of the main actors… a flatted fifth, indeed. I can imagine Garry Trudeau (who, in fact, has paid encomium to King's gifted successor, Richard Moores) as a ready pupil of King, enlisting tone and inflection rather than solar plexus addresses. The same benign aloofness enabled King to do authentic justice to sentiment (the pantomime of Walt keeping vigil during Skeezix's first serious illness). What emerges from a reasonably faithful reading of *Gasoline Alley* is that Frank King, evidently a profoundly sentimental as well as romantic man, perceived the sentiments — as well as a variety of cranks, vanities, resentments — as the property and topography of America's emotional and spiritual life. As such, they remained sacred to him; however remote or eccentric their occasional aspect. The sense of gentle, non pompous solemnity which he kindles in the strips about the national holidays during Skeezix's childhood remind me of Wordsworth in their unembarrassed, lucid acceptance of the feelings still contained in the commemorative rites of July Fourth and Thanksgiving Day. He conveys the sense of some untainted, residual sweetness that these people have retained from childhood.

I think that what managed to enchant so many readers of King's *Gasoline Alley* for so very long was the overwhelming refreshment of seeing taste and grace made manifest through the work of a humane imagination. King sounded the true resonance of taste — now a flouted and bedraggled term indeed, when seen at all — in a way perfectly intelligible, I believe, because it was humanly valid, to people who might declare themselves baffled by my words. You have a flow of small diversions, done with a luminous accuracy that represents the deepest meaning of "civility." The usual dry matter-of-factness of the dialogue's tone — Midwestern poker-pan — offers, as does its near neighbor in Hammett's prose, a reasonable American facsimile of wit. The athletic animation which the drawing, in its apparent effortlessness, captures; the energetic purposefulness which informs the figures even in long stretches of seeming repose; makes a kinship with sports cartoons and the fluent, no-frills competence of the best sports journalism, which must have engaged a heavy current of *Daily News* readers.

Apart from the supple and rangy graces of a near-aristocratic regard for elegance and property and well-being, which plays from the early years over its functional-looking, bony terrain, an unobtrusive, persistent respect for possessions and comforts informs King's style, and his evident sense of style, as much as it does the writing of a near-counterpart, the eighteenth-century Addison. Walt himself (his full name, Walt Wallet, is an image of snug prosperity) is something of a throwback to Addison's Mr. Spectator. He carries the whale-like swell of his belly as weightlessly as Oliver Hardy; and the tiny face, with its boyish forelock and sailor cap, seemed barely to emerge from his neck, lending a look of diffidence and discretion to the girth, and huge arms. Walt's image disseminated its mixture of well being and gracious bearing through the strip's succeeding decades, during which time he married the attractive and patrician widow, Phyllis Blossom. In the mid-Depression '30s, he could be discovered visiting Italy with her, and sending Skeezix to a posh boy's school. When Skeezix went on the road in 1937, it was as a hitchhiking lark.

It was probably King's reserved acceptance of the Wallets' happy times as a reasonable condition of their life — refraining, at the same time, from boosting or enshrining that way of life as the center of any imaginable, or worth-imagining universe — which continued and multiplied *Gasoline Alley's* readers during the Depression. He seems not to be showcasing any "values" or aphrodisiac for supposed American fantasies. He never highlights the convulsive clawings for wealth and power that furnished so many plot lines to Sidney Smith's *The Gumps*. The money is simply there. Why should it not be? King seems to ask. Walt was employed for a very long time by Mr. Ambrose Wicker at some work I have not to this hour clearly identified. The details of his work life are rarely seen (though the name Wicker enhances the impression of gracious leisureliness, with its suggestion of wicker lounge chairs on antebellum patios; an impression underscored by the Kentucky colonel sweep of Mr. Wicker's mustaches). And yet, yes: it was his acceptance of these circumstances that enabled Frank King to get on with the full-blown depiction of his world in the terms which were indispensable to him — the cranky, homegrown-eccentric, sometimes argumentative, sometimes rebellious personalities which cluster and posture and haggle in his foreground. They are the richest legacy, perhaps, of the *Spectator's* eighteenth century tradition of portraiture. When the bristly little Doc decides to go on a cross-country walking marathon in 1937, the defiant, eccentric angles of his wiry body as he treks along highways and over hills attired in plus fours and a huge cap, recall sporting drawings of Gilray or of Dickens's earliest artist-partner, Seymour, in the 18th and 19th century.

Walt embodied the sensible comfort and competence, Skeezix the restless enterprise and spasmodic waywardness in the saga of Midwestern America which begins — with Walt's discovery of Skeezix on his doorstep, St. Valentine's Day, 1921 — to glow in the forge of King's imagination. To think of Skeezix is to recognize the outstanding misunderstood truth which has attached itself to *Gasoline Alley's* reputation over the decades: to wit, that it is the first comic strip in which the hero grew up (a highly probable truth, as I say; yet, popularly misinterpreted, in order to smack *Gasoline Alley* with the stamp of Naturalism, a designation usually applied to many forms of creative expression by critics with the discrimination and gentleness of postage clerks stamping a "Special Delivery" fragile package). In the case of Frank King, the rubric is even less accurate, if anything, than it has proven in the instances of Frank Norris, Dreiser, James T. Farrell, and a variety of other artists. *Gasoline Alley* under King combined romantic exaltation of the individual with classical poise and reserve; as far as possible, in any case, from the squashing down of characters into patterns of habit, instinct and social circumstance which the term naturalistic, used of art, implies. (Can anyone, for sure, name any artist of any distinction who does adhere to these prescriptions of Naturalism?) To put it accurately, Skeezix, from his entrance in 1921 until the present, was depicted in the various phases of babyhood, childhood, adolescence, young manhood, and middle age. Yet, as became increasingly apparent in the late '40s, after his return from the army and settling into his own domesticity, the portrayal of an individual life in its entirety, with all its connotations for, say a novelist or dramatist, was not what King had in mind at all. The novelist's or dramatist's purpose would most likely be to confer form on their material through this frame — possibly, to marshal their contextual material, the setting, the pertinent lives of other characters, through the rallying music of a single consciousness, portrayed in some detail; and, very probably, to make us aware of the total quality of the individual's existence, in terms of significant changes which he or she undergoes, in terms of self-insights, self-projections; in short, through the overall pattern of psychological and moral salients which, at its end or the end of its depiction at least, we can see outlined through the life.

Now, what King was clearly aiming for in his biography of Skeezix was shaped not at all by the traditional literary forms I have cited. Skeezix's presence is crucial to his setting, to be sure — I have often heard *Gasoline Alley* referred to as *Skeezix*, as *Thimble Theatre* is popularly alluded to as *Popeye* — but he does not offer us any new critical perspective of his setting, as do Thomas Mann's or James T. Farrell's heroes, nor does the shape of his life acquire any of their lyrical or tragic inflections. In fact, once he reached young manhood, the whole "aging" procedure became curiously modified by King (and later by his successor) so that we follow for a while the growing up of his kid brother, Corky — Walt and Phyllis's child — and little sister, Judy (adopted like himself), and later of course, his children, Chipper and Clovia. The others, the older people — Walt, Phyllis, Avery, Doc, Mr. Pert, and the rest — seem virtually to have remained intact, although at least in their 30's at the time of Skeezix's advent. Walt has acquired glasses and some perceptible gray in his hair; Phyllis, a wrinkle or two. The rest appear to be such beneficiaries of Polly Bergen cosmetics as would instantly repay a two-page ad in the *National Enquirer*.

Patently, what King was seeking through this, his own recasting of the *Bildungsroman* was something uniquely answerable to the comic-strip medium, which is as alien to the traditional novel as it is to any other classic literary structures. The sustenance of the comic strip is sheer continuity, the endurance of its daily, hypnotic present tense. How can traditional form, itself dedicated to the illusion of finality through its own totality, be represented, much less honored in the comic strip? To assert or imply that it is, or ought to be, condescends egregiously to all sides, and, in this instance, particularly to Frank King: a comic-strip artist almost incomparably knowledgeable as to the nature of form.

What I believe he wanted — what he has presented us with — was, no more nor less than a poem, infinitely extendable, on the particular and archetypal aspects of a small-town setting. A poem that would represent neither a bazaar of folksy exotica, nor a waxwork of sins against various metropolitan morals, mores, and fashions; but which would, by inducting us into the rhythms of plausible daily life, kindle our reconsideration through imagination and love. And the growth of an individual through that setting offered the perfect meter, as it were, for the desired rhythm: seemingly poky, not infrequently lethargic, but also pricked out with quarrels, schemes, and small adventures.

Walt was the only man to adopt Skeezix, being the Unknown Quantity, a middling-prosperous bachelor, among the gritty professionals of the neighborhood. He looks, even, like an amiable cipher among his cronies. His easy curve of stomach, in white shirt, and the oddly delicate, half-formed-looking features, contrasts with the imprint of case-hardened age on the other men: Avery's bristly mustache, baggy pants and leather jackets and ossified-looking fedora (the nickel-nurser's habitual old clothes); Bill, rangy, pale, and barely animate, with his alfalfa-sprig of hair; Doc, with his immense, insect-like goggles, and contentious spike of goatee, and never-failing black bag. Among these boys of winter, Walt was Addison's Spectator, the man who looks on, who receives and ruminates, who acts at times the understanding foil (never butt) for his more sparky, volatile companions. Walt thus quietly detonated, for once at least, the popularly cherished image of the fat man as a walking vat of infantile greed and cowardice, or else of bluster and apoplectic frustration. He had made his adjustments, he had paid his dues, very early on. Thus, he appeared to us as an amiable priest of that rippling beauty which getting-on embodied for Frank King. Walt is a wonderful guide through *Gasoline Alley* terrain, because his tubby homeliness, and the gentle, candid dispatch with which King set him before our eyes, countervail the dangers of sentimental-pastoral prettification; while his cool, methodical, slightly phlegmatic personality keeps in our view the tone of a gentleman-chronicler. And when Skeezix is introduced, King evokes a kind of empathy seldom exampled among comic strips, in its cleanliness of feeling: the fascinated amusement and concern of seeing this efficient, tidy, decently confident bachelor put on his mettle a healthy seven times a week by a tiny boy. The way King's style plays against the sort of slam-bang immediacy, the comedy of frontal assault, which has been the specialty and affliction of comic strips from Outcault onward, is seldom turned to richer account than in the way his chaste, strong, smiling art sidesteps slapstick catastrophe when, say, Skeezix experimentally feeds Walt's shoes into the heating register, or has a black-face revel in the coal-bin. He is getting us to contemplate. He is tending our contemplation. When Skeezix holds the stage alone, in the Sunday page of 1923, King frames his dowdy, scattered, musing actions within the narrowest possible rectangles, adding up to a Bayeux tapestry of vignettes.

Skeezix becomes the Ariel, the animating spirit of the strip. Like Popeye in *Thimble Theatre,* he both confirms and opens the overall style and its possibilities. He is the agent for King's own rediscovery both of his country and of his art; and Walt himself becomes, more than ever, a projection of King as artist (in the Sunday episodes mentioned before, when he introduces Skeezix to various artistic manners, as though Walt and his creator were unlocking, simultaneously, another apartment of that craft which had formerly been confined to the garage and its environs). Day by day, too, the mastery of pantomime always evident in King's alertness to significant gestures and physical attitudes is focused in the little series of panels in which Skeezix, Walt, and Rachel are entangled with the duties of housecleaning, preparing dinner, or outmaneuvering Skeezix's little dog, Pal. There is a sparkling, unsticky joy in King's delineation of the actions and simple data of kitchen, bath, backyard, which reminds me of comparable details in *The Human Comedy* of William Saroyan, or in Saroyan's earlier short stories. Fantasy, too, is liberated. Walt has an anxiety nightmare about Skeezix and Rachel which is a fugue on the anxiety-based, ancient lullaby, "Rock-a-bye, Baby," marvelous for the way King turns his discreet use of line and space to eerie, funny solemn-absurd effects which are the quintessence of dream. When Walt tells the four-year-old Skeezix a cautionary tale about running away, King conducts us into Winsor McCay territory, an Expressionist city fairyland of looming smokestacks and drainpipes like jungle vines; his use of muted, nighttime colors, vertical compositions, the placement of Skeezix's pajama'ed little figure against chasm-like spaces, all matching the delicately ominous beauty and awe of McCay's best *Little Nemo* backgrounds. When Skeezix grows a bit older, the sequences of his play and adventures with the other kids — Spike, Spud, Gooch — are charged with air and weather and restless litheness. The mastery of shading which King is seen cultivating through the '30s lends a density of mood to some of his daily strips, the image's contemplation trapped, which for me, makes the much-praised ambience-nipping glamour of Milton (*Terry and the Pirates*) Caniff at that time seem rather tame, stiff, and period-enclosed. Consider those strips of autumn 1936, in which King catalogues the effects of a low,

November, Midwestern sun; or a still quieter study, in autumn of 1937, of Skeezix and his doubtful new friend, Tops, seen at a distance, beside a quiet lake. The only alteration in this image within the four panels that compose the strip are the changes in the water's pattern; and, an additional, gentle withdrawal from the boys in the final panel.

The overall effect of the Skeezix years, from 1921 until the 1940s, is of King joyously ransacking his own capacities and his nation's culture for new stanzas in his evolving *edda*, the expressive growth of the strip, and its images of America, paralleling Skeezix's own. *Gasoline Alley* looks, during these decades, like the comic strips favored by Hearst, with their prodigal opulence, the rich eclecticism of stylists like DeBeck, the mythic images of America promoted by Jiggs and Popeye. Each holiday is honored, for a rarity in American culture at that time, let alone its comic strips (Paul Goodman has eloquently bemoaned the expiration of the "occasional poem") as an invitation to King's imagination, rich in the suggestiveness of accumulated lore and dreams. During midsummer of 1932, Skeezix and Walt visit the site of the encampment at Valley Forge, and Skeezix becomes a bit-player in the Revolutionary scene, done in white woodcut style. New Year's Eve 1937 means a dialogue with Father Time; and a notable Halloween 1928 is occupied by Rachel, on a kitchen chair, patiently regaling Skeezix with all she knows about witches: an episode lovely in its distillation of graciousness and humor and King's (with Skeezix as his proxy) savoring of speech and imagination, and the ways in which our holidays could once invoke them at their best.

What becomes increasingly clear as I review King's '20s-'30s work is that the reverence to which I've been referring is never without a sizable measure of condescension. "Condescension" here means to me the will and corresponding effort, in someone confident of his own superiority, to extend himself to people, individuals or a class thereof, from whom he feels a distance not altogether to be bridged. It might be defined as the exertion of a gentleman — a word best understood, here, in its old-fashioned, eighteenth- and nineteenth-century sense, to extend himself where native instinct alone will not carry him. The word, to be sure, bespeaks a certain leaven of elitism (to use one of today's few authentic "dirty words") and arrogance, which, in many evangelical quarters, also carries its moral B. O. Yet, as I say, the detachment I have been trying to describe in *Gasoline Alley* is never far from such condescension, mainly implicit, in King's devout single-tracked attention to his people's ordinariness — occasionally he allows a chilling flicker of it in the amiable Walt. In the concluding panels, for example, of the Halloween episode described above, Skeezix asks Uncle Walt a question about witches, only to be assured that those are all Rachel's imagination. Walt's usual impeccable good sense seems a touch lofty here; more noticeable, perhaps, because it seems such a pat anti-climax to the enchanting wares of imagination — not hers alone — which Rachel has displayed for us. I think, too, of Rufus, the ubiquitous hired hand — the special protégé of King's successor, Richard Moores, and an exemplar of the differences in the two artists' styles. Under Moores's jovial grooming, Rufus and his white-whiskered crony accomplice, Joel, have become comic luminaries of *Gasoline Alley* natch'al kith 'n' kin of Shakespeare's rustic mechanickals. Much depends on one's tolerance for poor-white caprice; for me, two rereadings of *God's Little Acre* and the *Hamlet* a year are five or six helpings of blackeye peas. Yet, react to the humor as one will, Moores's treatment does represent an imaginative embrace, in contrast to which King's Rufus was a morose walk-on bearing, like a rusty hoe, the tag-line: "I don't know what it is, but I know I ain't gonna like it!"

And yet, these intrusions of condescension — they belong among the reverberations of the past two centuries which one can sense, time and again, in King's work — never, for me, outweigh, never vulgarize, the humane energy of his style or the creative breadth which, with the '30s, we can virtually observe as it extends at a day-by-day pace. Whereas earlier in the '20s he toyed with this and that painterly device on the Sunday pages — Skeezix's discovery that the world may be looked at in different guises, and from varying situations — we find him during the '30s implementing the fluency of perspective — a mobile actuality now, rather than a child's "Let's Pretend" supposition — by adapting the movies' camera set-ups, lighting (as incorporated in the use of shading, of silhouettes, and scenes like Skeezix's proposal to Nina, their bodies sculpted by moonlight and shadows of leaves). Basically, King's major appropriation from contemporary films was the premise of harmony between figures and their environment, and the shifting of perspectives to represent the restless shifting of perception and imagination. Whereas Moores utilizes the more drastic, showboating, fast-impact camera angles largely introduced to America in the '50s and '60s, King's cinematic models are Wyler and Cukor, and their prowling examination of the components in a superficially static scene. When Nina addresses a chiding, catty-sweet telephone conversation to the erring 16-year-old Skeezix (who was gallivanting at the Club Okedoke) we never see Skeezix, but we see Nina, in close-up, in every delicious shift of mood — teasing, scolding, aloof — which her body registers. It is a four-panel primer from King on the authentic expression, and use, of the erotic in art: not to compromise or diminish humanity, but to affirm it.

The coltish, mercurial élan, the willowy commonsense and competence of King's women characters — Phyllis, Rachel, Mandy; that delightful sapling of a girl, Walt's cousin, Dorrie, who crossed the eight-year-old Skeezix's path (regrettably) briefly; Nina; the girlfriends of Gooch and Tops — parade for us the spunk and generous volatility which Skeezix introduced to *Gasoline Alley*. They are notable exemplars, simply *as* women; for, notwithstanding the popularity during his early career of the "flapper" personality, the white-collar girl, and other prototypes, King distinguished his portraits by the sheer charm, residing mainly in their energy and wit and governed by their capacity for love, which he discovered in his women characters.

Again and again, I am caught by the way the candor and generosity of King's art admits the essential limitations of his imagination and, at the same instance, forestalls any sense of oppression or incompleteness because of it. Given the scope and resonance of his imagination, there is not a speck of philosophical vision, such as, even in its wayward and boring extremes, always gave an (occasionally loony) grandeur to Percy Crosby's *Skippy*. We must also return to Skippy or *Moon Mullins*'s Kayo, or any of a score of others, for the *anarchic* energy of a kid. Skeezix goes in for prankish or wrongheaded escapades, like the hitchhiking expedition, every so often (in fact, the older generation, like Doc, is prone to similar junkets and sallies, innocuous, boiling teakettle "rebellions," none of which would have proved unacceptable to the members of the Pickwick Club); but never, within my recollection, assaults or threatens his environment, *or thinks of doing so*. For that matter, evil of any variety gets the most piecemeal and scantling of treatment, even during the mobster and melodrama-mottled years of the Depression. Rather like Saroyan, King was content with token shadows: the boding appearances of a certain Mme. Octave, during the early '20s, who professes to be Skeezix's real mother, but is apparently entering her claim only to facilitate a profitable marriage. (The Madame's entrance does afford one delicious sequence in which she, a narcissistic opera *diva*, soliloquizes, depicted in her full-length mirror.) And, in late 1932, Punk, a tough little boy, whose back, the opposite of Madame's image, is permanently, defiantly turned on the viewer, brings an early whiff of Dead End violence to *Gasoline Alley*. Mainly, though, King opts for amusing minor imps — scamps and rogues — in his universe: illustrations of the inventive independence he elsewhere celebrates, gone slightly, sometimes ever-so-slightly, awry. They range from mere amiable liars, like Walt's cowpuncher friend, the shovel-chinned Squint (whom Walt and Skeezix unearth on a New Mexico excursion), or a wooden-legged old hobo who coaxes some food from the young Skeezix with his fustian history, in one Sunday page, or the minor rascalities of the penny-pinching — or plucking — Avery, or the Lilliputian sinners who flickered through the pictorial ballad of "The Phoney Dime," which held the bottom of the Sunday *Gasoline Alley* for a while during the late '20s. And there are occasional semi-skilled sidewinders like Tops, Skeezix's chum and self-delegated mentor of the '30s, with his turtleneck sweaters, beanies, topknot, and cupid's bow mouth, or later, in the '40s, Wilmer Bobble, a less personable and assured, but no less self-motivated version of Tops. High steppers whose feet seem invariably destined for pot-holes and cow-doilies, they offer, along with the rascalities which make them alter-types of the bemused young Skeezix, fairly endearing streaks of mischief: Tops is no psychopath, merely a cheerful indolent good-for-nothing; and, as such, quite as recognizable, and as welcome, as Mr. Jingle in *The Pickwick Papers*. Wilmer is still more abject; yet, neither gets a mite of excess credit from Frank King, that tight-handed steward of sentiment. Everything, meaning especially every threatened violation of its landscape, is contained and designated by the boundaries of his world; yet, afflicting us with none of the sense of being cheated, of being short-weighed in the reality issued us, which I reluctantly came to feel from Saroyan's larger work. The answer is, I suggest, twofold at least: first, that the universe of Skeezix and his garage vocation exists *more for the sake of its existence*, than for the sake of pleasing us, or stroking the fur of our philosophies, or tweaking our nostalgic muscles. The second part of the answer is that the universe of an art-work, in the convincing consistency it embodies, is not the issue of any consensus, or act of the Massachusetts legislature; but issues from the commitment of the artist to an incorporation of experience as near totality as can be managed; which, at the same time, even though it be deficient in this area or that of journalistic neatness, still bears the authority of it own space; meaning, the resounding spaces it can suggest, without depicting. Every portrait, every notation of *Gasoline Alley* walks erect with the authority which Frank King's frank, kingly imaginative assurance has delegated it. And, as I write, I am thinking particularly of Skeezix's days in the Engineering Corps, during World War II; thinking, with a kick in the rear, my own, which I have consecrated to some scornful remarks I once addressed to King's "bloodless" depiction of World War II. It seems to me now, and is confirmed by my present reading of Skeezix's army days, that those episodes are among the very few such of that period to find the source of a totally decent, totally cherishable pride in army life; founded, as always, in the hand-depicted holiness of craft, and the day-by-day joinings of one's life. The only shame one need feel may be, as in the present instance, at one's own stupidity in underrating these sequences.

Yet, it seems to me that the peculiar beauty and authority of Frank King's reserve, his plain-spoken dispatch, are lost to us today, as is, essentially, the humor of movies like *You Can't Take it With You* and *Topper*. The ferocious peremptoriness, the feverish wakefulness, of the last three decades, have untied knots which can never again be tied; to which the most convincing witness, perhaps is Richard Moores, one of the most brilliant and devout, and, from the bowels of his devotion, venturesome successors with whom a comic-strip author was ever blessed. Every difference of Moores's style from King's — the open-faced vivacity of the drawing's and situations' humor, the attention to engaging eccentricities of postures, the drape of overcoats or sag of stockings; the editorial-cartoon compression of story complications and resultant attitudes, within the individual panel, as underscored by Moores (highlighting of figures, and droll, mock-heroic treatment of space through compositions which mimic camera set-ups); all pay the most moving and vivid reverence to Frank King's art by translating and converting it, not a beat of the bardic strain fumbled or lost.

GASOLINE ALLEY—A FEW LITTLE ODDS AND ENDS

GASOLINE ALLEY—OFF TO AN EARLY START

GASOLINE ALLEY—THAT IS, ALMOST NOTHING

GASOLINE ALLEY—SMUDGE YOUR TIRES, WALT

GASOLINE ALLEY—MOIST GOING
WALT, DID YOU EVER SEE SO MUCH WATER BEFORE OUTSIDE THE OCEAN?
DOC, THERE'S THE ONLY NATIVE THAT HASN'T BEEN DROWNED!
WE'RE OFF OUR ROAD! CAN YOU TELL US HOW TO GET BACK ONTO THE LINCOLN HIGHWAY?
SURE. FOLLOW THIS ROAD OUT TO TOM KELLEY'S TURN LEFT AND GO ABOUT 3 MILE NORTH. YOU CAN'T MISS IT!
CAN'T MISS IT? SAY YOU DON'T KNOW US!
NOPE, YOU CAN'T MISS IT — YOU CAN'T GET OUT O' THE RUTS!
-KING-
NEVADA, IA.

GASOLINE ALLEY—IT TAKES TIME TO TIME A TIMER
BE BACK IN A MINUTE. JUST GOING TO RUN IN TO THIS FARM HOUSE FOR SOME WATER FOR THE RADIATOR
WHAT CAN BE KEEPING WALT?
HES BEEN GONE 20 MINUTES. HE MUST HAVE FALLEN INTO THE WELL
IF HE ISN'T SAMPLING THE FARMER'S APPLE-JACK HE'S TALKING POLITICS
YOUR TIMER POINTS WERE DIRTY. START HER UP AND LET'S SEE HOW SHE ACTS NOW.
-KING-
OMAHA, NEB.

GASOLINE ALLEY—THROUGH THE CORN BELT
WITH CORNFIELDS LIKE THIS YOU WOULDN'T THINK ANYBODY ON EARTH WOULD GO HUNGRY, WOULD YOU?
NO— NOR GO THIRSTY!
THEY'VE MADE A BIG INCREASE IN THE YIELD THROUGH HERE SOME PLACES TOO.
YES THE DEMAND HAS BEEN GREATER SINCE PROHIBITION
FERTILIZING AND SEED SELECTION HAVE DONE WONDERS!
WHY, SOME MEN HAVE MADE A REGULAR STUDY OF IT — GOT TO BE SORT OF CORN EXPERTS — I FORGET WHAT YOU CALL 'EM —
I KNOW — YOU MEAN CHIROPODISTS!
-KING-
HASTINGS, NEB.

GASOLINE ALLEY—A PAIR OF MISTS—OPTI AND PESSI
DOC, ONE OF THE FINEST THINGS ABOUT A TRIP LIKE THIS IS THAT WE STOP AFTER A DAY'S TRAVEL WITH ONLY A DUSTY CAR AND A LOT OF JUNK —
THEN TWENTY MINUTES' WORK —
AND WE HAVE A HOME, A FAMILY AND A FIRESIDE!
YES, AND NO NEWSPAPER! I WONDER WHAT THE CUBS DID TODAY!
-KING-
MC COOK, NEB.

GASOLINE ALLEY—GET IT ON THE WAY HOME, DOC

GASOLINE ALLEY—EVERY TOUR AN EDUCATION

GASOLINE ALLEY—WALT FORGOT

GASOLINE ALLEY—MRS. DOC ISN'T ABSORBING MUCH SCENERY

GASOLINE ALLEY—ALL CONVENIENCES

GASOLINE ALLEY—OUT OF HEARING, OUT OF MIND

GASOLINE ALLEY—THE BUNCH BACK HOME

GASOLINE ALLEY—HIS LAST CHANCE

GASOLINE ALLEY—HUNTING A ROOST

GASOLINE ALLEY—SHADOW MOVIES—2 A. M.

GASOLINE ALLEY—A MARKED TRAIL

GASOLINE ALLEY—GOOD OR BAD, A ROAD'S A ROAD

GASOLINE ALLEY—WANDERING ARCHITECTURE

GASOLINE ALLEY—THE SPIRIT OF THE WEST

GASOLINE ALLEY—ITS RATTLE IS WORSE THAN ITS BITE

GASOLINE ALLEY—WALT CAN QUALIFY

JAMES SWINNERTON, R.I.P. (1875-1974)

The chill sweetness of Victorian literature flavored the comic strips of James Swinnerton from the earliest I have seen — the lustful sallies of the Tammany-spirited tiger cub, Mr. Jack — to the adventure and inquires of that diminutive Gulliver-in-reverse Little Jimmy, whom Swinnerton introduced, in Hearst's *New York Evening Journal*, at the turn of the century, and who attended the end of Swinnerton's career — the little boy ever watchful, reflective, marveling — in the early '50s. Little Jimmy's watchfulness was through eyes that were not of mere childhood, but of Nature peering through the child's gaze. Mr. Jack's funny, perky decorum (Mr. Jack tipping his beaver hat and bowing to a likely looking little tigress) repeatedly found itself in convulsive, comic confrontation with the rough addresses of the familiar world. The watchfulness *and* decorum of Swinnerton's vein of mystery was inherent in the way his children and small animals would see — as we were shown — the world anew. Flickering but persistent in Swinnerton's young work are side-glints of the vision, garden-size but unflinching, that guided the verse of Robert Louis Stevenson, Ralph Hodgson, Walter De la Mare or even the rustling, intrigue-scented Wonderland of Henry James's *What Maisie Knew*.

However, any comic strip's claim to style must emerge from the way it faces the challenge of perpetuity. Swinnerton's poetry drew a thick, gritty texture from the neighborhood where Big and Little Jimmy advanced their careers; the rank, sporty jauntiness of the *Journal's* sports section. Mr. Jack's ill-starred cockiness, his slangy swagger, announced an affinity with the grinning, in-the-know repartee-spurting dog men of the sports section's amiable and youthful patriarch, Thomas Aloysius Dorgan (remembered as cartoonist and emblem-forger of the 1920s style by his acronymic, TAD). TAD's cartoon community comprised a doggy elite: his urban wits, con artists, stooges, and foils, whether canine (as in *Silk Hat Harry's Divorce Suit*, and the raffish excursion of Judge Rummy, Fedink, and TAD's average guy, Mr. Bunk) or human, as in *Indoor Sports* and *Outdoor Sports*, all shared an aristocracy of scoffing criticism and a congenital satiric identification of everyday weaknesses and errors. All exchanges made in TAD's coin of the realm: memorable, freshly-minted slang phrases like "Baloney," "Give 'im the office," "He takes the fur-lined bathtub," and such, flipped from animal and human mouths, and from TAD's cavorting colophon-signature.

These features of TAD's work bespeak, of course, that brilliant man's distillation of a style, and a *sense* of style, that made articulative, usable, and as I infer, bearable, the world of the early twentieth century in which he chiefly strove and thrived. So, to be sure, does the work of Swinnerton; however (as noted in the essay, *Jimmy and Company*), it employed some of TAD's architecture — skepticism, reflex-swift observation, inherently gentle playfulness — but constructed its own edifice, with the flares of nursery mischief, and interpreted by Swinnerton's extraordinary vision of small, casually-presented oddities and occasional miracles of the familiar world. Swinnerton's style was more a fortress of serene scrutiny, full of eye-slots for the double-circle eyes of Jimmy and his friends; a fortress against instances of horrendous shyness (as of the stammering Englishman, Mr. Batch, and the floundering suitors of Jimmy's pretty cousin), and against the incessant mating maneuvers of Mr. Jack.

Yet, it was a fortress wonderfully erected in Swinnerton's understanding, and possession, of innocence. He is one of the few American artists who lasted into the middle phase of the twentieth century, whose work bears the term "primitive" as a rightful legacy, and not a ragamuffin's ball costume (patches by Gucci) nor as an ID badge at a convention of incompetences; and one of the still fewer number whose primitivism was not a greased slide into mere parochialism and creative stagnation. The very least (yet basic) accomplishment of his art was a storytelling rhythm that seemed to monitor the very pulse of folklore: in which the generous deployment of space between and around his figures, the quaint and solemn delineation of their careful, ceremonial gestures within that space (also, the explosive flurries of action, chases and scuffles) function as in the distribution of lines of poetry. When Little Jimmy and his entourage returned, in the late '20s, to Swinnerton's native Southwest, to encounter and take part in the lore and magic of the American Indian, the cadence of fairy tale and, sometimes, verse becomes irresistible.

The prevailing tone that he conferred on his comic strips was one of kinship with nature. His affection for the squat little kids who cavorted and fought, but also watched and questioned in his episodes, was too candid — and his regard for their freedom and initiative and self-respect too deeply lodged — for the manipulation, the dalliances of sentimentality ever, ever to show themselves. He knew children to be born matter-of-fact, the heirs of precision. A clear consistent stream of influence might be traced, I think, from *Little Jimmy's* grave and independent style to both *Peanuts*, with its patina of chic knowingness, and to the bright, even-toned, and regrettably forgotten comic strip of the 1940s: Crockett Johnson's *Barnaby*. Robert Louis Stevenson comes to mind as a comparable poet-journalist of children's stillness in his verse about the little boy digging holes in the sand.

Although Swinnerton ventured into fantasy during his American Indian episodes — the confabs of the medicine man with prairie dogs and bears; the mystic drum-beaters and the tree men — he never vainly presumed to use imagination in order to cosmeticize his original perceptions, the way in which the child and the world exchange their gifts of newness. The tree-man, with branches sprouting from fingers and toes, is no stranger or more droll than a tiny Scandinavian husband-to-be, his suit a wondrous imbroglio of wrinkles, his mustaches drooping disconsolately as he dangles like a charm-bracelet from the arm of his jovial fiancée. I must add here that Swinnerton, through his style's disarming plainness and deliberation, was able to deliver some of the most extraordinary ethnic portraits to be found in the medium — of the Scandinavian couple described above; the little Scottish boy who battles Jimmy for the honor of his kilts; and perhaps the most startling of all today, a towering black man named Sam, whose comic affliction, and unfailing agent of disaster, was his instinct to laugh, loudly and unabashedly, at thc grotcsqueries and contrariness of white folks. In such depictions, whatever Swinnerton knew and/or sensed of social circumstance was kept well to the rear; what delightfully stuns me with each rereading is a near-reverent curiosity that is sire to respect on Swinnerton's part. The shyness that recurs as the subject of his laughter, and seems so obviously a formative agent of his art, became also a conditioner agent for his patient, inquisitive wondering — though neither sentimental nor credulous — study of his fellow man. The distinction of Swinnerton's ethnic sketches — the utter freedom from embarrassment or fear or patronizing, obligatory kindness — is supplemented by the warmest, most encompassing, yet clear-eyed fellowship.

Always, the comic strip itself was armature for Swinnerton's poetry; its bluntness, crassness, and intermittent gusto furnished him, I think, with the medium for depicting innocence in all its shadings and mutations — often gauche, occasionally cruel, not so infrequently havoc-wreaking. I remember one startling 1910 strip — it was displayed once or twice at the Whitney — of Jimmy and some of his friends mocking a deranged man, who chants, grinning: "I am a lark! I am a boid!" However, it was also a medium for the temper that *Little Jimmy* embodied more often — patient, pragmatic, tough-minded, yet deeply civil — and expressed his striving to maintain it.

What folly to regret that such an artist never produced a novel, or story-sequence, or series of sculptures! He saw form for what it was: not a vehicle or vessel of sentiments, but an identity in itself, which, at best, embraces all other forms. He honored it as such. God maintain his soul.

— Based on reflections at the time of Jimmy Swinnerton's death (1975).

JIMMY AND COMPANY

JAMES SWINNERTON AND LITTLE JIMMY

Any form worthy of survival is a form that can be exploited: i.e., handled, stretched, mishandled, its boundaries tested and shifted. Form in itself is the illusion of fixity given to that which is mutable and plastic — the encounters of practice with eventuality. In time, if permitted, practice will outweigh eventuality, its very thickness creating its own supplement to experience. At such times, form congeals; and at such times an act of defiance and sacrilege is indicated.

James Swinnerton, whose career breasted that of American comic strip art, offers a kind of one-man instruction course in boundaries, and how much mobility they can be permitted while continuing to maintain themselves as boundaries. His *Little Bears* (California cubs which later, in deference to New York City's political climate when he moved East, became *Little Tigers*) was a single-panel cartoon feature, peopled with the toy-like little animals in various settings and pantomimes. From there to the block format (two panels on two panels on two panels of his *New York America* and *Journal American* years); from the nursery-like charades of the bears and tigers to the miniature lecheries of *Mr. Jack*; to the gravely humorous, all-encompassing childhood of perhaps his most-famous feature, *Little Jimmy* (done eventually in the across-the-page "strip" format which he helped to evolve) — throughout this little chronicle of cartoon history and technique, Swinnerton holds to the frames and ceremonies of illustration. Through this holding of outposts, he retains a hypnotic fluidity of space within the odd, heatless sunlight that pervades his drawings. There is an insidious fluency, which infiltrates not only compositions, but characters and situations.

Although the half-century and some-odd-years' career brought its own simplifications, corner-cuttings, Swinnerton's drawing at its most memorable presents a face of almost doll-like blankness to the world. Large-headed little animals (their minikin bodies sporting either costumes or contemporary styles); large-headed children, whose faintly mask-like faces, with their double-circle eyes, increase the haunting uncertainty as to their actual age. These kids, like the tigers and bears, have tiny noses and bird-bill mouths; mouths which regularly, however, fan out in smiles of surprising virtuosity for such simple-looking arcs: they can be apologetic, or amicable, or — often — of a lunar self-complacence. In conversation, the people lean towards each other as though their heads were magnetized. Some of Swinnerton's most amusing panels result from these children running about on their stumpy little legs, like turtles dancing. And throughout Swinnerton's career — possibly his most notable and enduring trait — all personae speak with quote-marks enclosing their dialogue: the emblem of Swinnerton's shy, comic decorum.

The last thing one should expect of this Kewpie-like repertory, this gently archaic style, ought to be an almost total lack of sentimental coyness; and this is what Swinnerton continually achieves. Genteel and courtly and sedately middlebrow he is: but, withal, James Swinnerton is totally immersed in his creation; meaning that the gentleness and gentility and formalism are all Swinnerton's earnests of his own presence in his work; meaning that this embodies last-ditch resistance to that waste and shriveling — the emotional mold — that we usually call sentimentality, or cuteness.

Little Jimmy is full of sweetness and good manners, but it is also full of orneriness, demandingness, people who yank and wrench at their betters' brute endurance, let alone patience, like a salesman demonstrating latex underpants. And *Little Jimmy*, with all its just-short-of-prissy quietness, is a signal achievement, I think: a comic strip supposedly centered on a little boy — more contemplative than Skippy, less chillingly ambiguous than Orphan Annie — through whom we see an adult world of willfulness, boorishness, lechery and tiny violences trafficking.

Throughout the various configurations of his panels, Swinnerton deploys almost-empty space as austerely and suggestively as, say, the earlier sculpture of Robert Morris. He evolved throughout his career a horizontal, mural-like composition, in which the background — California desert or small-town street — runs flat as a tape behind the figures; and the figures themselves seem etched as much as drawn, in a methodical, all-but-shadowless line, whose main function seems to be to emphasize the space between the characters and between the characters and settings. A fierce balance of patience and anxiety seems to prevail in Swinnerton's drawing: I constantly receive an image of him musing over every line, like the chessplayer over his next move. Each panel, true to illustrative principles, catches an action at its central point, in suspension, rather than the process of action. Practically no speed images — whizzing lines and such — nor illusory effects; every action sequence is centered in the placement and attitudes of the figures.

The effect of such etching-like impaction is a series of minute episodes which are almost over as soon as they begin; and which typify the somewhat stiff-kneed dance rhythm that permeates the whole of Swinnerton's work. One receives from such work, not the interlocking actions of *Moon Mullins* but a procession of tableaux, whose participants appear time after time in the same eye-level, frieze-like arrangement; sometimes several of them struggling on through one ribbon-like panel. This stretching of time and space, day after day, leads one to wonder how much can happen, when such limited space is so attenuated. And, indeed, the flickers of action that occur, like little camp fires spotted down a canyon, are definitely of secondary interest; the main concern being the odd, seeming-lethargic rhythm that Swinnerton sustains, with its lizard-like movements of covert alertness.

Throughout his life as a cartoonist, Swinnerton seems to have gripped jealously the conditions of his freedom in the earlier years of the *Examiner* and the *American* and the *Journal*: those years in which the drawings of Swinnerton or T.E. Powers or McGurk or

Tad Dorgan were still treated as accompaniment or ornamentation to the newsprint terrain which bounded them. It was, I think, this very second-class existence that may have guaranteed the artistic freedom of the comic strips and panels of those decades, from the 1890s through the middle '20s. It was precisely being regarded as a mere illustration, gloss or doodle, that, I would propose, liberated the American cartoon — not merely the editorial cartoon, but the progressively-diluted comic — by safeguarding it against *form*.

Swinnerton's own illustrative techniques represent not a form but a means of location, of constantly orienting himself for the maximum freedom of space and of imagination. And so did Swinnerton's contemporaries — T.E. Powers, with his skittish stick-figures; Dorgan's smirking political terriers; McGurk with his mock-elegant satirical sketches — make free with the whole terrain of informal observation that their classless class afforded them; not to mention the terrain of paper, the undictated visual surface which was still available to them. This is not at all to suggest that they weren't as bound by deadlines and page-space, by demand for regimented production, as much as their successors. But, looking at their work today, from among the withered pods of so much desiccated comic art, I can feel an imaginative rapport with the world at large. Apart from the obvious advantage of permitting occasional social-political comment (which, however, then as now, only the most daring used to much advantage), this freedom allowed the artist to rally his own anxieties, cranks, obsessions, and appetites, impressing them into a daily or weekly idiom, which were, at best, more teasingly evocative than out-and-out funny.

Reading *Little Jimmy* or *Mr. Jack*, you can re-encounter that primary communion of hand, pen, and paper that injected a child's apprehension of art into the beefy sports and politics of the old dailies. I have no precise idea of how far his influence may have reached. But I can detect his close rapport with men Like Frank King (*Gasoline Alley*) and J.R. Williams (*Out Our Way*); or, in its sedate seriousness, Crockett Johnson's popular '40s strip, *Barnaby*. In all of them, diverse as their voices are, the southwestern or the midwestern sense of frontier space merges with the imaginative limbo of sheer blank paper.

In Swinnerton's comic strips, people are constantly making advances that seem to be rejected more often than accepted; and resorting to little ceremonies, rituals and protocols, which are repeatedly capsized by some gnarl of human waywardness. One of Jimmy's adventures out west (a landscape to which the strip returns, eventually permanently, as did its author) involves the harassments of an Indian medicine man, a healer who cures the hornet stings of a bear, only to be importuned by the bear to relieve his mate's cold. The hornets reappear to rescue the beleaguered shaman; but this time, demand the cure of grandfather hornet's rheumatism in repayment. As we last see him, he is appealing to the earth spirits, whose emissary, a prairie dog, is explaining to him, in turn, that the hornets are not their domain; now, if they were mud wasps…

In another episode Jimmy meets a little Scottish boy, whose explanation of his kilts ("These are nae skurruts…") seems totally implausible, and results in a scuffle, which Jimmy wins. In the next day's return match, however, the Scottish boy triumphs; and Jimmy admits that the kilts would probably answer, if buttons were sewn on them and the legs divided. The young Scot buys him an ice cream on this handsome concession.

The enchanting clarity of such episodes comes from the clarity of Swinnerton's own commitment to them. Like the greatest of children's artists, Sendak or Krauss, he does not compromise his eye with either optimistic gookiness or cynicism. Everyone who can or will read these simple, though faintly mysterious characters, can get Swinnerton's message: that people or animals do return to their habitual natures, good or evil; that in so doing they run counter to many dictates of propriety or considerateness; that some such occurrences are not to be avoided; and that we should look forward chiefly to mending fences with wherever enough lumber is left us.

Yet, *Little Jimmy* is by no means entirely a child's comic strip, except to the important extent that a child's directness, diffidence, and anxieties are central to Swinnerton's art. Here again, he practices his art without bending it uniformly to the tone of any medium or the prescriptions of a form. Nor is he one bit concerned, as is Charles (*Peanuts*) Schulz, or Mell (*Miss Peach*) Lazarus, with creating a coy little pavilion world of "childhood" that is as precious and as adult-directed as anything out of the Victorian era. He was invested in relating his fable-like stories through the childhood-molded vision of a fairly complex and vulnerable adult.

So we have him from *Little Jimmy's* opposite number: *Mr. Jack*, a possible, more upper-class, grandsire of R. Crumb's Fritz the Cat; a pint-sized roué in silk hat and frock coat, flourishing a ubiquitous walking stick. Mr. Jack is a little tiger, as are the girls he squires, their fathers, and his circle of head-waiters, policemen, butlers and sporting fellow-bachelors; each diminutive adventure is like a spray of New York City's swank, raunchy, tenderloin atmosphere, in the early days of the century. The typical refrain of Mr. Jack's adventures is paying court — usually to some lovely tiger-girl, occasionally to some bootleg hooch. The portrayal of his escapades is more concentrated, linear and strictly pantomimed than *Little Jimmy*: but with some wonderfully funny riffs of sheer design and timing (one essentially — and typically — weak gag is reharmonized by a feline beauty, swaddled in furs, whose single visible eye keeps shifting position). But their common current is that same strange interplay of shy decorum, all-but-mute sardonic humor, and unexpected flurries of sheer wildness that give *Little Jimmy* its constant purr of fascination: that endless suspension between the rigors of illustrative convention and the protean wildness of line.

Especially in the'20s and '30s, *Little Jimmy* is full of animals; who, while not the complete ensemble as in *Mr. Jack*, are important featured performers. They are the strip's pantomimists, its Id-figures: Jimmy's burly, Edgar Buchananish bulldog, Beans; his little friend Pinky's rooster; a Californian bear cub. Less inhibited even than the children, these animals enact the potential wildness of line that Swinnerton sparingly allows himself, subverting his own formalities. One notable character, during January of 1917, was a handsome Siamese cat owned by one of the boys, which would get high on catnip. During such trips, it would commit such unfeline outrages as stealing the uniform off an organ-grinder's monkey; or else, stroke its long, curling whiskers with the characteristic Swinnerton smirk at zenith.

Little Jimmy gives us, I suspect, James Swinnerton's most amusing and beguiling evolution of that hesitant, quirky, harassed rhythm that he was developing throughout his and Jimmy's and the American comic strips' careers: that rhythm which is the true content of Swinnerton's work, and the work of his best contemporaries and successors. *Little Jimmy* is often a series of interruptions, postponements, distractions, the tilting of formality. In one series of episodes, Jimmy's cousin, Cora (as good a looker as Swinnerton's little tiger-girls, and through almost equally economic means) is being visited by a series of beaux, who send Jimmy on a variety of errands, from which Jimmy is repeatedly diverted; once, an old codger conscripts Jimmy — and, eventually, the boy friend — to help him out with his daily crossword puzzle; at another time, a dog fight lures Jimmy, and he comes back with a pocket handkerchief instead of the sheet music requested.

The strip was far more text-laden than *Mr. Jack*; but the words themselves ran a sort of interference; dropping like a scrim curtain between the reader and what is going on. People — boys, mostly — untiringly comment on or interpret the action which we see; giving that action itself, simple as it is, a magical effect of suspension and of focus.

Little Jimmy is, at last, almost like an *esquisse* of every American comic strip; from the great, blank, ever-accommodating southwest desert in which the cast eventually made its permanent home, that desert which was the frontier of art; to the theme of interruption, postponement, endless delay: the theme of childhood's fantasies and frustrations, with which Swinnerton made his gently restless peace. And this ever-interrupted, ever-suspended rhythm, more than gags or excitement, is the content, the sustenance, of comic strips, of which James Swinnerton was the constant frontiersman; using the inherited furniture of illustrative art to set the outposts of his own space.

JIMMY—HE HASTENS TO GET A TOWEL!

JIMMY—HE BRINGS PAPA ANOTHER COAT!

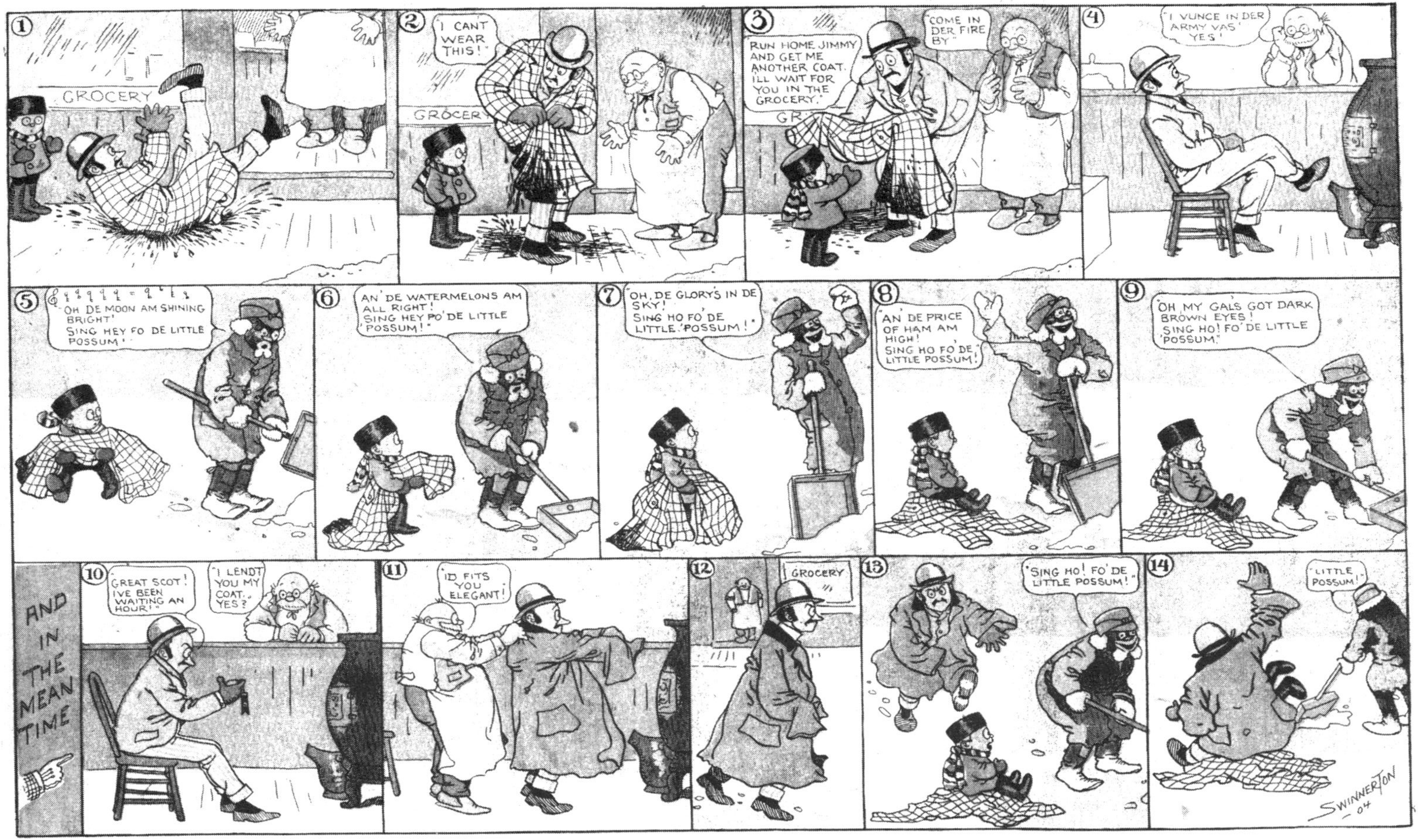

DEAR, SWEET LITTLE KATY! WILLIE JONES, TOO!

JIMMY—HE STOPS THE NOISE!

1
FUNG
BANG
BIFF
BING

2
"RUN UPSTAIRS AND TELL THE LADY PLEASE NOT TO MAKE SO MUCH NOISE. PAPA HAS A HEADACHE."

3
OH! OH! OH!
"BE VERY POLITE JIMMY!"

4
"REMEMBER YOUR MANNERS JIMMY!"

5

6
WELL! IF IT ISN'T DEAR LITTLE JIMMY! COME RIGHT IN. IM GIVING A PARTY TO MY LITTLE FRIENDS."

7
"CHILDREN THIS IS LITTLE JIMMY. YOU MUST MAKE HIM JOIN YOU IN YOUR INNOCENT GAMES"

8
"LITTLE JIMMY WILL YOU NOT JOIN US?"
"ISN'T HE POLITE"
"YES THANK YOU"

9
BANG!
"YOW!"
"HOORAY!"
"WHOOP-LA!"

AND IN THE MEAN TIME

10

12

13

SWINNERTON '04

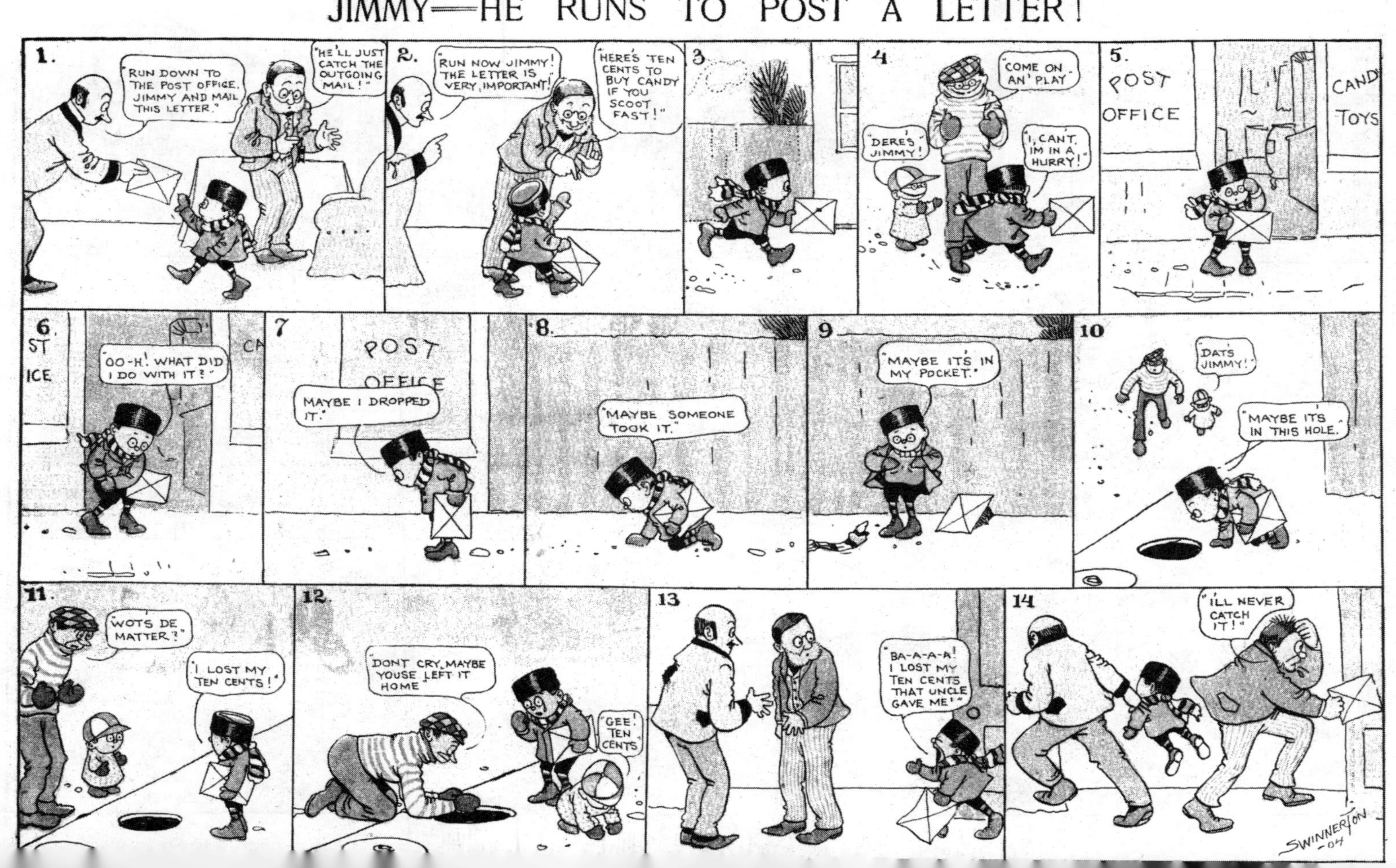
JIMMY—HE RUNS TO POST A LETTER!
1.
"RUN DOWN TO THE POST OFFICE, JIMMY AND MAIL THIS LETTER."
"HE'LL JUST CATCH THE OUTGOING MAIL!"
2.
"RUN NOW JIMMY! THE LETTER IS VERY IMPORTANT!"
"HERE'S TEN CENTS TO BUY CANDY IF YOU SCOOT FAST!"
3
4
"DERE'S JIMMY!"
"COME ON AN' PLAY"
"I CAN'T IM IN A HURRY!"
5.
POST OFFICE
CANDY
TOYS
6.
ST
ICE
"OO-H! WHAT DID I DO WITH IT?"
7
POST OFFICE
MAYBE I DROPPED IT."
8.
"MAYBE SOMEONE TOOK IT."
9
"MAYBE IT'S IN MY POCKET."
10
"DAT'S JIMMY!"
"MAYBE ITS IN THIS HOLE."
11.
"WOTS DE MATTER?"
"I LOST MY TEN CENTS!"
12.
"DONT CRY, MAYBE YOUSE LEFT IT HOME"
"GEE! TEN CENTS"
13
"BA-A-A-A! I LOST MY TEN CENTS THAT UNCLE GAVE ME!"
14
"I'LL NEVER CATCH IT!"
SWINNERTON -04

MR. JACK!

1.
"PLEASE MUM THERES A BOOK AGENT LADY TO SEE YOU"
"SHOW HER IN. HORTENSE"
2.
"I HAVE HERE A LOVELY SET OF THE WORKS OF THE POETS AT TEN DOLLARS A SET"
BIRD!
3.
"PST-T-T!"
4.
"ISNT THIS A LOVELY LINE, JACK- "THE SUN WAS SLOWLY SINKING IN THE SEA—"
5
MEET ME AT THE CORNER IN HALF AN HOUR I'LL BUY 20 SETS
6.
"YOU WRETCH!"
SWINNERTON

JIMMY—HE RUNS FOR EGGS!

JIMMY—HE LEARNS ALL ABOUT GEORGE WASHINGTON

WHY DONT YOU START?
I'M WAITING FOR JIMMY TO BRING MY GOGGLES.
START
13
COMIC SUPPLEMENT OF THE
JIMMY
Chicago Sunday
AMERICAN
FEBRUARY 12th 1905.
COPYRIGHT 1905, BY THE AMERICAN-JOURNAL-EXAMINER. ALL BRITAIN RIGHTS RESERVED.
"BOO!"
SWINNERTON '04
JIMMY—He Rushes to Get Mr. Jones!
1
I'LL CLIMB THE TREE AND IF I CAN SEE THE AUTOMOBILE RACE. I'LL BOOST YOU UP."
2
3
"I SEE THEM!"
4
5
RUN FOR HELP JIMMY! QUICK! ASK MR JONES DOWN THE ROAD TO COME! HURRY!"

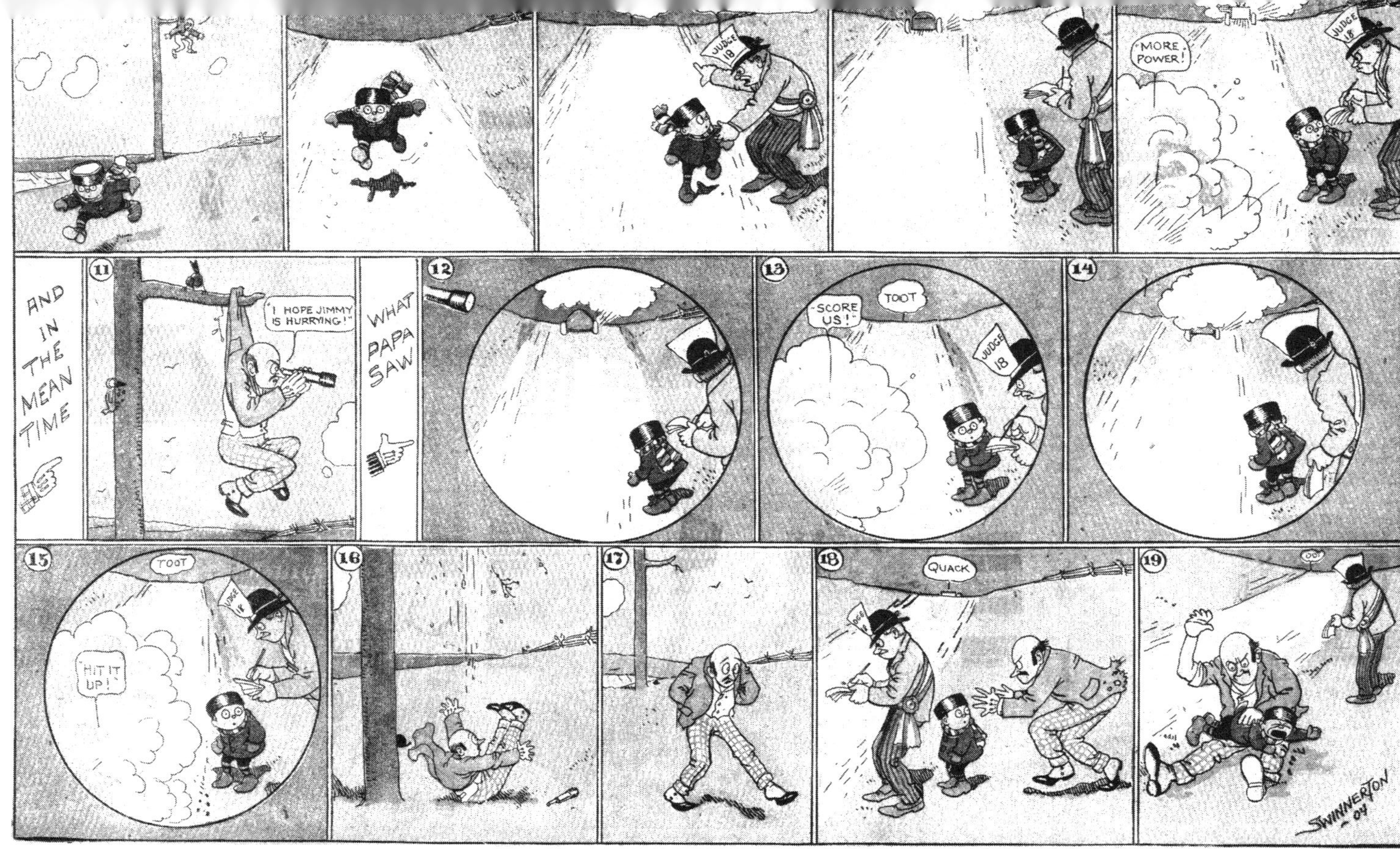
JUDGE 18
"MORE POWER!"
JUDGE 18
AND IN THE MEAN TIME
11
"I HOPE JIMMY IS HURRYING!"
WHAT PAPA SAW
12
13
"SCORE US!"
TOOT
JUDGE 18
14
15
TOOT
"HIT IT UP!"
16
17
18
QUACK
19
SWINNERTON -04

COMIC SUPPLEMENT OF THE
BOSTON AMERICAN.
FEBRUARY 26st 1905.
COPYRIGHT 1905. BY THE AMERICAN-JOURNAL-EXAMINER
ALL BRITAIN RIGHTS RESERVED.
SWINNERTON -05-
Jimmy! And Dear Katy! And Sweet Willie Jones!
1
"HE'S GOING TO TAKE ELECTRICITY FOR HIS RHEUMATISM!"
"MAMMA, WHAT IS PAPA DOING?"
2
"DR. GREEN IS A GREAT DOCTOR, I FEEL BETTER ALREADY."
Z-Z-Z-Z
"WHAT A FUNNY NOISE!"
3
"OUCH!"
Z-Z-Z
4
"RUN FOR DR GREEN QUICK, JIMMY! I CAN'T LET GO!"
5
"HURRY JIMMY!"
"QUICK JIMMY!"
6
7
"HELLO JIMMY!"
"TUM INSIDE!"
8
"COME IN AND PLAY BAND JIMMY!"
9
"HELLO JIMMY! NOW CHILDREN RUN AWAY AND PLAY I WANT TO READ"
"LOOK UNCLE. JIMMY'S HERE!"
"TEE HEE"

HOORAY! WE'LL SING THE JUBILE-
ZANG
ZANG
BAND!
TACKLE HIM!
I DOT IT!
ITS MY TURN!
TEE HEE
14
CLEAR OUT OF HERE, YOU LITTLE NUISANCES!
AND IN THE MEAN TIME
15
JIMMY HAS BEEN GONE HALF AN HOUR. I'LL GO FOR THE DOCTOR MYSELF!
16
17
18
IT'S EASY
19
WHERE ARE YOU GOING DEAR?
ONLY TO FIND JIMMY!
20
NOW GO HOME AND STAY HOME!
21
TEE HEE!
SWINNERTON -04

BOARDING HOUSE DAYS AND ARABIAN NIGHTS

THE LIFE AND IMAGINARY TIMES OF MAJOR HOOPLE

Aside from 1313 Wump Street, where the Mullinses and Plushbottoms dwell, probably the most memorable boarding house in American comics strips was *Our Boarding House*: Hoople Manor, as presided over by Martha Hoople, its redoubtable manageress, and, of course, Major Amos Hoople, its chief ornament; monumental fountainhead for the subversive current of fantasy that one could always sense playing amid the ailing wallpaper, rump-sprung sofas and armchairs, yesterday's cooking smells and hangdog boarders. The author, Eugene L. Ahern, easily matched Frank (*Moon Mullins*) Willard for appreciating and rendering the stodgy, dawdling, hand-in-pocket, near-torpor of such a place, where it seems perennially to be Sunday afternoon: the men shuffled about in vests and pullovers, toothpicks or cigar butts drooping from jutting lower lips. Except for the ineluctible Martha, and an occasional maidenly, middle-aged schoolmistress type — inevitably frightened off, within five minutes of her visit, by the Major's more sanguinary big-game-hunting stories or the misunderstood eccentricities of some guest — the cast was largely male.

Although Major Hoople was a classic target of domestic wit for his failure to get a job, I cannot recall, offhand, seeing any of the boarders at regular jobs, or even *en route* to one: The only regularly functioning souls at Hoople Manor appeared to be Martha and Jason, the Negro handyman. The standard facial expression was a Ned Sparks stare of bilious doubt, which, one felt, would deepen to incredulity were the other person to say anything remotely new or important. The telephone-booth cubicle of Ahern's weekday format — a single panel a day — emphasized the listless, late-afternoon atmosphere of dawdling talk; for the panel-a-day format must rely on talk, rather than on the contiguous action of five- or six-panel strips.

The personae of Hoople Manor appeared to be made of the same wrinkly, over-padded faded-genteel fabric that composed the drapes, the armchair and sofa covers; thanks largely to Gene Ahern's drawing-line — unshaded, phlegmatic, yet strikingly weightless-looking — which dwelt like a vagrant upon folds and crinkles and the bulges of bellies. Here, I think, Ahern had the edge over Frank Willard, who relied mainly on his two reigning families, with an occasional paying guest introduced for plot-kinks. Ahern created a little constellation of boarders who, though basically the same throughout *Our Boarding House's* career, were nevertheless always reshuffling, always being infiltrated by newcomers.

The oldest fixtures included Clyde, a Midwestern type, with scanty cowlick, lantern jaw, and an air of dour tolerance; Buster, who looked like an aging Joe College, a quizzical woodchuck in his eternal pullover sweater, with a stare of disarming innocence that inevitably accompanied the lethally deflating questions about the Major's fabulous tales.

There was my favorite of the steady boarders, Twiggs: a bald-headed, glowering-browed little snapping-turtle of a man, with a snapping-turtle's mode of address ("I might have passed you, going head-down in a blizzard!" is Twiggs's reply to a visitor's query about having met him before). In later years, the household was variously augmented by the Hooples' irascible neighbor, Mr. Morgan; and Aunt Clara, Martha's sister, with her acerbic candor. There are the Major's counterparts: Two-gun Terry, an imposing, square-shouldered figure of the frontier West, who, however, in a haze of red-eye whiskey, would take any innocuous stranger for a member of the gun-slinging Beeler Boys — a brotherhood surely as various, and wide-spread, as that of the Mafia. There was the Major's brother, Robin, a streamlined and more larcenously purposeful edition of the Major, with the slicked hair and the sleepy eyes of a riverboat gambler. And, unforgettably, there was the physically prodigious Earl of Shankham ("Don't call me no Oil — I'm Junior, see?"), former wrestler and teddy bear stuffer. (Junior's wistfulness for nursery-school pursuits extended to playing with toy trains and chewing bubble gum. He tried shooting marbles with the local kids, but gave up, disillusioned, when he discovered they were playing for keeps.)

All of these presences served, on this or that occasion, as chorus members, foils, adversaries, or co-plotters, for the boarding-house's Juno and Paycock. Major Hoople, by the time I became aware of the comic strip in the '30s, had become the emblem and practically the main architectural feature of the place. It is difficult to realize that the Major was ever lanky (as illustrated in Coulton Waugh's *The Comics*), a decade before; even harder to comprehend that one time he was merely one more boor, and worthy butt, amid the satiric conventions perpetuated in this country by Clare Briggs and Thomas A. ("TAD") Dorgan and H.T. Webster and the *non-pareil* J.R. Williams. His later, heavy-weight metamorphosis owes a little to W.C. Fields, and probably, almost as much to J. Wellington Wimpy. But Gene Ahern's loving, dallying delineation of the Major was his alone: beginning with the turreted Turkish fez, with its drooping tassel: past the fatuous, self-congratulation of the beady-bleary eyes, around the regal bulb of the nose and the twin promontories of the chins; down, down, down over ledge after ledge of vest-wrinkle and natural jut of that splendid Gothic pile which unites his chest with his beer-belly.

Here I must interject that, although I have been referring to the Hooples and their menage as though their names and appointments remained intact for most of their careers, this is not strictly so. About the middle of the '30s, William Randolph Hearst and King

Features acquired the services of Gene Ahern, but not the rights to the title and characters of *Our Boarding House.* So, devotees of the Hooples were faced with the anomaly of the man responsible for the Hooples' corporate identity and vitality, transferring his talents to a near-duplicate of the boarding house and its inmates, while the comic he had originated was continued, very competently indeed, by the NEA Service. Ahern's transplanted strip was called *Room and Board*; the Hooples became the Puffles, with the Major now the Judge. These changes proved, at best, unsalubrious, and, at worst, annoying, like the discovery that a former long-time girlfriend has gotten a totally superfluous nose job — which, in fact, was what befell the Major; his imperial beezer, in transit, was deflated to an unimposing snub nose (out of deference to the judiciary?). While, almost as devastating, his secondary regal symbol, the fez, was replaced by an assortment of sporty berets and tams. Martha (now Norah) was the chief casualty, however; she lost about 60 pounds of her bulk, thus relinquishing her look of buxom stoicism (and sibling-like complement to the Major) for the appearance of a harried drudge. Nevertheless, Ahern's cardinal virtues not only remained intact, but prospered.

In a universe of talkers, Hoople had a vocabulary to match his sumptuous profile: not of words only, but of exclamations and interjections — a steam-calliope-full of splutters and snorts and chortles. In addition to the ever-present and all-purpose "Egad!," I recall "Fap!," "Faw!," Tush!," "Splltt!" (for grievous frustration), and "Hrummf-hakkaff!" which was a favorite of Arthur Godfrey, for some reason. Ahern is the only artist I can currently remember who invented a new punctuation mark, and one at that with its own personality: the sign ⋜ to denote fuming bafflement.

Martha Hoople gave newly vivid meaning to the phrase "better half," for she resembled the Major enough to be his sister, as befits one hemisphere to another. Together, she — pragmatic, prosaic, and stoic — and he — lethargic, grandiloquent, and fantastical — made up a quite compact world. And her character so imprinted her physical traits that she could not have been mistaken for the Major had she put on his fez and vest and striped trousers. Her double chin was a flying buttress; the line of her mouth, a bow-string of resolution. Her nose was smaller, in keeping with her responsible role; her aproned bulk was stout in every sense, where his was fat.

Theirs was actually one of the happiest marriages I recall from American comic strips — especially those of the '30s, with that miasma of ever-more-viperish hectoring and needling which infected so many of the even secondarily domestic strips, like *Barney Google* or *The Katzenjammer Kids*, and reached its nadir in the '40s *Blondie*-plagiarisms, *Dotty Dripple* and *The Berries*. Compared with any of these, how gallant and even sweet seems the Hoople household's motif of simply putting up with one another — this of course, with all Martha's salutations to her husband of: "You big barn owl!" and occasional brandishings of her rolling-pin; or with all the Major's orchestral mutterings about how it's a throwback to the feudal times, spllt — hak-kaff! — when he is run to earth long enough to be set raking leaves or washing dishes.

The peculiar, unobtrusively charming harmonies of *Our Boarding House* went considerably deeper than the Hoople marriage theme. For, in Gene Ahern's hands, it was all about the theme, not so common as one might suppose, of the interdependence of reality and fantasy, with neither ultimately prevailing or being given preference; each, rather, needing and supporting and furthering the other. The quotidian dowdiness of *Our Boarding House* was, as I have noted before, under recurrent assault, mainly whenever the inhabitants opened their mouths. For out of unwieldy, if beguilingly candid-looking drawing, Ahern delivered a sinuous, gleaming freshet of dialogue — the partial legacy of TAD's dapper, tight wisecracking dialogue in *Indoor Sports* and *Silk Hat Harry's Divorce Suit;* and of Raymond Chandler's tropical-worsted phrases and *bons mots*. It was a river at which every member of Hoople House dipped his tin cup. The Major's larcenous brother Robin unblinkingly announces that one of his sure things "finished behind the track-sweeper." "I'll wilt his ear!" promises the outraged Neighbor Morgan; while Aunt Clara informs a would-be pianist that, "There are 85 keys in that piano besides the three you're annoying!"

Ahern, it seems to me, had an impeccable understanding of wit as, essentially, an effort to be extraordinarily precise under pressure. And apart from the quips and digs — which had become common, for better or worse, in American comic strips by the 1930s — the Ahern dialogue was a conduit of the characters' *sub rosa* fantasy lives. When Aunt Clara recommends to Mr. Morgan that he ask the zoo to rent him a beaver (to saw down the Daliesque fence carpentered by the Major) you feel that she would be ready to call the zoo herself, or at very least wishes that she might be.

One of the unremitting beauties of *Our Boarding House* was Ahern's shuffling, in his various characters, of child-like reverie and sophistication. Two of the strip's most knowing figures, surely (I say "strip" advisedly here; for generally, they appeared on Sundays, when *Our Boarding House* ran about 12 panels) were the Major's nephew, Alvin, with his moon-face, naïve cowlick, and quizzical stare, suspiciously like Boarder Buster's; and his smart-aleck pal, Leander (more burly than Alvin, with a bullet-head, Brillo-pad poll, and frog-mouth with which he would announce his role in the strip by regularly addressing the Major as "Uncle Bulgy — I mean, Amos"). I can remember dimly when Alvin seemed wholeheartedly to accept the Major's yarns about charming Bengal tigers by singing the "Last Rose of Summer" in his peerless baritone or, as the pride of Scotland Yard, uncovering espionage agents working out of a fish-and-chip house by passing code messages through the alphabet soup. Still, Alvin's diplomatic powers may have ripened even then; later on, he makes less a secret of his skepticism and, at times, boredom. Yet, Alvin (and Leander, too, in his more saturnine way), shows the type of common worldly kindliness toward Alvin's uncle — more than indulgence, really — that the household shares, because they realize that his nonsense is basic to their lives beyond any mere need. It was more than Romance the Major embodied; romance, for me always implies a hierarchical choice, being presumably "superior" to reality. What the Major supplied was fantasy indigenous to reality, a dimension of reality. The most case-hardened boarders would find themselves investing in the most unworldly commodities — like the magpie whose single utterance, supposed to guarantee astronomic success, was: "Use Sand-Blast Toothpaste!"

This impounded fantasy of the Sunday *Our Boarding House* featured not only the Major's opulent tall tales, fully illustrated, but Gene Ahern's companion strips: the surrealist jubilees, *The Nut Brothers*; and over Judge Puffle's *Room and Board*, *The Squirrel Cage*. Like certain other notable "secondary" comic strips — for example, Chic (*Blondie*) Young's slapstick ballet, *Colonel Potterby and the Duchess — The Squirrel Cage* distilled the shaggier impulses of its author, like a kind of satyr-play. They were the most out-and-out surreal comic strips I can recall, barring possibly *Krazy Kat* or Lyonel Feininger's *The Kin Der*

Kids. From one panel to the next, not only would the landscape shift with demented virtuosity, but the costumes and very persons of the two principals, the Nut Brothers: Ches, with his blond topknot, and Wal, with his flat head and scrubby mustache. They would disport themselves in 1890s bathing suits, admiral's uniforms, the burnooses of bedouin sheiks; or appear with their heads emerging from giant turnips, barber poles, or hammers and nails. Strangest and most engaging of all, the daft volatility of the top strip was, somehow or other, dominated by the aridly deadpan tone of a Hoople boarder wondering whether dinner would be a rerun of last Sunday's lamb.

The emblematic figure of *The Squirrel Cage* — emblematic even of a shabby sweetness and wistful lunacy, not only of *Our Boarding House*, but of the '30s during which it flourished — was neither Ches nor Wal Nut. He first appeared as an adjunct of one of those dreamlike highways, which, indeed, might have figured in the dreams of the Hooples's tenants. He was a hitchhiker, wearing a red beret, ankle-length black overcoat, and apron of white beard; and he stood in the approved hitchhiking position, with canted thumb; but what came out of his mouth was not the approved phrase, "Going my way?" but the never-translated and, patently, untranslatable inquiry/comment/appeal: "Nov shmoz ka pop?" So popular did this hitchhiker become that, for a little while around 1938, he became the virtual protagonist of *The Squirrel Cage*, which gradually moved from surrealism into Oz-like whimsy. His dialogue was augmented by a few no less cryptic phrases. I have no memory or notion of whether he ever got his ride, or of where it took him; but if he did, there is no doubt about where he stopped over.

SOME DAY NEXT WEEK DURING YOUR LUNCH HOUR, DROP IN TH' RUMMLEY ART GALLERY TO SEE AN EXHIBITION OF GOOFY MODERN ART! — TH' MAJOR HAS ENTERED A STATUE HE MADE OF PUTTY, THAT LOOKS LIKE HE DID IT WHILE FALLING DOWN STAIRS! — HE AN' I ARE PLAYING A GAG TO WORK A LOAD OF LAUGHS OFF ON TH' NUT EXHIBITION, — HE'S S'POSED TO COME FROM FINLAND AN' I'M HIS MANAGER, — HIS WORK IS LISTED UNDER TH' NAME OF "YILSTADJ" — SO GO INTO A HEADSPIN OF RAPTURE OVER HIS STATUE!
JUST DOIN' IT FOR A LAUGH, EH? — WELL, TH' BOTH OF YOU MAY WIND UP TRYIN' TO LAUGH A DESK SERGEANT INTO LETTIN' YOU PUT UP SOME HAY FOR BAIL!
I'LL RUN IN AN' SEE IT! — I'LL GO INTO ONE OF THOSE ARTISTIC TRANCES, AN' START RAVING OVER TH' STATUE UNTIL THEY TRY TO SELL IT TO ME, — THEN I'LL REGAIN MY COMPOSURE!
GENE AHERN.
BUILDING UP HAND-PICKED ADMIRERS
REG. U. S. PAT. OFF.
©1929 BY NEA SERVICE, INC.
3-9

OOF-FF ~~
~~ YOB SKOLL ~~
KOPPS JAD
VUMZ ROOR
DILLINGSKOLL!
~OH-OH~
OH!!

OOP, ~~ WAT
IS MATTAIR
WEETH ZE
GREAT YILSTADJ?
~~ HE GROAN, ~
~~ SOB, LAK IN
BEEG ANGUISH! ~~
~~ SPEAK, ~~ IS HE
GOING SWOON
WEETH A FIT?

GREAT HEAVENS, MAN,
~~ HIS MASTERPIECE,
THE STATUE!! ~
~~ YOU HAVE IT
FACING THE WEST,
~~ AND IT SHOULD
FACE THE SOUTH-
EAST! ~~ QUICK,
TURN IT AROUND,
BEFORE YOU CONFUSE
IT'S ART VIBRATIONS!
~~ AND THE STATUE
MUST REST ON
ANTIQUE ROSE
VELVET! ~~
~OH, THIS
IS
AWFUL,
SIR!

GENE AHERN

BALLYHOO
ART
TEMPERAMENT

©1929, BY NEA SERVICE, INC.

REG. U. S. PAT. OFF.

3-11-

GENTLEMEN, — IT IS THE WORK OF A GENIUS! — THE MAN HAS IMBUED THE FOURTH DIMENSION IN IT! — THAT IS WHAT MAKES ITS VAGUENESS SO FORCEFUL!=

IT IS POETRY UNUTTERED! — THERE IS NO LIMIT IN ITS SCOPE TO OUTDISTANCE THE RAYS OF MORTAL IMAGINATION! — THE ESSENCE OF THOUGHTS TO COME, ARE ON THE THRESHOLD OF RELEASE IN THIS WORK!

I SEE IT AS A SYMPHONY BEFORE THE PROCESS OF COMPOSITION! — THERE IS HARMONY AWAITING TO BE ASSEMBLED! — MELODY MUTED IN COLD FORM!=

THE WORK IS BY FAR THE FINEST EXAMPLE OF SUBCONSCIOUS EXPRESSION!= — IN IT IS A SPECTRUM OF ETHEREAL EMOTIONS!= — VERILY, GENTLEMEN, THE MAN WEARS THE MANTLE OF GENIUS!

GENE AHERN.

THE JURY

©1929, BY NEA SERVICE, INC.

REG. U. S. PAT. OFF.

3-12

© NEA Service, Inc., 1929

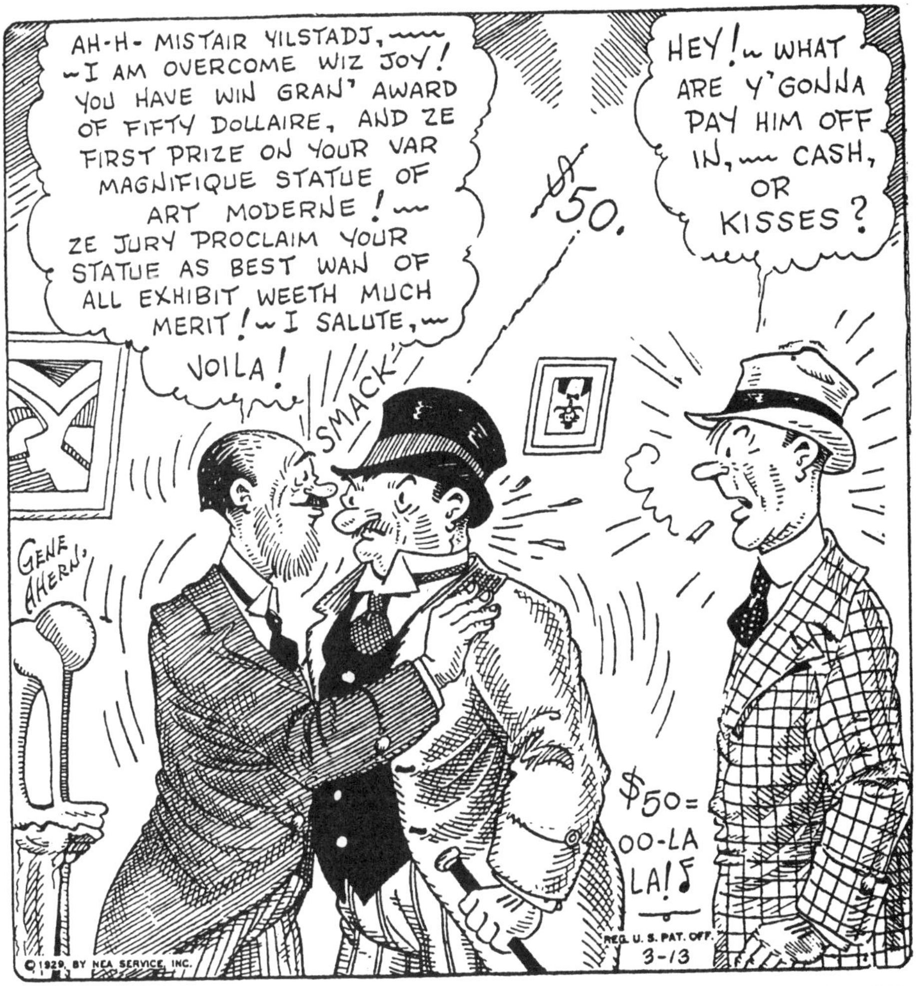

AH-H- MISTAIR YILSTADJ, — — I AM OVERCOME WIZ JOY! YOU HAVE WIN GRAN' AWARD OF FIFTY DOLLAIRE, AND ZE FIRST PRIZE ON YOUR VAR MAGNIFIQUE STATUE OF ART MODERNE! — ZE JURY PROCLAIM YOUR STATUE AS BEST WAN OF ALL EXHIBIT WEETH MUCH MERIT! — I SALUTE, — VOILA!

SMACK

$50.

HEY! — WHAT ARE Y'GONNA PAY HIM OFF IN, — CASH, OR KISSES?

$50= OO-LA LA!

GENE AHERN,

© 1929, BY NEA SERVICE, INC.

REG. U. S. PAT. OFF.

3-13

YES SIR, — THE JURY OF MODERN ART CRITICS VOTED THE FIRST PRIZE ON MY STATUE, — AND AWARDED ME $50. IN CASH! — NOW, LET ME HEAR YOU ATTEMPT TO SCOFF THAT, — EGAD! — FURTHERMORE, THEY SAID MY STATUE WAS THE UNMISTAKABLE WORK OF GENIUS! — — MARK THAT, — THEY HAIL ME AS A GENIUS!

TH' WORD GENIUS TO-DAY, DOESN'T MEAN ANYTHING! — IT'S A RUBBER TITLE THAT WILL FIT ANYBODY! — — MEAN TO SAY YOU CAN WRITE YOUR NAME UNDER MIKE ANGELO'S? — — YOU COULD ON A BUM CHECK!

SAY! — DON'T FORGET YOU MADE THAT NIGHTMARE STATUE JUST FOR A LAUGH, AN' TO RIB THIS MODERN ART CRAZE! — YOU DID IT TO PROVE THAT ANYBODY COULD DO IT! — — AN' NOW YOU'RE TAKING A BEND ON BEING A GENIUS!

GENE AHERN.

PUTTING ON THE PUFF

3-14

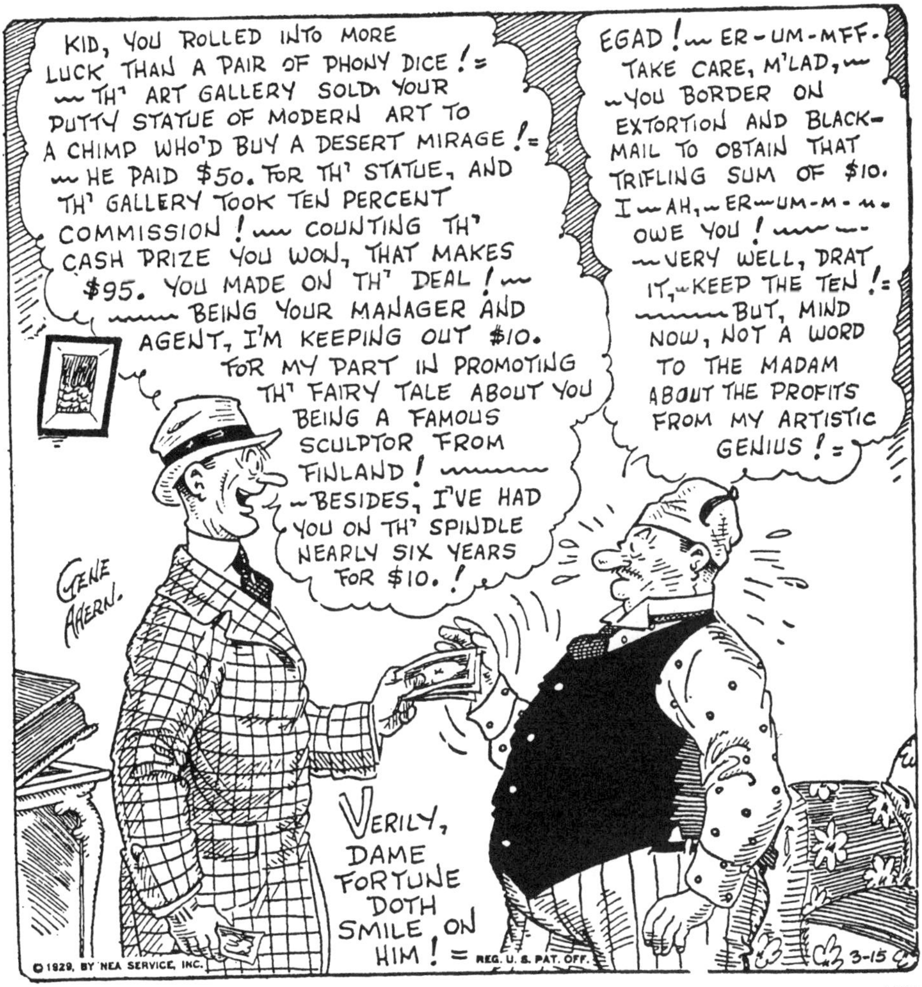

KID, YOU ROLLED INTO MORE LUCK THAN A PAIR OF PHONY DICE != — TH' ART GALLERY SOLD YOUR PUTTY STATUE OF MODERN ART TO A CHIMP WHO'D BUY A DESERT MIRAGE != — HE PAID $50. FOR TH' STATUE, AND TH' GALLERY TOOK TEN PERCENT COMMISSION ! — COUNTING TH' CASH PRIZE YOU WON, THAT MAKES $95. YOU MADE ON TH' DEAL ! — — BEING YOUR MANAGER AND AGENT, I'M KEEPING OUT $10. FOR MY PART IN PROMOTING TH' FAIRY TALE ABOUT YOU BEING A FAMOUS SCULPTOR FROM FINLAND ! — — BESIDES, I'VE HAD YOU ON TH' SPINDLE NEARLY SIX YEARS FOR $10. !

EGAD ! — ER-UM-MFF. TAKE CARE, M'LAD, — — YOU BORDER ON EXTORTION AND BLACK-MAIL TO OBTAIN THAT TRIFLING SUM OF $10. I — AH, — ER — UM-M-M. OWE YOU ! — — — VERY WELL, DRAT IT, — KEEP THE TEN != — — BUT, MIND NOW, NOT A WORD TO THE MADAM ABOUT THE PROFITS FROM MY ARTISTIC GENIUS !=

GENE AHERN.

VERILY, DAME FORTUNE DOTH SMILE ON HIM ! =

 REG. U. S. PAT. OFF. 3-15

© NEA Service, Inc., 1929

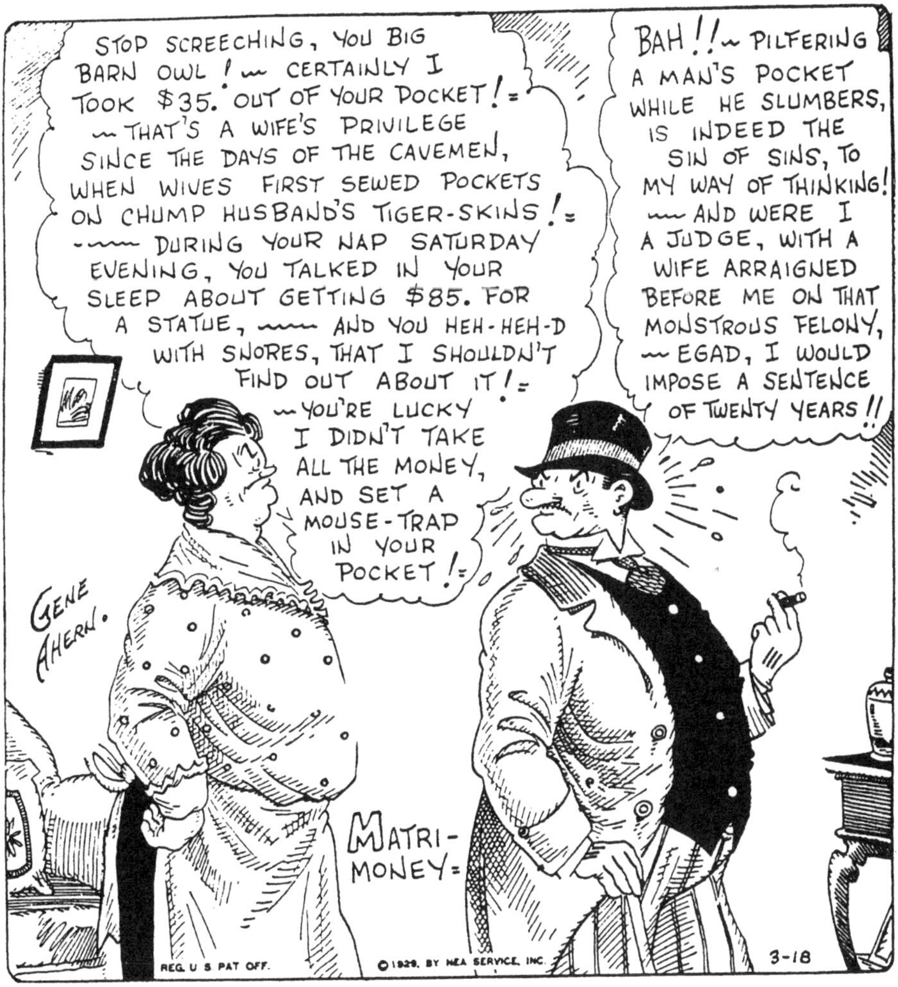

STOP SCREECHING, YOU BIG BARN OWL! — CERTAINLY I TOOK $35. OUT OF YOUR POCKET! = — THAT'S A WIFE'S PRIVILEGE SINCE THE DAYS OF THE CAVEMEN, WHEN WIVES FIRST SEWED POCKETS ON CHUMP HUSBAND'S TIGER-SKINS! = — DURING YOUR NAP SATURDAY EVENING, YOU TALKED IN YOUR SLEEP ABOUT GETTING $85. FOR A STATUE, — AND YOU HEH-HEH-D WITH SNORES, THAT I SHOULDN'T FIND OUT ABOUT IT! = — YOU'RE LUCKY I DIDN'T TAKE ALL THE MONEY, AND SET A MOUSE-TRAP IN YOUR POCKET! =

BAH!! — PILFERING A MAN'S POCKET WHILE HE SLUMBERS, IS INDEED THE SIN OF SINS, TO MY WAY OF THINKING! — AND WERE I A JUDGE, WITH A WIFE ARRAIGNED BEFORE ME ON THAT MONSTROUS FELONY, — EGAD, I WOULD IMPOSE A SENTENCE OF TWENTY YEARS!!

GENE AHERN.

MATRI-MONEY =

REG. U. S. PAT. OFF. ©1929, BY NEA SERVICE, INC. 3-18

OUR BOARDING HOUSE

By Aher

LUCKY FOR YOU, THAT Y'WASN'T IN THIS JOINT A HALF HOUR AGO, OR YOU'D BE IN TH' TANK NOW, WITH TH' REST OF THEM OWL CLUB MUGS! — WE PULLED A RAID HERE AN' TOOK THREE LOADS OF 'EM AWAY IN TH' MARIA, FOR PLAYIN' STUD, SHOOTIN' CRAPS AN' HAVIN' A CASE OF SNAKE SHELLAC!

EGAD, OFFICER, IS THAT TRUE? — BY JOVE, I'LL TENDER MY RESIGNATION TO THIS DEN OF INIQUITY! — MY WORD! — AND I THOUGHT IT WAS A GENTLEMAN'S CLUB! — LUCKILY, I AM JUST A NEW MEMBER AND I THANK YOU, OFFICER, FOR INFORMING ME THAT THE OTHERS ARE ROGUES AND KNAVES!

Gene Ahern

HE'S JUST PRESIDENT OF THE CLUB

REG. U. S. PAT. OFF.
© 1931 BY NEA SERVICE, INC.

11-28-

OUR BOARDING HOUSE

By AHERN

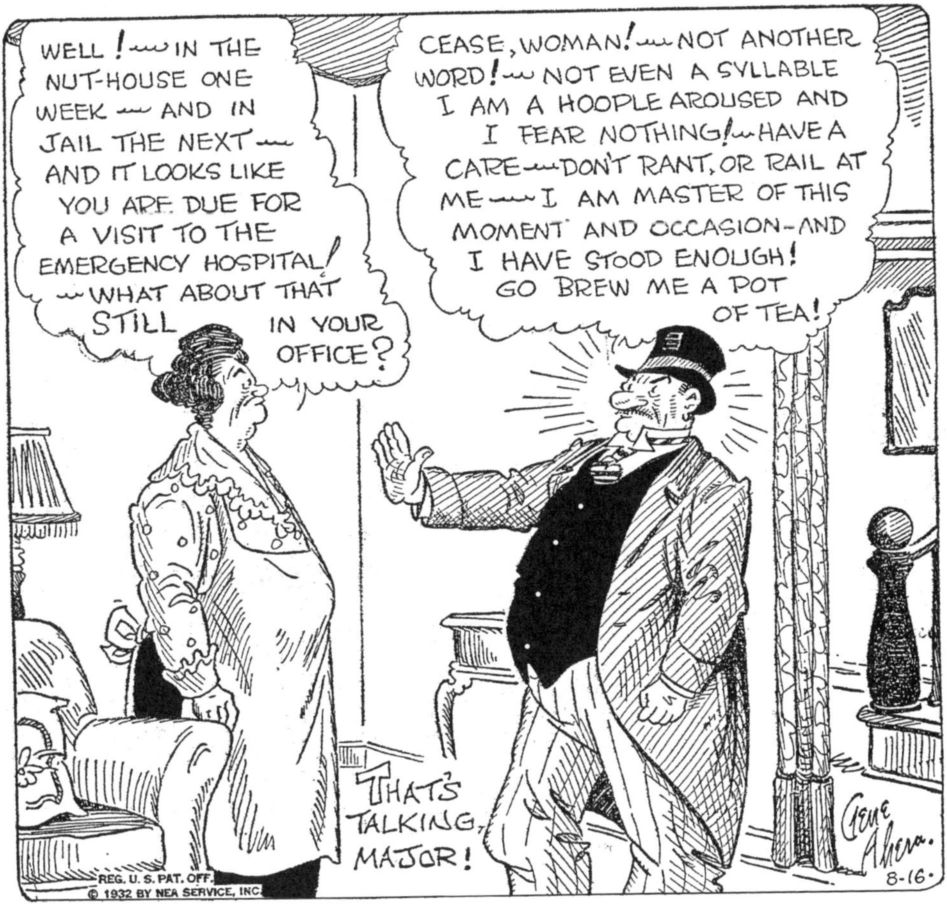

WELL! — IN THE NUT-HOUSE ONE WEEK — AND IN JAIL THE NEXT — AND IT LOOKS LIKE YOU ARE DUE FOR A VISIT TO THE EMERGENCY HOSPITAL! — WHAT ABOUT THAT STILL IN YOUR OFFICE?

CEASE, WOMAN! — NOT ANOTHER WORD! — NOT EVEN A SYLLABLE I AM A HOOPLE AROUSED AND I FEAR NOTHING! — HAVE A CARE — DON'T RANT, OR RAIL AT ME — I AM MASTER OF THIS MOMENT AND OCCASION — AND I HAVE STOOD ENOUGH! GO BREW ME A POT OF TEA!

THAT'S TALKING, MAJOR!

Gene Ahern. 8-16.

OUR BOARDING HOUSE

By AHERN

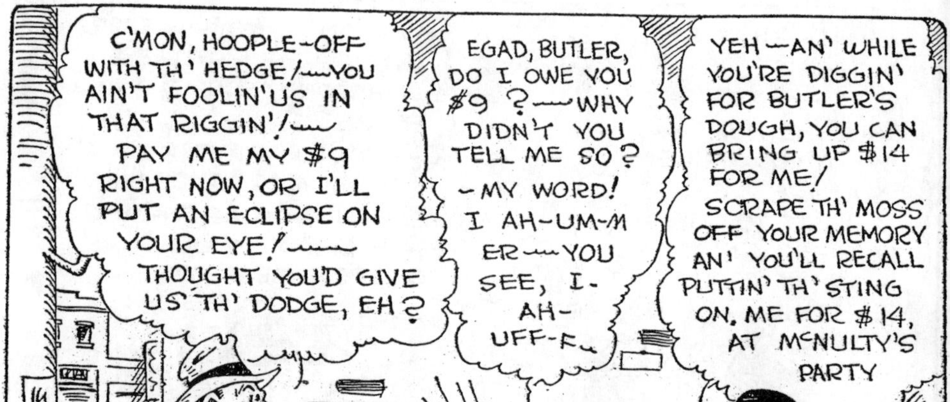

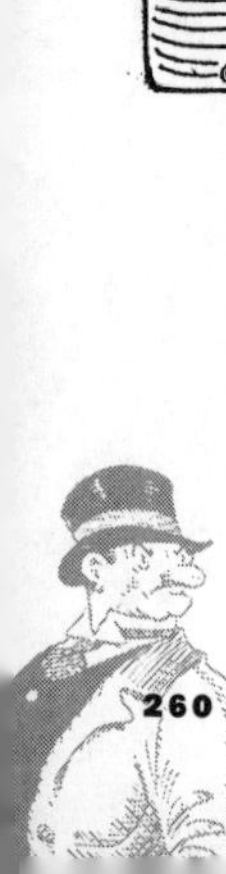

C'MON, HOOPLE–OFF WITH TH' HEDGE!— YOU AIN'T FOOLIN' US IN THAT RIGGIN'!— PAY ME MY $9 RIGHT NOW, OR I'LL PUT AN ECLIPSE ON YOUR EYE!— THOUGHT YOU'D GIVE US TH' DODGE, EH?

EGAD, BUTLER, DO I OWE YOU $9 ?— WHY DIDN'T YOU TELL ME SO? –MY WORD! I AH-UM-M ER— YOU SEE, I- AH- UFF-F.

YEH — AN' WHILE YOU'RE DIGGIN' FOR BUTLER'S DOUGH, YOU CAN BRING UP $14 FOR ME! SCRAPE TH' MOSS OFF YOUR MEMORY AN' YOU'LL RECALL PUTTIN' TH' STING ON ME FOR $14, AT M^cNULTY'S PARTY

Gene Ahern

PAY UP, MAJOR!

9-6

OUR BOARDING HOUSE . . . WITH . . MAJOR HOOPLE

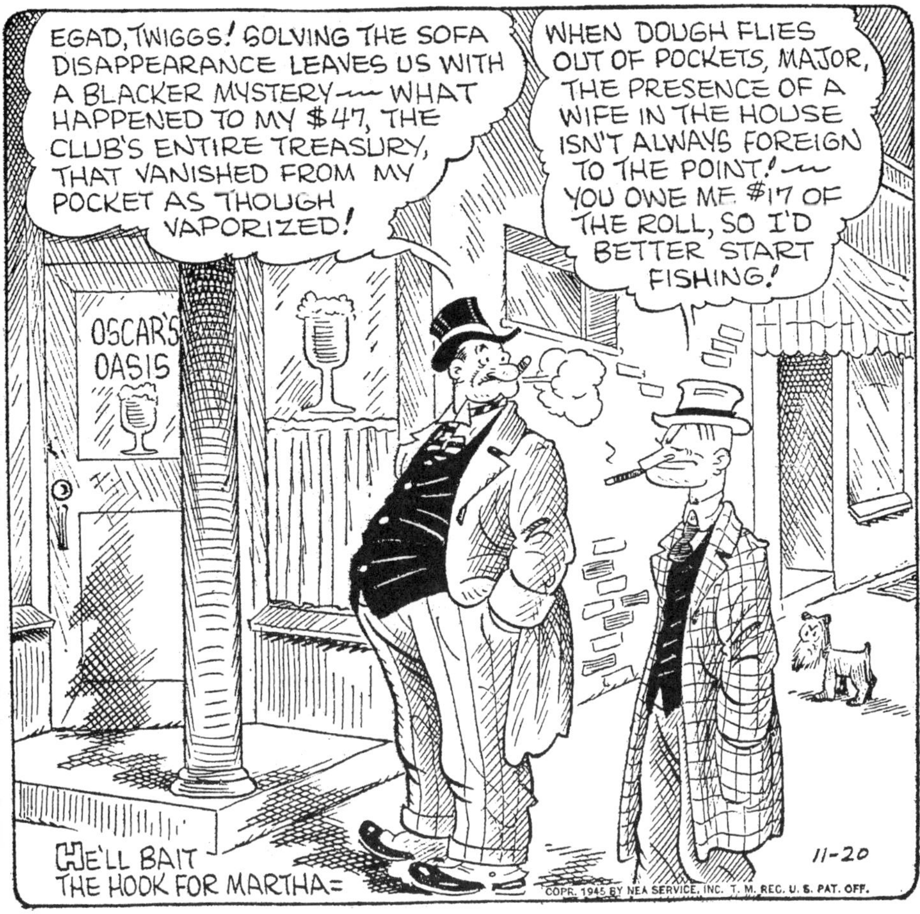

EGAD, TWIGGS! SOLVING THE SOFA DISAPPEARANCE LEAVES US WITH A BLACKER MYSTERY— WHAT HAPPENED TO MY $47, THE CLUB'S ENTIRE TREASURY, THAT VANISHED FROM MY POCKET AS THOUGH VAPORIZED!

WHEN DOUGH FLIES OUT OF POCKETS, MAJOR, THE PRESENCE OF A WIFE IN THE HOUSE ISN'T ALWAYS FOREIGN TO THE POINT!— YOU OWE ME $17 OF THE ROLL, SO I'D BETTER START FISHING!

OSCAR'S OASIS

HE'LL BAIT THE HOOK FOR MARTHA=

11-20

"DADDY"

ANNIE! I'VE FOUND YOU AT LAST-

LITTLE ICON ANNIE

"WHO'S THAT LITTLE CHATTERBOX?"

The celebrated eyes of Little Orphan Annie and her supporting cast were pupil-less holes, until, in the mid-'40s, Harold Gray, in one of his spasmodic tenders of cordiality toward his public, outfitted them with erratically situated pupils — with the effect of junkies' eyes: a sort of tokenism which neither Gray's early frontier spirit, nor the sensibilities of *Little Orphan Annie's* readers could endure. Mostly, however, the characters of the strip were obviously masked figures; and were also undoubtedly peering into a space beyond their own, or the readers,' immediate accommodation.

Those empty eyes were a symbol of the black, measureless space which was the comic strip's cardinal element (and I look forward to the day when Leonard Starr, whose stint on *Little Orphan Annie*, under the show-biz title *Annie*, was the most respectful and amiable pastiche yet of Harold Gray's strip, will find himself capable of quietly jettisoning a convention which has nothing at all to do with his own breezy, square-jawed style). The circlet eyes of Starr's version are merely a mildly inapropos, gently perplexing signature retained from a now-browning document. But the eyes of Harold

Gray's figures were the central marker of his style, and his metaphysic: the distance of people from each other and the customary, yet frighteningly detachable, masks they wear. They are symbols, too, of the darkness in which Gray continually lodged them, even at noonday; the black apertures that were the usual doorways of living room or library; the sense of a sky that was a ceiling, even in depictions of full daylight. And they are eyes which are both observant of, and terribly inaccessible to, the world-at-large; eyes that indeed amount to appropriate mirrors of a bleak, denuded, miserly world, replete with matter for shock, terror or simply misgiving beyond words.

They are transmitters of the world, and they are masks of the world. Compare and contrast these with the figures of Modigliani, with those imperturbable circlets which link the figures, their diffuse and complacent sensuosity, to the abstraction of Modigliani's own drawing; which John Held, Jr. was to mimic successfully: patient, mock-languid, solicitous of the mating-dance between his funky-erotic light and color, and his showoffish-serene, desultory-seeming design. In Gray there is no abstraction whatsoever. Bare as his drawing may seem — and be — the lean compositions and the stony pace wield their own heft and texture. The world in which his little orphan moves, in her charade of nineteenth century Victorian convention, is one of the most wintry imagined by a comic-strip artist; a continuous study in distance, silence, and cold light; light that exhibits much and reveals little. It is light which seems, itself, a mask: the headlights on a winter road, which pick out the feathery fringes of shrubbery, the furrows and dents of the road immediately ahead, and the stoic, phantom shape of a cast-iron dog which forecasts the doom of the dog-hating hit-and-runner, Elmer Pinchpenny. It improvises grim sculptures from the figure of "Daddy" Warbucks, disguised as a common seaman in one of the numerous alternative lives he leads away from Annie, in a waterfront café, awaiting news from the underground. It — the light — frames and portrays, and spotlights illusions, like the bewitching aureole which surrounds Punjab's menacing abracadabra with his vanishing-cloak. Gray's light seems more often a partner of the darkness than its dispeller.

Gray's grim architectonics emphasize what the long and ever-more-dreary succession of Little Orphan Annie's would-be guardians (and, Lord help us, in one or two instances, reformers) and even the

genial and talented Leonard Starr, have, willfully or helplessly, failed to perceive: to wit, that *Little Orphan Annie's* scaffolding, the "Hark!"s and "Yi"s, and "Arf!"s (the latter appropriated by Popeye) all belong to the charade aspect of a classic-paced epic whose tone is doom-laden almost beyond articulation.

"*We* think it's a pretty good old world, don't we, Molly?" besought "Daddy" Warbucks in Al Capp's late-'40s parody, *Sweet Fannie Gooney*, addressing his appeal to a near-supine scrub-woman who obliged with "Lovely, Sir… lovely!" — which is a wonderful Capp image of dumb, impervious callousness, such as he produced with much virtuosity in his "liberal" days. It hardly, however, nicks the tempest-weathered tissue of the original; for Capp, as much as any of the others — as much as his brother, Elliot, who took Annie's narrative in hand (with Tex Blaisdell's images); as much as the deservedly forgotten concocter of the ghastly Saturday TV-styled version which called halt to Annie's Annie-tators, as much as Starr — was flummoxed by the enigma of Harold Gray's style. That style carried the very brand name of elusiveness; dealing, as it does, in and with, the unseen, i.e., the world in its immensity, which is always hovering at, issuing ominous rumbles or screams from, the strip's peripheries — those edges which are crucial in Gray's envisioning, the fringes of a world whose characters are constantly peering off the limits, the boundaries, toward vistas which are reflected in classic Gray shorthand: fingers that trembles at chins, fatuous grins, or empty eyes that become popping ciphers of curiosity, bemusement, or horror.

A typical view of Annie, which has furnished forth some of Gray's most eloquent, suspenseful sequences, has her spying out a town to which, in one of her periodic, acquiescent exiles from "Daddy," she has newly come. Gray achieves fugitive panoramic effect, a little mosaic of his own fascination with cities and their casual, piecemeal phenomena; from the repeated views of Annie in the foreground, lower right or left-hand corner, the panel's vertical border paralleled by the wall of the building against which she is standing, commenting, ruminating, popping out little squib-like judgments about the tiny figures that we see as from the back row of some airless movie house, as they walk or gesture in aimless-seeming abstraction. Or sometimes Annie walks along those implacable walls dabbed with shadow, of some brick building or stone country-fence beloved of Harold Gray, nibbling tidbits of insight from the near-impervious blankness of a city. It was the inanimate, or near-inanimate, aspects of a city, it seems to me, which fed Harold Gray's visual — not imagination, but appetite and gloomy élan.

The jaded, yet alert, chance-reckoning tone of Annie's monologues (some of the driest, most downright prose to be found even in those monologue-possessed days of the comic strip) make an impeccable, an indispensable, text to Gray's inchmeal pantomime. Throughout these reconnoiterings, Sandy is silent and without discernible personality, an avatar more tactful than even the Asp, as against the obsequious gallery-bids of other comic-strip mutts, like a gangster's bodyguard. Small cause for marvel, that, in the Fritz Lang-domesticated territory through which the two move. Sandy's presence emphasized the eerie counterpoint of chatter and silence that Gray establishes and repeatedly recalls during the monologues of Annie and others.

Sandy's reticence emphasized the staid, formal weight, as of an unceasing ceremony, that distinguished the movements of the characters, like the figures of a primitive frieze, and even the progression of events. The hypnotic rhythms of Harold Gray, which have often been haphazardly identified as "suspense," consist of just this, I think: the way he attenuates and *scales* action, grading it against a lowering, excruciatingly heavy sense of time. Gray's puritanical delight lies in those *longueurs*, those prospects of waiting and routine, which are as sweat-boxes to other comic-strip artists, panicky-solicitous of their fans. Annie and Sandy lost in the woods, or Annie sweating out in all senses a sojourn in the orphanage, her home-site, under the cronish reign of Miss Asthma, seem to excite a zest in Gray for seeking out prickles of suspicion, moody curiosity, or reflections on the mechanics of survival, which supply the genuine texture of these long-haul ordeals.

Even the moments of "relief" — that is, Gray's slapstick with its vengeful, demeaning overtones (Miss Asthma mistaking Annie for a ghost, tumbling downstairs into a laundry basket) — are peculiarly deadened, with no funny or terrific resonance. The foreground is pre-empted by a different sort of suspense, geared to the sheer blankness of expectancy from one day to the next, and spiritual attrition which Gray's rivals, from Hitchcock down, have shown no understanding of, or predilection for. At the same time he is able

to suggest a buried, impounded violence, violence as possibility, in his figures' girths, their litheness or inertness; and able to portray the imminence of such violence — a motion begun, a character barely curbing his or her savage response. He can discern and analyze casual, innocuous-seeming gestures or tableaux — like a small-town dude fingering his tie or Annie at her school books under the lamplight — with a dream-like insistence, a muted electricity, which suggest the paintings of Cornells Rutenberg.

Threading these various vignettes and glimpses is the feeling to which I think Gray's major power can be traced: that of his forging a double perspective — the formality of fifteenth-century "primitive" painting, or the classical stage, with the gruffness, wariness, soreness, and sometimes startled gentleness of the voice which never for any length of time releases us. Referring to primitive painting, I mean the peculiar intent upon lodging figures within their own space, conveying an authority to that space, which Gray achieved in his loving address to rooms, desks, tables, books, or dishes. Such space and the composition which it seems to dictate holds priority over the action in Gray's world, rather than the reverse (the foregrounding and amplifying of action) to which comic strip after comic strip, from *The Katzenjammer Kids* to *Kerry Drake*, have accustomed us; and commonly, tended to inundate the factuality of action in delectable cataracts of color and design. Gray is as free of these and other erotic shenanigans, and felicities — plot invention, richness of detail — as any such artist I can remember.

The surfaces of his stories are hard-stitched, of a didactic intensity, which has as its background pessimism of the deepest sort. The "storytelling" aptitude for which I have heard Gray, with cheerful inanity, praised again and again is the valid product of this quality, and forms our awareness of a text — Annie's words, the juiceless, deliberate words of all — which actually holds together a "plot" of minimum invention and variety of movement. Here, the time-killing *longueurs* and muttered running commentaries, the compulsive chewing-over of, say, Sunday's revelation or catastrophe on Monday (Tuesday anticipating Wednesday; Wednesday resuming, etc.) do their moony parts toward furthering Gray's brooding rhythms, and also keep to the fore his favorite narrative element — the chorus of gossips, gulls, and gawkers. The general impression of a Gray episode is not an exciting or beguiling accretion of plot complications, but rather his own hammering, into the beaten bronze of a fable, a little coin-patter of intrigues, scandal, retribution; all giving the impression of resonance, of emotional plenty, through those gravid shapes, and those mulling, obsessive soliloquies.

But the most insidious single effect of Harold Gray's art is the impression of staid-looking surface which may, at any time, be peeled or torn or simply curl away, like those decals, then called "transfer pictures," which Ovaltine, sponsors of the *Little Orphan Annie* radio show, issued at one time. This is another contribution of the gossips, with their Monday morning hash: They keep the pot boiling, and at the same time, present a satiric counterpoint/contrast to the wold's tribunal, with which Harold Gray identifies his readers implicitly — The Voice of the People any *Daily News* editorial page will attest. That tribunal is like a constant murmur, which we hear ventriloquially through this character and that. A murmur to which the characters, even when alone, seem impelled to respond, in some of the leanest yet — I'm tempted to say "musically" — expressive monologues in comic strips: hectic arias of explanation, self-exculpation, prophecy, apprehension; almost totally devoid of the wise-cracking plumage, which the *Gumps*, say, could always assure. In that strip, the rhetorical preenings of Andy Min, Bim and Tilda represented a kind of wealth, a triumphant preemption of style as honor, even amid lower middle-class doldrums. Likewise the slingshot-paced ripostes of *Ella Cinders*: Even the browbeating (everybody else's brow, unlike *Annie's* personae) stepmother was not begrudged — "You're so lazy," she barks at Ella at one point, "You remind me of the man who invented the Model T Ford so he wouldn't have to empty out his pockets."

Each character of Gray's is seen within a monkish cubicle of his or her own loneliness, a stark presence underscored by the storm cloud cross-hatching, the packed speech balloons which hang like joyless blimps above them: the awareness of events proceeding *through* them, of their bleak histories exerting a tensile insistence of their own, which you never felt when Min and Andy were jumpily hustling their speeches along, hoping the reader could hold out for another panel or so. Everybody's got his budget, folks. Gray's panels are never lethargic, never simply dawdling. There is a constant crackle in the air around them, as a short-wave speaker about to broadcast long awaited, perhaps long-dreaded news from the front. There is here depicted, as everywhere else with Harold Gray, an awareness that what many eschew as boredom is positive calcium in the tissue of life itself.

This has to do with Gray's belief that the best discoveries we can expect are piecemeal — never expect the wall to split asunder, as far as our fellow humans are concerned. I can recall, prior to the settling in of Maw Green, a top-strip entitled the *Private Life of...* (a shoe, a flower, a ghost): the "private life" of which consisted not of Hans Christian Andersen rhapsodies by any means, but the plain record of what one might expect to befall any of these objects, or entities. The sense of history being immured within a retaining wall of evidence, and beyond that, blankness, is what enfevers Gray in the "private moments" of his own characters. These are moments of release — not at all for the imagination, but for the watchful eye.

The bare carpentry of the "little orphan" fable was sufficient armature, it seems, for the dry fatalism, the dour wariness, which really preoccupied Harold Gray. It also kept Annie, that smart little stepper, on a constant pavement-strip of cold journalism quite separate from the professed sentimentalities of her sufferings in the orphanage (from Miss Asthma, or derisive little peers like Monk), her snubbing and frigid persecution by Mrs. Warbucks, and her two sinister-clownish protégés — porcupine-haired Selby Addlebert Piffleberry, whose acronymic affords Gray and Annie many a day's vengeful laugh; and the marionette-like Count De Tour, with his physical resemblance to a defrocked Jack-in-the-Pulpit plant, tubular duck trousers and painted-looking hair and monocle. But most of such narrative lumber, and the smarmier aspects of Annie's and "Daddy's" (so she always called him; those inverted commas remained to the last) affinity were briskly and, to all evidence, willingly, put aside as soon as possible in favor of Gray's medley of journalistic watchfulness, knowingness, and morose foreknowledge.

The conventions Gray was compelled to sustain, like the small-town nostalgia, were treated with the most vinegary regard via depictions of termite-cabals: righteous biddies, male and female, or fledgling psychopaths like "Pig Eye" Mack: Sinclair Lewis challenged on his own turf. The Silos (who, by the way, became regulars on the radio-show, which insistently and with some commercial heart-flutters, perhaps, anchored Annie to Simmons Corners) never appeared much after their initial introduction; indeed, most of Annie's acquaintances, surrogate parents and beneficiaries seem tacitly to accept, on her departure, that they will seldom, if ever, see her again. They become readily inured to their loss.

Annie's true vocation is that of the child spy, her picaresque passage one of life-long, itinerant espionage; that of, for sure, spying out at the adult world. In this pursuit, she — as Harold Gray's agent — confirmed and articulated an image of this world, an "adult world" which even her adult reader might deem inaccessible. It seemed aloof, authoritative, massively dark, imbued with sinister eminence and touched with that spirit of Eld which Edgar Allan Poe, projecting himself in the "real world," discovered in the mysterious crew and captain of "Ms. Found in a Bottle." Annie's occupation is to squint out and pry open — not with the method of a journalist or private eye but with the random sniffling and peeping of an outsider — the occasional quartz-glints of this intrigue, or that secret, or some guarded vulnerable passion which sometimes traced the flinty faces of these adult structures. Most of all her spying reveals these to be exactly as they seem: the pantomime, the glimpsed group scenes, such as images of Big Business clustered around what appears to be the identical Spanish oak desk with identical Renaissance inlay, before the identical French windows, on every occasion; a repetition which yet, like the images of a dream, or the tableaux scenes in D.W. Griffith's historical films, is pitched to an absolute evocation. In other words, adults as stage-managed by a child, who sees *all* ages past the corridor of the immediate next few years as a common lunar landscape. Gray's narrative rhythms so prevail through his depictions of these wielders and connivers that one hardly notices the paucity of detail; or, more accurately, Gray's lack of interest in, and cursory handling of, such detail. The same applies to his depictions of menial labor, of which he is professedly enamored. Although you can sense that he knows, say, something of driving a truck, or working in a general store, or peddling papers, the details themselves take on no inventive life. It's the routine, and the endurance it exacts, and the space left for Annie's watchfulness, that engages him most. (Was ever an artist more distinguished by those things in which he is not interested?) The world of rich observation seems to recede under Gray's touch as though the visual was being slowly, subtly absorbed by the aural.

Was there ever a comic-strip artist who exhibited so little pleasure in — and even, granting Harold Gray's faith (whatever it may have been) its full allowance of heterodoxy — so little *faith* in the drawing act as such, at least as conveyor of visual data, as a transmitter of visual intelligence? When Annie, on short commons in the forest, encounters Sandy returning from some private dinner trove, she exclaims: "You not only look different — you are different! You're as tight as a little drum!" I am here, however, to attest that not only does Sandy not look a particle different from his usual self; I doubt seriously that the Continental Op, elbow-to-elbow with Sherlock Holmes, could discern any difference; and I don't believe any, at least in *visual terms*, was intended. It is not merely a question of Gray's drawing style being unable to accommodate certain facts, as is true of many realistically oriented styles. It seems a matter of Gray's drawing being oriented to the exclusion of, or the most budgety skimping on, most of the sensuous detail which is often the comic-strip author's essential syntax. I feel, looking at a *Little Orphan Annie* strip, that the panels are riddled with secret pinholes, not readily accessible to my eyes, through which the crucial facts of each episode might be divined, and not too clearly, at that. I also experience the slightly chilling sensation of Gray's voice declaring: "These particulars are not so important: time will wash them out anyway. Why not take time's side?" I can remember a New Year's 1937 Sunday page in which Annie describes human relationship as resembling "A kind of river." The characters and scenes of *Little Orphan Annie*, graphic and resonating though they are, seem, at the same time, constantly on the point of submerging in a Mississippi of words, of text. And, as the strip proceeds into the '40s, '50s, and '60s — and the importunities of a still more brutal journalism than that of the '30s — the supporting personages seem half-faded into journalistic prose (like the hapless walk-on, "that nice Mr. Sam Smith," stomped to death by teenage thugs) upon their initial appearance.

In this I find Gray the most credible witness I know, or can easily imagine, against the critical hashish-dream which declares the comic strip to be a "purely visual medium," a phrase which makes as little sense when applied to film, including the silent ones, the best of which made unrestrained and consistently intelligent use of text. Gray's images are inseparable from his text; they at once enact and counterpoint his text, as they are committed, in league with his text, to the theme of history, including the most personal, writing itself day by day, for the eyes of posterity, and the judgment of the world. His cautious, skimpish, austere art reminds one of Jean-Marie Straub's and Danielle Huillet's fine films; in which, as in *The Chronicle of Anna Magdalena Bach*, the image and text work virtually as one, each supporting and abiding by the other. In both these ashen artists, the text is like an immense scroll, which is ideally regarded as unwinding itself through eternity. Like Straub, time after time, Gray, especially in the later Annie episodes, becomes enamored of images repeated — or, a single image prolonged — in panel after panel, in a way which engraves the event upon the attention of the reader. A daily strip will feature Annie, in bed, overhearing conversation among five little children about their bickering parents. Or, on a Sunday page, shortly before Gray's death in the late '60s, he features the back of Annie's head as she listens to two predatory disaster engineers named Tar and Knuks quarreling, framed in the window facing her. Even in 1936, when Annie is selling flowers on the East Side with a "Lady from Another Day" named Ginger, Gray achieves one of his treasured effects, the stream of a social panorama via few figures, and the commentary — philosophy-salted as usual — of Ginger and Annie, a vest-pocket transcription of the kind of syndicated column which ballooned the fame of Runyon and Winchell, with the last-panel sign-off line: "Buy a flower, Mister?"

The little-girl body which Annie trotted though these various episodes was, of course, a mere dolly-truck for a spirit which once belonged to Odysseus, or Melmoth the Wanderer. A not-too-remote cousin of Maisie in Henry James's *What Maisie Knew*, Annie, however, brought not a particle of a child's vulnerability to her nosing into the crannies of adulthood. When she would bewail the "death" of "Daddy" Warbucks in one of his many periodic liquidations (after which, like the durable corporation he was, he'd reorganize himself) Annie's grief, though sincere, was also unquestionably ritualistic. (Gray tried to vary this in the early '40s in one of Annie's last bids for "little girldom" by dispatching her into a catatonic trance, whereupon she was mothered back to her standard of sanity by a frigid old spinster, who was earlier impervious to Annie's worldview. I persist in thinking: so unconvincingly was this collapse of Annie's — on the basis of her previous history — that the whole thing was a brilliant, extemporaneous set-up designed to prevail over the aged stalactite with shock therapy while gaining some repose during which she, Annie, could reorient her plans for the future.)

The most instructive comparison/contrast awaits the interested reader between the far-reaching plateau of age (not precocity) on which Annie builds her campfire, and Skeezix's dry, graceful acquisition of age, done as a low-keyed tone-poem, in Frank King's *Gasoline Alley*; during which all of Skeezix's gaucheries, escapades, and indecision are drenched in a style represented by an unerring grace of perspective that bespeaks King's loving, watchful detachment; usually the equivalent of a few yards away from his subject. The style of Harold Gray was more akin in *its* detachment, and in Gray's hungry embrace of formula, to some long-hallowed classical rite. To have Annie "grow up" as did Skeezix would have been inane to the verge of obscenity. Annie was as old as ever she need be — she and the hero of *The Tin Drum* might have exchanged pointers — or did they? — within two years after her appearance, in 1924, in the tow of Mrs. Warbucks. Gray knew what he was doing when he burned down — in a brilliant, scarily drawn Sunday page November 18, 1928 — Miss Asthma's orphan asylum, of Annie's infancy, and all records of her parentage. She was frozen in time as a priestess, a perennial caretaker of the musing, disenchanted voice which held the world as eternally, basically static — a view not so much pessimistic (although certainly that) as wary, assessing, not always ungentle.

I know of no other comic strip that is so governed by such a view, and mood, and consistency of will enacting both over and over. It's the only one I am aware of which can be described as "philosophical" without reference to the nature or quality of the philosophy; for, whereas a strip like *The Gumps* enlisted, at times, an ad hoc philosophizing, dishing out views and aphorisms from its steam-table, *Little Orphan Annie* offered a perspective of the world, and an attempt to assemble and summarize one's experience of that world which is embodied in the very drawing; especially in Harold Gray's proclivity for, espousal of, structure. As in primitive painting and the classical work that issued form it, the laws of space and distance and balance are presences in themselves. The furniture, whatever its paucity of sensuous allure, assumes in its own glowering, stolid bulk, like the settings of Fritz Lang in their Expressionist menace, the dimension of a character. One is dealing with a strip in which the true protagonist is the Law: not only the "law and order" which is regularly and derisively cited by his liberal critics (and which, according to any careful reading, Gray himself regards with a very doubtful eye) but the laws of structure and space, which dictate, say, the usual pedestrian distancing (always in equivalent of a "Medium CS" on camera) and centering of actions, the "normal-eye view" of figures. When Gray, on very rare occasion, adopts an "angle shot," an interpretive perspective, it's invariably a view from above (Old Jake standing outside his grocery store on the East Side); which accords with Gray's frosty affection for buildings, for stone surfaces, and the cities which house them.

He never within my memory employed the opposite, a fact brought home to me by it use in his successor's work, in depicting skyscrapers, for example. Gray's esteem (narrow-eyed) for power is no such yokel's veneration. He is short on hope, though surely not without faith, as far as worldy power is concerned. Yet the bulk of whatever affection he can yield is for the cities as maps, or as tapestries, of those chip-like portraits and vignettes, which are his basic vocabulary as a comic-strip author. The prospect of "private lives" appearing and reappearing out of their various warrens and the thought of their respective routines being shredded and strained to be more connecting-wires, animated both his admiration and — hard upon that — his thin but whip-supple inventive resources.

Annie is heard, or seen, time and again, voting her preference for cities because "Folks leave you alone"; and, on the other hand, skirting the advance of "snoops," benevolent or not, in small towns. (I suspect that Gray objected to small-town prying, first, because it was likely to succeed; and second, beyond even his obvious reverence for privacy — among his few unqualified venerations — he was aware that such success was futility itself. In his view, there is no "inner life" which the world will not, somehow, or other, discover and invade. It meant that there are no irreducible secrets, no personal holy-of-holies, which are not, in some way or other, on constant display; and, by his estimate of their general intelligence level, well beyond the perception of gossips.) Gray's 1931 adventure, which transported Annie and "Daddy" head-on into the Depression, has a range and unpredictability of incident which is not locked into the Nautilus chamber of Gray's accustomed plot architecture; a redolence of both suspense and poignancy (both translated into Gray's familiar terms discussed above, only ingrained with more specific topical reference than usual); and a stream of cranky, picturesque figures —

the original Maw Green, with her shrewd, stoic monkey face, before Gray gave her the bottom-of-the-page Irish Wit and Wisdom concession in 1931; J. J. Shark, the financial bulldozer (Gray's declaration that, yes, there are *evil* capitalists, and, more of a surprise, perhaps, to desultory, or Gray-hunting, readers); Old Jake, the straw-hatted and vested Jewish merchant, arms folded as he stands beneath his awning; best of all, perhaps, Flophouse Bill, "Daddy's" dwarfish guardian angel after he is blinded on the first day of his truck-driving job. Bill's stumpy figure scores a repeated, gritty impact, which, like his fellow neo-Dickensians, is enriched by its action upon, and benefit from, the concrete-tenement street setting in which he is continually seen. "Daddy" himself is accorded one of the last humanly vulnerable appearances in which we will see him: destitute, betrayed by his fellow free-enterprisers led by Tom Bullion and J.J. Shark; slouched at the kitchen table of the flat he and Annie are sharing, worrying about his age. Here, the delicacy and gravid economy of Gray's drawing can give untoward poignancy to the forward droop of "Daddy's" bald head, and the way his arm lies upon the table, speaking his near-disintegration as a man in a single panel. The plainness of the room is oppressive; only in *The Bungle Family* have tables and chairs looked so unyielding — all combining to reduce the charade-like sense of Gray's manipulating on outsized "typical" situations, like those depicted in 1930s post-office murals.

On the other hand, the city scene itself seems to release, to lend a fermenting excitement to, Gray's compositions, which here feature a sense of sheerly gratuitous existence, at least as far as theatrical mechanics are concerned: the scene of "Daddy's" truck kissing an "El" upright, as he swerves to avoid a Breughel-like kid stubbily chasing a ball, while peddlers and passers-by look on, move gingerly toward the arena of action. The life in such a panel seems to cluster and rally, rather than straggle toward the scene's peripheries, as in many of Gray's depictions.

Such an episode, which features one of Gray's most forceful and vivacious dramatizations, also demonstrates his adherence to classical, melodramatic types and story-lines, with a different application — lean and dogged, charged with his sense of, in Paul Goodman's naïve-sounding but hard-to-match phrase, "How it is with him." Other artists would either opt for burlesque (Hershfield,

Kahles, etc.) or, as would Chester Gould, translate the clichés — those of situation, at least — into one's own visual vocabulary of *things*: tools, machines, facilities, contraptions. For Gray, I suspect, clichés had a value and authority of their own, and he redeemed them with the *visual* authority, which he brought to bear upon them. By that rearrangement of priorities with which the best painters and poets are familiar, he gave preferential place to *outlines*, which, in panel after panel, the theme of people's presence and ongoing histories are graven into their immediate and projected situation. This action of etching, of engraving, is exactly what cliché, in Gray's usage, performs. His style performs, not the conjuration of new stories, but the translation, and re-establishment, of old ones — an act of engineering which all-but-uniquely defines comic-strip style.

There emanates from Gray's most characteristic work, as a result, a curious sort of spellbinding which actually gains force from the two-dimensionality of its terms, as presented with Gray's reticent intensity: the feeling, as with films of King Vidor, Ince, or Griffith, that we are rediscovering the actuality, in terms of singular immediacy, of these stock situations, which are being inscribed, as it were, before our eyes. Every gesture to the smallest — and Gray has conjugated a small vocabulary of tight, minuscule, emblematic actions: raised finger, flat-handed dismissal, a fist descending upon, rather than merely pounding, a desk — carries a sort of epic weight. The electricity extends to the simplest outlines, as well — the frizzes and elf-locks of Annie's hair, rising in terror or dismay; the *kris*-edge line which underscores key words.

The deployment of clichés also pertains, I think, to a dexterity that Gray, self-confessedly not overly sentimental, offers in "obligatory" sentimental moments, with no obvious curveballs — calendar excerpts like Thanksgiving dinner, Christmas, and New Years, etc. What he communicates in these milestone events (milestones beneath which better artists have often been discovered pulverized, with Cherry Heering seeping from their veins) is, I feel, a purification of the sentiment that comes from respect; which forms a kind of cement kiln for sentiment, for the ceremony itself, and for the hand-over-hand rope which all such observances provide for lives in which daily history more often than not seems an unending, and bottomless, crevasse. The seasonal strips in which these rituals occur seem, somehow, more *earned* than many others, by virtue of the way Gray's stories, soap opera or dime-dreadful plots notwithstanding, manage to convey the sheer pressure and abrasive power of such aforementioned histories. He sees the sentiments attending them not as commodities to be delivered, but as gentle gods, requiring only proper, courteous genuflection. And we may never forget that, here as thoughout most of his work, the word "obligatory" is Harold Gray's nearest synonym for "devout."

But in terms of any generous sentimental scale, of any imaginative nurturing by such sentiment, Gray offers only a series of thin, expertly placed, recorder-notes. In that weird armature of a relationship with Annie, "Daddy" Warbucks is permitted most of his human confusions, lapses, and resignations between 1924 and 1932; thereafter, he is often exposed to danger and proves most convincingly vulnerable to it; but never again does the strip reflect any considerable curiosity on Gray's part about "Daddy's" susceptibilities, the traceries of his sentimental self. Married to a hard-thrusting parvenue who "adopted" Annie as an obligation to a Lady Bountiful stature, "Daddy," with a bullet-shaped head (in obvious salutation of his name's still-fresh associations) also distinctly signaled our recollections of Jiggs, with his snub-nose, circlet eyes, and trap-mouth. On the death of Mrs. Warbucks (preceded by repentance; a rare dispensation from Gray) "Daddy" lets himself be towed off his usual astute course by a gold-digging fiancée named, if you please, Trixie Tinkle, who tries to dry-dock Annie with a cleaver-jawed harridan named Miss Treat, who commands a reformatory. For Gray, however, most such permutations of "Daddy's" human weakness are exhausted by the '30s mid-point; after which even the association with Annie becomes increasingly, and to the obvious relief of both, a partnership. Their dialogues (Annie giving out with: "Gee, 'Daddy,' y' don't mean the law really can…") are increasingly socratic, increasingly serviceable to Gray's somewhat droning, somewhat grating, journalistic voice.

It seems to me that attempting to pose extrapolations at any length on the premise of a comic-strip author's "philosophy" likely leads one into the recurrent dilemma of Yosemite Sam in the Bugs Bunny cartoons, who discovers himself treading air, about a yard past the cliff-edge. I feel nostalgia for a parachute right now: but, grabbing for the nearest mountain goat's nose, I would add hastily that, to me, the general feeling conveyed by *Little Orphan Annie* is of a world over which Harold Gray can imagine only the most limited control, by himself, or anyone else. An island world, sure enough fringed by thunderous breakers, with sea-monsters repeatedly observed beyond the five-mile limit. The tote-bag of driftwood attitudes which he and his Annie, and "Daddy," have shored up against the evil weathers is remote from any such hermetic fortress of reaction as he has been taxed for maintaining. The attitude which can be inferred from a comic-strip is the operative factor, or, none at all; and Gray's attitude, to any one-eyed reader using that single eye with minimal discretion, comprises the most profound (and very far from smug) distrust of even the latitude of the law — not that of the legislature alone, but that of the cosmos encompassing — which is the major stanchion of his faith. This law is embodied, for Harold Gray, in the ubiquitous line that boxes spatial relationships, limits perspective, and imbues every action, large and small, with its peculiar, dreamlike, and awful finality. But the function of that line and the law that it depicts, is of a retaining wall, or as the leanest sinew of faith imaginable. It is not anything that brings assurance and hopeful concoctions to his imagination. It represents the minimally reasonable means by which we are to go on, if we are to go on at all.

All such can return with undiminished formidable effect in alternate episodes: the Devil-as-fool is the Devil nonetheless. For, while Gray's deeply anti-Manichean soul cannot tolerate a presentation of absolute, undiscountenanced evil, and would show all personas as subject to the coteries of experience, his didacticism holds that evil inheres in evil *attitudes*, which amount to folly, begetting fools and villains both: which one, at which moment, depending on the red-black eventualities of life. From the Waring blender of his theatrical zest, these factors emerge as a dexterously plied vaudeville, strengthened by something additional: the novelist's avidity for scouting out as many aspects of persons and events as possible. Thus, if the renegade banker, Mr. Mack (himself a resident of the Scots community of Bluebell, but suspiciously non-Caledonian in his slicked-back hair and spectacles and van dyke beard), engages lawyers named Stein and Gold for his defense as a bank robber, Gray will present us, at loving length, with old Jake, the benign Jewish shopkeeper, and Uncle Al, the true-blue pawnbroker. In 1935, a sequence about an ethics-flouting cobbler named George Chiselopolis is intercut with the Flag Day beatification of another immigrant, named Tony (whom I initially mistook for Curious George). In these instances, as in those cited above, the term "obligatory" is transmuted (as it was not when Dickens confected the Good Jew, Raiah, as palliative for Jewish protesters of Fagin) by Gray's own instinct for panorama and the sensation of a mural-like diversity, which yet adheres to basic archetypes, or stereotypes; and his inclination to keep the reader off-balance as far as his, Gray's, predilections are concerned.

The actuality of the tabloid universe is a Great Wall of China to *Little Orphan Annie*, casting its immense shadow in due course, after the trial years of the mid-'20s. The extraordinary moral/political/cultural avalanche of the '40s unloaded upon most popular artist in this country an unprecedented imagery. It was also an affront to many long-forged armors of the popular imagination, and hastened insensate bureaucratic hardness. All this was as nothing to Harold Gray save opportunity for enlarged latitude and increased encouragement of candor — for all such offered mere corroboration of views which had been in his strip for a very, very long time. The hideous world that Annie and "Daddy" always knew was so self-evident that Gray and Annie could not mask their benign disbelief, not untainted by amiable scorn, at those good and worthy people (usually given names like Fumble or Fuddle), who failed to reject its injunctions. Such a world merely assumed its sovereignty, struck its colors, more openly. An account from *Little Orphan Annie's* highlights of the '40s alone reads like an endlessly unrolling scroll of atrocities; many of them, to be sure, directed against the heavies. A conniving banker literally springs himself out of jail, over the wall, only to be impaled on a Bengalese tiger trap fashioned by Punjab. In a grinding succession of all-black panels, a detail of Soviet agents, infiltrating "Daddy" Warbucks's fortress, are trapped by the automatic lock on his vault and slowly suffocate. On still another Sunday page, a body of journalists is ushered by the doting, unwitting mother of a small-town-bred-psychopath into his "private zoo" (where he has been conducting amateur vivisection) and are shown staggering out, retching, against a background of bile green.

Gray's imagery of violence, his rhetorical economy of violence, demonstrate, throughout his career, a collaboration of mordant poetry, and an apprehension of "taste" that surely dwelt bone-deep in his relation to his wok. It had to do with a respect for actuality itself, and for the distances that one's regard for actuality (occasionally known as "inhibitions") impose and a hard, stringy humility, never entirely lacking in him at his sententious worst, regarding what is sheerly mysterious and uncontrollable, let alone unthinkable, in this world. Beside the factual horrors of Gray's universe, the productions of the comic-book coterie seem (more than ever, that is) the work of slickly misanthropic, flashy, essentially craven undergraduates. How strange to realize that he almost comes abreast in this — his visual recognition of violence as a hole in the world, as a negative effect, the terrible removal of human presence, no matter how obnoxious — with those anti-violence advocates whom he devoutly despised.

Like Rudyard Kipling, Gray saw the only refuge within the generally intolerable turbulence of this life, as an island of the elite: those who had access to the inner darkness of the universe, and, at the same time, were empowered to overskip the barriers of man-made law. One such clique is that of the outlaw elite, the managers who stand somewhere apart from the law, and who are blessed, not by their outlawry, but the grace with which their admiration and affection for Annie carries to them. They are not above the Law — which must after all safeguard our sanity, since much else it cannot do — but, rather within an enchanted circle. Racketeers like Nick Gatt, political bosses like Big August; Tom Take, the neighborly kleptomaniac of Cosmic City, with his smiling Mercury profile; Shanghai Peg, flinty-benign approximation of Long John Silver; and, incipiently of course, "Daddy" Warbucks, munitions manufacturer and lone wolf of finance. They, with "Daddy" at their center, are the curators of our fantasies, our hopes of power and justice and certainty beyond the Law's Versailles-maze of non-certainties, which, today, many yearn for if only in our lost power to envision them. Such imagining, like Gray's sentimental interludes, are barricaded by the bleakness of his world-view, of which he has been the insistent mason all throughout Annie's career.

As a dancing Platonic shade of our responses to actuality and the central emblem of such, possibly Gray's closest approach to sheer elation is the white-whiskered Mr. Am: a neighbor of "Daddy" Warbucks, introduced in 1935, who, "Daddy" confided to Annie, was reputed to have lived "thousands of years"; who chucklingly acknowledged, in a most spectacular courtroom interview, that he had sold sword and shield to Alexander the Great, and been *intime* with Aristotle, Plato, and Socrates, "the wise-cracking syndicated columnists of their day." Mr. Am's very special guest appearance on earth could only have been sustained for its short duration by the near-manic (beneath its midwestern poker-pan) mixture of gravity and audacity which was Harold Gray's. So, too, his sense of drawing as a ritual of invocation and conjuration: like all such mystical acts, sufficient unto itself for the adhesive qualities it achieves, from this day to the next; of whatever intelligibility we can salvage from life. In the drawings discussed above, as in all his work, Harold Gray says in effect: "What would you have of me, who must sweat out the same world as you? To permit myself, and you, the false hope of some vision in which the law of this world is loving partner with justice, would be more than a false hope; it would blaspheme against the actuality of my work, which is the imprint of God's handiwork, from pillar to cornice. I can, however, offer you, and myself, a little of that magic which builds a small provisional bridge, a formula which offers a fresh look at how-things-are, such as has always consoled, in the world, the poor in spirit."

For all the contrary reasons which come trouping daily before me, I must nurse my regret that they, the domesticators and elegiasts, could not have let *Little Orphan Annie* withdraw, along with her creator, into her taciturn, eccentric legend. For he died after setting forth the ultimate homecoming, Annie's entry into her particular Promised Land: an antebellum-style Southern mansion, presided over by a naïve, serene grandmotherly mistress, discreetly and peripherally menaced by two white-trash scoundrels named Tar (a chiseling lawyer) and Knuks (superintendent of a prison farm, slightly recast from the Arkansas death-camp of then-recent headlines). The mansion was staffed with liveried servants, tinted the most discreet of pinks for the Sunday page, who deferred to "Miz' Annie" at every point. What a closing act for the opera which Bertolt Brecht and Kurt Weill never made.

LITTLE ORPHAN ANNIE — The Slender Thread of Life

LITTLE ORPHAN ANNIE — Coming Back—to Wha

LITTLE ORPHAN ANNIE—"Sittin' On Top O' The World" — By Harold Gray

LITTLE ORPHAN ANNIE — Annie Stops the Sh

LITTLE ORPHAN ANNIE: *The "Croaker"*

LITTLE ORPHAN ANNIE — Half Victory

LITTLE ORPHAN ANNIE: *The Cold Facts*

LITTLE ORPHAN ANNIE—A Few Rays Of Sunshine — By Harold Gray

LITTLE ORPHAN ANNIE—We Meet Again

By Harold Gray

LITTLE ORPHAN ANNIE—A Mystery

By Harold

LITTLE ORPHAN ANNIE

A Pleasant Thought

LITTLE ORPHA NANNIE—When A Cloud Obscures The Sun

By Harold Gr

LITTLE ORPHAN ANNIE

LITTLE ORPHAN ANNIE One Man Who Won't Give Up

LITTLE ORPHAN ANNIE A New and Bigger Game

LITTLE ORPHAN ANNIE—The Problem By Harold Gray

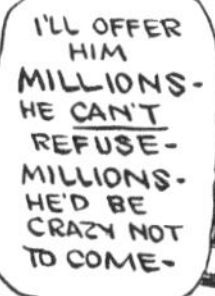

LITTLE ORPHAN ANNIE **Oliver Has an Idea**

LITTLE ORPHAN ANNIE: Au Revoir

LITTLE ORPHAN ANNIE **"There's Always a Way to Forget"**

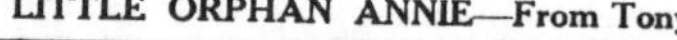

LITTLE ORPHAN ANNIE—From Tony **By Harold Gray**

LITTLE ORPHAN ANNIE—Aw, Leapin' Lizards

By Harold Gray

LITTLE ORPHAN ANNIE

'Aw, Leapin' Liza

LITTLE ORPHAN ANNIE—Irresistible Sandy

By Harold Gray

LITTLE ORPHAN ANNIE

Watching and Waiting

I GOTTA HUNCH DADDY'LL SHOW UP SOON- HIS CAR'LL COME DOWN THAT ROAD, MOST LIKELY- HE MIGHT COME THE OTHER WAY THOUGH- BETTER GO LOOK OUT THE FRONT DOOR ONCE-

LITTLE ORPHAN ANNIE — Personally Conducted

LITTLE ORPHAN ANNIE: Nerves

LITTLE ORPHAN ANNIE — The Examination

LITTLE ORPHAN ANNIE — The Long Chance

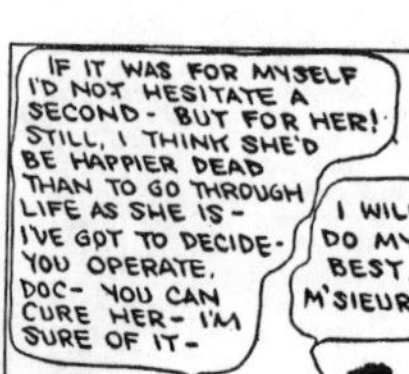

LITTLE ORPHAN ANNIE — Right or Wrong?

LITTLE ORPHAN ANNIE Encouraging The Doc

By Harold Gray

LITTLE ORPHAN ANNIE—Minutes That Seem Hours

By Harold Gray

LITTLE ORPHAN ANNIE —Shadows

By Harold Gray

LITTLE ORPHAN ANNIE

LITTLE ORPHAN ANNIE: The Crisis

LITTLE ORPHAN ANNIE—The Turning Point

By Harold Gray

LITTLE ORPHAN ANNIE

Monday Tells the Sto

LITTLE ORPHAN ANNIE—The Last Hope Gone

By Harold Gray

LITTLE ORPHAN ANNIE

The Bitterness of Sorr

LITTLE ORPHAN ANNIE

Confiding in San

LITTLE ORPHAN ANNIE

Some Time, Perhaps

LITTLE ORPHAN ANNIE

Will Annie's "Tomorrow" Ever Come?

LITTLE ORPHAN ANNIE

For "Daddy'

LITTLE ORPHAN ANNIE—"There's A Great Day Coming"

By Harold Gray

LITTLE ORPHAN ANNIE—On The Way

By Harold Gray

LITTLE ORPHAN ANNIE

Company

LITTLE ORPHAN ANNIE

A Safe and Sane Thanksgiving

FOOTSORE AUDACITY

B. KLIBAN

Amidst a garage sale, or Bartholomew Fair, of violent novelty and contrived outrage, it is the rediscovery of bedrock actuality that deeply involves, shocks, persuades. So among the works of his numerous contemporaries, and many of his own, certain flinty, morosely resigned, and scabrously funny drawings and cartoons of B. Kliban emerge — lending a distinctive, ashen thread to the caravan of his five increasingly popular collections: *cat*, *Never Eat Anything Bigger than Your Head and Other Drawings*, *Whack Your Porcupine*, *Tiny Footprints*, and most recently, *Playboy's Kliban*. In this latter collection, featuring a number of full-page color drawings, two discoveries interested me: first, how very many Kliban cartoons I had viewed, never identifying them with the work of his preceding books; and second, how, in fact, both the addition of color and the intervention of *Playboy's* chic-raunchy, whimsically perverse manner converted the stiff, disconsolate gawkiness of Kliban's most memorable drawings into the cuddly clumsiness of children's — or for that matter, adults', viz. *Playboy's* recurrent ads — inflatable dolls. The saddled and bridled blonde nude, exclaiming to her nude, mustached and bespectacled buckaroo, "How come you never take me anywhere?" involves a Kliban *motif* of the books — role-changing among persons, animals, machines — but the nursery-exotic hues, the urbane line, the wax-smooth contours, make the resemblance seem almost as anachronistic as the cigar-flourishing Martin Luther, in the drawing "Martin Luther Declines Statehood" (*Never Eat Anything Bigger*, etc.).

I am referring to style here as a sense of location and of terrain: the landscape which subsumes the artist's total sense of that concreteness which, indispensably, underlies, and buttresses and affronts his imagination. In Kliban's work, especially, that work which declares him an original comic artist, this sense of landscape, a city landscape, rubble-strewn and pothole-ridden, turd-bedecked and litter-bangled, is an indispensable sort of subversion to the facility which we see in the *Playboy* collection, and in rather too much of the additional work. Like the work of Philip Guston, to whom he bears an unobvious, yet, I believe, deep kinship, Kliban's work pays a shrugging, grim-lipped sort of tribute to the persistence of the *literal*, to the irreducibleness of things, of presences both natural and man-made, which refuse to be any other than themselves; and to the ridiculous, yet apparently inescapable, labor involved for the human imagination in trying to make of them anything else. There is an awful, hilarious mixture of deference and resignation in those drawings which depict, for example, a Dreiserian trio: a jacket-draped, crop-headed hulk of a man; with the eyeless spectacles and beak-nosed countenance acquired by Kliban from Steinberg and the Parisian zanies, Siné and Chaval; flanked by a shirt-wasted, bee-hive-coifed Easter Island replica, and a blob-faced, sausage-curled barmaid, or retired Madam, under the caption: "The Victim's Family." For once, the wavering we feel between laughter and something else, the ambiguity, is not stoked by the evasion of what we know to be terrible, through a cowardly mechanism of "camp" disdain; but rather though Kliban's frontal address to the *content's* ambiguity; and especially the fearsome absurdity involved in the very premise of doing an illustration — whether a drawing, or a news photograph — from so mysterious a content of grief, pain, and what appears to be a lifelong habit of stoicism or inertia, which now serves its purpose; all forced into the compounded indignity of iconography, which is emphasized by the dead-white space surrounding and highlighting the trio and, here as throughout his best work, the suture-like, gracelessly deliberative line in which Kliban has inscribed them. Their stodgy ugliness does not deflect or modify by a particle the impact of their true awfulness, the *secrecy* of their affliction; focused by our realization that the incremental ugliness of a corporate lifetime has been compounded and charged and fixed by the cruel formalism of the illustrator's or photographer's art. The "something else" to which I have referred above turns out to be, in fact, the very threshold of awe: the source of that authentic grotesquerie of which Kliban is among the few American masters, and the hinge upon which his most formidably edged satire revolves (as distinguished from the lesser editorial cartoon-like hackings, like that of the George Grosz-like decadently shriveled "Industrialist" feasting on a platter of human hands).

Like Guston — like a host of American artists from the past few decades — Kliban hones his comedy, and his style, against the stonewall of a content which seems impervious to both. Style, forsooth! Kliban's is one of the most nearly invisible styles among present-day American cartoonists; and this, despite the eclectic flickerings throughout his work of various other artists: Siné's preoccupation with cats, clergy, and cloaca (as well as his frequent sportive cruelty with all of these, and with Siné's legless men, whose counterparts are found in Kliban's galleries of "crazies" and "feebs"). The madcap pedantry with which Virgil I. Partch beatifies the pun, and the cliché (one of Kliban's "Polar Puns," which richly deserves exile thereto, has a sport-jacketed, Ascot-tied walrus intoning "You walrus hurt the one you love"). Steig the Earlier's psychoanalytic jottings, from the *Lonely Ones* (the guy in *Tiny Footprints*, crouching on a shelf, opposite a can labeled "Paranoia") and Steig the Later (the leafy baroque trio of creeps representing "Deformed Car Salesmen" [*Never Eat Anything Bigger*]); and, to be sure, in his most richly gloomy, starkly willful drawings — those composing a mini-novella, "The Turk," in *Whack Your Porcupine* — the forlorn elegance and brooding caprice of Thomas Nast. None of these derivations, or appropriations, shows to me the chameleon slavishness, the vagrant echo-snatching of those hack virtuosi for whom style is the total content, and indeed, actuality. Rather, it is Kliban's total awareness of, one might say his benign obsession with, his immemorial terrain and context, the circumstances which he *cannot escape*, which deflect the dangers of eclecticism. The abundance of white space which he deploys (it always seems a *rumpled* whiteness) obliterates the textures, graces, everything save the monumental gawkiness of his figures, and highlights the arid, stitch-like line which seems to have walked, footsore, over every eighth-inch of the drawings, as across acres of asphalt, to pick up a welfare check, say.

The use of space emphasizes as well the fatuous or malign city faces which are the medallions of his art— the tease-curled, flabby-chinned women's faces (you can almost smell the talcum) or the ravenously, vacuously grinning mouths (the debutantes and executive secretaries); and, the treasure of Kliban's skill and morose cruelty, a certain indelible city face, or configuration of features: black stripe of eyebrow within adultery-distance of the hairline; eyes which are at once feral, moronic, and chronically, pitifully suspicious; cheese-wedge, or tuber nose over an abject, drooping pock-mark mouth and, Kliban's signature touch, the speckling of either a bad shave or bad and long enduring acne. We are not always encouraged to examine closely, or to speculate about, Kliban's details, any more than those that our glance skims on our daily walks. These faces, and the bodies of which they are bewildered tenants, are condemned to their own dreary gravity: the ungainly bolster-like torsos, which fart and lurch, the buttress-like legs, which seem to urge them toward renewal of some long-lost kinship with architecture. Like the people in Segar's *Thimble Theatre* — another deeply melancholy, frustration-steeped "comic" work — the characters in Kliban's illustration and cartoons seem constantly on the point of becoming one with their austerely noted, stone-faced backgrounds. The most poignant and wickedly amusing single fact of their continual earnest, mulish parade, is their common *structure*; with its implicit, ineffaceable comment on all structure, or all faith in structure, human-made and natural. What is least avoidable, in Kliban's humorous metaphysic, is what is most absurd; as here, the structure itself, for all manner of linkings and agglomerations, throughout our enterprises; and the virtually insane act of consecration which such structures usually embody. In this regard, he may or may not be an atheist; that question is, in fact, not to the point, which is, rather, that he sees religion — the profession, the iconography of religion — as an interesting and perplexing phenomenon amidst the entanglement of persons and things: iconography dissolving back into the objects which induced it. "The Holy Filament" is an electric light bulb (votive?) which is cradled by the Virgin Mary. Who among us, Kliban might be implicitly asking, can deny the possibility? There emerges here a hazardously poised double potentiality of savagery and whimsical bemusement, which informs some of the most mysteriously playful of Buñuel's films; and so, too, "*El Cuaderno de la Virgen*" (the Virgin exhibiting a marble-papered composition book: a not-unimaginable class poster in many a contemporary parochial school); or, the Miracle (#3 in a typically uncompiled series) of the "Virgin Mary's Appearance to a Foreign Car in Denver." His drawings of monks and their crucifixes suggest a slapstick transliteration of Calderón de la Barca's *Devotion to the Cross*: monks putting their change in cruciform coin banks (Monk Bank); or, using them to hammer on the ceiling when disturbed by the noisy prayers of a neighboring religious; and — Kliban's sinewy grimness re-emerging — consign their discarded crosses to a heap labeled "Monk Junk."

Most of these are relatively gentle; Kliban's most intense agnosticism, also fascination, being reserved for the aforementioned structures, an instance in point being buildings: which, informed and maintained as they are by humankind's ridiculous will, are thereby informed with almost-animate identity, as plainly as Kliban can discern it. The Steinberg-like drawing "Fred's House" features a pyramid section, with some token clapboards, windows and a chimney added, from which is emerging Fred — according to the inscription on his flank: an abstraction of the pyramid section, with a token face and legs added. The salient point, whatever Kliban's momentary intention, is, I should say, not the cornball projection of the satirist's cliché about the occupants being "cannibalized" by their houses, but the mysterious, vagrant identity of a building itself. You could just as easily interpret the drawing by saying that the house has begotten its own "Fred." And the devilish challenge to the myth-making imagination, which Kliban acknowledges in the mini-gallery of buildings to be found throughout *Never Eat Anything* and *Whack Your Porcupine*. The Contaminated Pork Building (Cincinnati, OH); the Clown Building of Tulsa, OK (a dippy fun-house shape, attracting no major notice from the clown passers-by); and the Orifice Building of Hartford, CT, whose undulant form is riddled with all the anatomical entrances and exits. (The drawing exudes an eroticism, earthy and surreal, not to be found among Kliban's burlesques of pornography.)

The preposterousness of all such structures (which are also miniature accounts of Dos Passos-like concision of the cities in which they are placed) lies with the action of the human will, the *willfulness* of its impositions and games, and the never-to-be-house-broken caprice of the human imagination, which sees all sorts of links and affinities where none exist; interacting in these grotesque, absurd, and mock-heroic presences. The imagination is always headed for death, for dissolution back into the gravel, shale, and mine of the actual, which coax it forward, except when the batteries of the will turn it to invention. Philip Guston sees invention as absurd, is reflected in the junk that it leaves behind, and the pertinacity of that junk in continuing to exist. Kliban sees invention as absurd more, I think, because of the *process* involved and because of the way such process allies itself with the processes of history and of mythology. He is not, on this account, a Surrealist, as I interpret that enterprise and label, because he does not see the inanimate as convertible, as subject to the cosmetics of the imagination. For what should probably count as a semi-final word by Kliban on the "magic of objects," see "A Visit to the Spoon Museum." The incongruity which the Surrealists like Ernst or Klee profess to see as a culture for all sorts of yummy little miracles, Kliban sees as a given of the most ordinary existence, in somewhat the same way as Ernie Bushmiller of *Nancy* renown, who self-declaredly drew his inspirations from the Sears Roebuck catalogue. "The Original Venison Receiver" (a guy in a headset tuned in on a steak) is no Surrealist's conjuration; but rather, an all-too-literal, foreshortened statement about the perverseness of the human imagination, as expressed in human resourcefulness; and the way in which the invention, its purpose, its operation, may all be oxidized, made unintelligible, to us by the velocity of history, the peremptory dispatch of years and of centuries. Human invention seen as an ongoing, unstoppable rubbish collection, joining and deploying the natural and inorganic, flesh and metal and wood, in unions which only the process of decay can legitimize. Kliban's presentation of such marvels is as foursquare, non-erotic, and non-if-not-anti-"imaginative" as any flea market. His virtually single-minded aesthetic care, it strikes me, is the amount and nature of the space in which these incongruities are to be realized: the fascination of their juxtaposition. Kliban's depiction of "God," in *Whack Your Porcupine* — an old man with rake and bag over his arm, seen from the rear as he ambles down a beach from which tiny human heads are sprouting — is one of the few discernible self-portraits; unless we assume, perhaps justifiably, that he projects himself into all portrayals of art as fully and (regrettably indispensable) encumbrance: as something which take its place among the undertows and deadweights of reality. A typical artist, in Kliban's unconventional pantheon, is Alice, of whom the caption confides to us "Just give Alice some pencils, and she will stay busy for hours." Alice is engaged in trying to join the pencils, point-to-eraser; her efforts accompanied by a smile, a fan-light of vacuity, which assures us, if the caption did not, against her frustration or boredom.

The tough, matter-of-course, prosaic set of Kliban's comic intelligence is what, I feel, enables him to encompass various facts of human cruelty, manipulation, mulishness, through a vocabulary of slog-footed incongruity and deflation, without lapping at the troughs of Torquemada righteousness, or scatological bombast. He really has no, or little, portion with most of the "underground comics" macks and messers, including the best, like R. Crumb, Gilbert Shelton, and Spain Rodriguez. I recall, however, my automatic instinct of disesteem and, indeed, dismissal, on first viewing, in the window of a Sheridan Square bookstore, blowups from *Never Eat Anything Bigger*, of the bewhiskered customer at a restaurant ordering an elaborate continental meal, "And bring some shit for my fly" (an immense pet seated opposite him) or, of "Wendell, the Class Fool," producing some intricate Rabelaisian music with his fingers through his nose; or Alice, our lady of the pencils. My general inference was, as I remember, of a sour, tired recap of gestures, grimaces, and attitudes, which Crumb and Company had not only exhausted, but, in too many instances, were engaged in running up and down the same blind alley. My captious mistrust was, I suspect, underscored by the arid, seedy look of Kliban's line; fit medium, it seemed to me, for the pedestrian pokiness of the amateur, dawdling among the leftovers of the underground cafeteria. "Who needs it?" was the sum and substance of my reaction.

It now seems to me that I was right about some of the strains in Kliban's work which continue to give me trouble; but

wrong in my emphasis. What I found so objectionable in the examples I saw was, I realize now, not Kliban's kinship with the underground schleppers and slurpers; but, in fact, the very thing — the *middle-aged* aspect of the drawing — which gave it an edge over the Crumb contingent in its increasingly compulsive, and decreasingly compelling, carryings-on. All those mucky humors and rank exhalations which the Crumbs and Crumb-snatchers have treated as the alchemical agents of "creative freedom" Kliban, with weary matter-of-factness, treats as facts. As those occurrences which measure off, which, yes, adorn in one way or another every day of our lives, which make their entries in the vocabulary of our common imagination, humor, sentiment; but, indeed, as occurrences only, as kinds of punctuation in the continuing syntax of our existence: an ongoing sort of context, which Kliban recognizes eminently well through his linking of drawing and text in his first three collections.

The basic self-frustration of Crumb's recurrently brilliant work has always seemed to me to lie in its romanticism: the greedy insistence of his cartoons, with their cushiony Max Fleischer/Betty Boop contours, the teeming busyness of their backgrounds, the explosive offhandedness of catastrophe and/or copulation — upon the premise of the comic strip as a magical sausage-casing, which can accommodate everything: the traditional strips' raffish, elliptical visual language, their crisp storytelling dexterity, and the putrid fondant that Crumb dispensed from his funky cornucopia: all indispensable gooks which the older strips, format-corseted and sensibility-hobbled, had been constrained to omit or to present in subliminal images, like the "glue" with which the Katzenjammer Kids would bedeck their household and themselves. Crumb treated these sticky verities as images in themselves, whereas they were not images, but only facts: incapable of liberating any imagination by or of themselves, and hardly by virtue of Crumb's boisterous showboating; but only as the style which displayed them could make them articulate, and meaningful, and in so doing, reintroduce the readers to the entire world. Crumb's masterly portraitures of semi-competent, sometimes vulnerable rogues (Fritz the Cat, Mr. Natural, Those Cute Little Bearsie-Wearsies) and the contemporary broken-field paper-chase of semi-mystical ideals (Mr. Natural, again; the Sacrificial Burger, in "Hamburger Hijinks") never birthed such a style, in my opinion; and the hyperbolic monotony of his approach, for all his inventive élan, exhilarating rascality and visceral good cheer, ultimately narrows rather than expands the sensuous range, the imaginative latitude, of the comic strip; in great part, by stripping from it its precious vocabulary of disguise.

Kliban's drawing, Kliban's humor, embodies a one-hundred-eighty-degree turnaround from the romanticism of Crumb and his Crumb-pets; without, I might add, restoring that sensuous vocabulary that their "liberation" sacrificed; but offering instead, at least, a tenable, realistic point of view, a stance toward the world-as-given. He is far more crass than any of them, with their summer-boys-camp scatology, and tree-house swashbuckling, simply in the way he confronts art, and nature, with an attitude which is informed much less by any particular animus, than by a resignation, which amounts almost to nullity. This last, I think, furnishes many a crucial poser for anybody interested, as I am, in locating and verifying Kliban's distinction as a comic artist. What I originally sensed about his "amateurism" obtains just here, I think: the (or so it may appear) self-abnegating slumpishness in his acceptance of his terrain, including apparently everything which nature, his fellow humans, destiny, and his muse (who probably resembles Alice of the pencils) have handed him; and, certainly, among the givens of art, his consciousness of working through a medium of portrayal, among data which the partnership of text and image have delegated to him.

He favors illustration, I think — and can use it as both agent and foil for his wry, enigmatic comic tone — because illustration leaves as nearly as possible *intact* the landscape for which he is acting as medium. Illustration is the form that provides him with maximum opportunity to celebrate the balkishness of nature toward any attempt at poetic plastic surgery, guru glamorizing or canonizing, or sentimental garlanding. (Kliban's *cat* is at once a warmly playful and bemused witnessing of the cat, and an irreverent jam-session on the subject of "catolatry" in general; which he keeps in equilibrium by treating the cat both as well-loved but impenetrable animal; the only non-caricature Kliban drawing I have seen, of his own several cats, is here, and as ambulatory design.) The aromatic ragout of loneliness, squalor, and dream-like improvisation that we get from the brazier of the captionless little series called "The Turk," in *Whack Your Porcupine*, takes the suggestive tang of its gloomy face from the honor it pays to the art of illustration as such (The Turk, portly, soot-countenanced, dressed in an increasingly-begrimed pin-stripe suit — the emblem of Kliban's flashier losers — is a distinctly less-endearing M. Hulot; always engaged in negotiations eccentric and/or lecherous, making forlorn and erratic excursions). "The Turk" presents some of the freest field I have yet seen in his work, wedding illustration to what he can observe and infer about the ungarnerable, unclassifiable tag-ends of human existence, the freakish intrusion of life (a face peering around a restaurant's kitchen door, a spectrally indistinct female form behind a bead-curtain); and, along with this, illustration's capacity for cabining mood, period, and a variety of secretive presence within the marvelous cachet of an unguessable age; such as we find in the work of Gustave Doré or Frederic Dorr Steele; which is captured in a way few photographs can duplicate, through the illustration's double act of commemoration and spying.

This is the reverse side, of course — this homage to portrayal — of Kliban's mordant jibing at iconography: how it savages privacy (as in the "Victim's Family," or the acolyte's ultimate questions of the Buddha: "How much do you weigh, and what's your favorite color?"). Yet, the perverse alterations which such depiction works on the subject tantalize Kliban; and the invisible, ubiquitous, Boyg-like audience which it conjures (which never deserts some person's grazing ground of awareness) entrap something like his love, I believe; probably because the "audience" itself can beget such mysterious and near-magical glimpses, on occasion.

Yet nothing I might find to say about the ambiguity, the reversibility on occasion, of Kliban's work lays to rest the feeling of flatness, or more disturbing, *blankness*. The suggestion of total abandonment to a smug so-what, as from the Village Sage holding up the cigar store with the nape of his neck, and a few clever hand-holds. The worst sort of attention, no doubt, which one can accord to any artist, is to ham-string whatever is native-eccentric in his work by a wiring of so-called "theme": a pseudo-literary continuity, a synthetic persona, spliced from tendencies, or occasional preoccupations or attitudes, or (very likely) misguided editorializings in this work or that. So I have been constrained to nudge myself against doing with Kliban. Yet, the salient point would seem to be that (a) Kliban's long suit involves a denial, or evasion, of style, by which I mean a long-range imaginative traffic with experience, rather than posing, or lolling against, or strolling up and down in front of a stonewall of accepted experience; and (b) that his operative attitude, far from self-effacing, is, in fact, the testimony (which I infer from numerous inflections, not to mention his free-booting borrowings from other artists) of a well-nurtured and well-muscled self-regard, which sets the seal of prerogative on such close-to-the-chest playing. None of which is to deny Kliban's ego full validity, when it work positively for him; but only to suggest that his quota of strengths, and the noteworthy best with which he sometimes uses them, makes me wonder, what medium, or vehicle, he might find to permit them more leg action than has engaged them so far. (*Tiny Footprints*, a book from Workman Publishing, offers here no revelation, or particular encouragement.) The material, sometimes quite funny, is also very preferential of a gag-oriented, patly-designed, curdled whimsy of the *Playboy* model without the rag-tag venturesomeness of the more openly pedestrian work. Yet, wondering on all this, I must wonder also about the practical, never mind the aesthetic sense, of either recommending or prophesying new forms for an originality which, like most such, is housed squarely in the here-and-now of its existence. All-but-immobile resignation: "Here I be, and what I am I going to do about it? And thus I wonder, as any critic must, at my possible over-impatience with this huge, stolid cat's refusal to come and eat from my hand.